The *Philomena* of Chrétien the Jew
The Semiotics of Evil

LEGENDA

LEGENDA is the Modern Humanities Research Association's book imprint for new research in the Humanities. Founded in 1995 by Malcolm Bowie and others within the University of Oxford, Legenda has always been a collaborative publishing enterprise, directly governed by scholars. The Modern Humanities Research Association (MHRA) joined this collaboration in 1998, became half-owner in 2004, in partnership with Maney Publishing and then Routledge, and has since 2016 been sole owner. Titles range from medieval texts to contemporary cinema and form a widely comparative view of the modern humanities, including works on Arabic, Catalan, English, French, German, Greek, Italian, Portuguese, Russian, Spanish, and Yiddish literature. Editorial boards and committees of more than 60 leading academic specialists work in collaboration with bodies such as the Society for French Studies, the British Comparative Literature Association and the Association of Hispanists of Great Britain & Ireland.

The MHRA encourages and promotes advanced study and research in the field of the modern humanities, especially modern European languages and literature, including English, and also cinema. It aims to break down the barriers between scholars working in different disciplines and to maintain the unity of humanistic scholarship. The Association fulfils this purpose through the publication of journals, bibliographies, monographs, critical editions, and the MHRA Style Guide, and by making grants in support of research. Membership is open to all who work in the Humanities, whether independent or in a University post, and the participation of younger colleagues entering the field is especially welcomed.

ALSO PUBLISHED BY THE ASSOCIATION

Critical Texts
Tudor and Stuart Translations • *New Translations* • *European Translations*
MHRA Library of Medieval Welsh Literature

MHRA Bibliographies
Publications of the Modern Humanities Research Association

The Annual Bibliography of English Language & Literature
Austrian Studies
Modern Language Review
Portuguese Studies
The Slavonic and East European Review
Working Papers in the Humanities
The Yearbook of English Studies

www.mhra.org.uk
www.legendabooks.com

RESEARCH MONOGRAPHS IN FRENCH STUDIES

The *Research Monographs in French Studies* (RMFS) are selected, edited and supported by the Society for French Studies. The series seeks to publish the best new work in all areas of the literature, language, thought, history, politics, culture and film of the French-speaking world and to cover the full chronological range from the medieval period to the present day. Proposals are accepted for monographs of up to 85,000 words, while proposals for 'short' monographs (50,000–60,000 words), a traditional strength of the series, are still welcomed.

Editorial Committee
Diana Knight, University of Nottingham (General Editor)
Robert Blackwood, University of Liverpool
Jane Gilbert, University College London
Shirley Jordan, Newcastle University
Neil Kenny, All Souls College, Oxford
Max Silverman, University of Leeds

Advisory Committee
Wendy Ayres-Bennett, Murray Edwards College, Cambridge
Celia Britton, University College London
Ann Jefferson, New College, Oxford
Sarah Kay, New York University
Michael Moriarty, University of Cambridge
Keith Reader, University of Glasgow

PUBLISHED IN THIS SERIES

20. *Selfless Cinema? Ethics and French Documentary* by Sarah Cooper
21. *Poisoned Words: Slander and Satire in Early Modern France* by Emily Butterworth
22. *France/China: Intercultural Imaginings* by Alex Hughes
23. *Biography in Early Modern France 1540–1630* by Katherine MacDonald
24. *Balzac and the Model of Painting* by Diana Knight
25. *Exotic Subversions in Nineteenth-Century French Literature* by Jennifer Yee
26. *The Syllables of Time: Proust and the History of Reading* by Teresa Whitington
27. *Personal Effects: Reading the 'Journal' of Marie Bashkirtseff* by Sonia Wilson
28. *The Choreography of Modernism in France* by Julie Townsend
29. *Voices and Veils* by Anna Kemp
30. *Syntactic Borrowing in Contemporary French*, by Mairi McLaughlin
31. *Dreams of Lovers and Lies of Poets: Poetry, Knowledge, and Desire in the 'Roman de la Rose'* by Sylvia Huot
32. *Maryse Condé and the Space of Literature* by Eva Sansavior
33. *The Livres-Souvenirs of Colette: Genre and the Telling of Time* by Anne Freadman
34. *Furetière's* Roman bourgeois *and the Problem of Exchange* by Craig Moyes
35. *The Subversive Poetics of Alfred Jarry*, by Marieke Dubbelboer
36. *Echo's Voice: The Theatres of Sarraute, Duras, Cixous and Renaude*, by Mary Noonan
37. *Stendhal's Less-Loved Heroines: Fiction, Freedom, and the Female*, by Maria C. Scott
38. *Marie NDiaye: Inhospitable Fictions*, by Shirley Jordan
39. *Dada as Text, Thought and Theory*, by Stephen Forcer
40. *Variation and Change in French Morphosyntax*, by Anna Tristram
41. *Postcolonial Criticism and Representations of African Dictatorship*, by Cécile Bishop
42. *Regarding Manneken Pis: Culture, Celebration and Conflict in Brussels*, by Catherine Emerson
43. *The French Art Novel 1900-1930*, by Katherine Shingler
44. *Accent, Rhythm and Meaning in French Verse*, by Roger Pensom
45. *Baudelaire and Photography: Finding the Painter of Modern Life*, by Timothy Raser
46. *Broken Glass, Broken World: Glass in French Culture in the Aftermath of 1870*, by Hannah Scott
47. *Southern Regional French*, by Damien Mooney
48. *Pascal Quignard: Towards the Vanishing Point*, by Léa Vuong
49. *France, Algeria and the Moving Image*, by Maria Flood
50. *Genet's Genres of Politics*, by Mairéad Hanrahan
51. *Jean-François Vilar: Theatres Of Crime*, by Margaret Atack
52. *Balzac's Love Letters: Correspondence and the Literary Imagination*, by Ewa Szypula
53. *Saints and Monsters in Medieval French and Occitan Literature*, by Huw Grange
54. *Laforgue, Philosophy, and Ideas of Otherness*, by Sam Bootle
55. *Theorizing Medieval Race: Saracen Representations in Old French Literature*, by Victoria Turner

www.rmfs.mhra.org.uk

The *Philomena* of Chrétien the Jew

The Semiotics of Evil

❖

Peter Haidu

Edited by
Matilda Tomaryn Bruckner

Research Monographs in French Studies 59
Modern Humanities Research Association
2020

*Published by Legenda
an imprint of the Modern Humanities Research Association
Salisbury House, Station Road, Cambridge* CB1 2LA

*ISBN 978-1-78188-929-9 (HB)
ISBN 978-1-78188-930-5 (PB)*

First published 2020

All rights reserved. No part of this publication may be reproduced or disseminated or transmitted in any form or by any means, electronic, mechanical, photocopying, recording or otherwise, or stored in any retrieval system, or otherwise used in any manner whatsoever without written permission of the copyright owner, except in accordance with the provisions of the Copyright, Designs and Patents Act 1988, or under the terms of a licence permitting restricted copying issued in the UK by the Copyright Licensing Agency Ltd, Saffron House, 6–10 Kirby Street, London EC1N 8TS, *England, or in the USA by the Copyright Clearance Center, 222 Rosewood Drive, Danvers MA 01923. Application for the written permission of the copyright owner to reproduce any part of this publication must be made by email to legenda@mhra.org.uk.*

Disclaimer: Statements of fact and opinion contained in this book are those of the author and not of the editors or the Modern Humanities Research Association. The publisher makes no representation, express or implied, in respect of the accuracy of the material in this book and cannot accept any legal responsibility or liability for any errors or omissions that may be made.

Trademark notice: Product or corporate names may be trademarks or registered trademarks, and are used only for identification and explanation without intent to infringe.

© Modern Humanities Research Association 2020

Copy-Editor: Charlotte Brown

CONTENTS

Acknowledgments	xi
Caught in the Co-text of History: An Introduction to Peter Haidu's *Philomena* Project MATILDA TOMARYN BRUCKNER	1
Preface PETER HAIDU	19
Introduction — History, Potentiality, and Dialectical Reading	21

I Identity and History 29

    (i) Christian the Goy 29
    (ii) The Twelfth Century *à rebours*? The Convert's World 43
    (iii) 1096: A Holocaust? 55

II *Philomena* and the Semiotics of Evil 63

    (i) (Re)presentation: Narrative 63
    Excursus I: 'Courtly love' vs the Twelfth Century 66
    (ii) Episode 1: On Beauty and the Desirability of Evil 71
    Excursus II: Tyranny, a Detour Through John of Salisbury's *Policraticus* 88
    (iii) Episode 2: Resubjectifiction, Semiotics, and Class Transcendence 96
    Excursus III: Alterity, Cultural Relativism, and Universalism 106
    (iv) Episode 3: Vengeance, Justice, Universalism 113
    (v) Epilogue: *auctor ex machina* 123

Conclusion — Chrétien de Troyes: Singular Universal 127

Appendix: Counting Jews in Medieval History 137

Bibliography 143

Index 155

For Rachel and Noah Haidu

ACKNOWLEDGMENTS

On 17 April 2017, the day after noted jazz pianist Noah Haidu gave a concert at Birdland in memory of his father, I met with Peter Haidu's daughter, Rachel Haidu, art historian and experienced academic, to investigate what we could find on his computer. With affectionate friendship, my first thank you goes to Rachel and Noah who gave me permission to work with Peter's manuscript in whatever way I thought best for securing publication. They supported me with their knowledge and enthusiasm throughout the process of editing: I am sure their father would have wanted to dedicate his last book to them.

Among the many documents on the computer's desktop, there was a draft of acknowledgments Peter had waiting for publication, and although some of it is no longer appropriate, I include the first and last paragraphs here, as I feel that we have indeed become collaborators serving a common goal.

> This book could not have reached its present form without the contributions of two readers of earlier drafts, Matilda Tomaryn Bruckner and Daniel O'Sullivan. Their readings are triumphs of sinuous, elegant attentiveness, always ready to move with a thought even contrary to their own positions, in the warmest contribution of a generous charity beyond faith or agreement. There are moments in this text that are truly co-authored.
>
> Both Tilda and Dan have my warmest gratitude.

I express here my own heartfelt gratitude to Peter Haidu, mentor and friend, for placing his trust in me to complete his work after his death.

Colleagues and friends who helped move along the project, including Sarah Kay, Caroline Palmer, Daniel O'Sullivan, Virginie Greene, Simon Gaunt, and Larysa Smirnova, all deserve my thanks. Their specific contributions are gratefully acknowledged in my introduction.

I owe special thanks to the Office of Interlibrary Loan at Boston College for their indefatigable speed in locating needed books and articles, and to the Boston College Association for Retired Faculty which generously awarded me financial support for the bibliography and index.

Lastly, I would like to thank the editors of Legenda, Diana Knight and Graham Nelson, who have been unfailing in helping me bring this book to publication, from the delicate process of submission and evaluation to the nitty gritty of multiple proofs. It has been a great pleasure working with them.

MATB, Newton, MA, March 2020

Poetry is always a site of thinking, a truth procedure.
Alain Badiou

Spleen is the emotion that corresponds to
catastrophe made permanent.
Walter Benjamin

In epochs of distress and improvisation,
some are killed just for a night, others for eternity;
a bird-song of entrails.
René Char

INTRODUCTION

Caught in the Co-text of History: An Introduction to Peter Haidu's *Philomena* Project

Matilda Tomaryn Bruckner

> I think [...] that one who writes ends up, whether he wants to or not, entirely in his writing. The author is always there, in the text, which therefore contains everything needed to solve the mysteries that matter. It's pointless to consider the ones that don't.[1]

Over the years of our friendship and what Peter Haidu called 'our personal tradition of reading each other's manuscripts', he became convinced that Chrétien de Troyes, the twelfth-century author who most constantly brought us together, was a converted Jew.[2] That conviction deepened as he worked on his final book project during the last decade of his life. Until the beginning of February 2016, when Peter sent me some six hundred pages, I knew nothing specific about the nature of his book, nor did I fully understand the complicated and multiple reasons behind what he acknowledged as conjecture on Chrétien's double identity that can neither be proved nor disproved.[3] Yet that conjecture, taken seriously, allowed him to produce an unprecedented, extraordinarily powerful reading of *Philomena*, Chrétien's youthful translation of Ovid's tale from the *Metamorphoses*.

'Et de la hupe et de l'aronde | Et dou rousignol la muance' [the transformation of the hoopoe and the swallow and the nightingale] figures last in the list of works Chrétien gives in the prologue to *Cligès*, his second romance (or, as Peter would

---

1   Elena Ferrante, *Frantumaglia*, trans. by Ann Goldstein (Rome: Europa, 2016), p. 205.

2   'Would you be able & willing to take the time to continue our personal tradition of reading each other's manuscripts? I think I'm ready to cut the cord on "Chrétien de Troyes' Wedges: Chrétien the Jew Writes Rape, Poverty, Extortion from Labor, and Messianism in Twelfth Century Romance"? I'd like your reactions, as well as any suggestions on what to do with it: c'est pas évident' (email dated 1 February 2016). Our tradition of reading began when Haidu directed my doctoral dissertation (even after he left Yale to teach first at the University of Virginia and then at the University of Illinois at Urbana-Champaign); it became a mutual exchange in the years thereafter.

3   At one point, Haidu expansively imagined his working title as 'Chrétien de Troyes, a Jew, Invents European Literature by Writing Dispossession, Rape, Poverty, Forced Extortion from Labor, and Messianism in Twelfth Century Romance as Subtractive Universalism', then added: 'Which no sane publisher would accept' (email dated 16 February 2016).

prefer, 'verse novel'), traditionally dated *c.* 1175–1176.⁴ Probably composed in the 1160s, *Philomena* was included in the *Ovide moralisé* by an anonymous fourteenth-century author who explicitly credited Chrétien, naming him twice as translator, before and after transcribing his narrative of rape and revenge.⁵ The author/translator himself signed his work at the midpoint: 'Ce conte Crestïens li gois', a signature that will be amply commented in Part 1.⁶ Although there is no absolute certainty of attribution, the two editions of his collected works include *Philomena*, and most scholars accept the identity of 'Crestiens li gois' with the romancer who signed his name as 'Crestiens de Troies' in the prologue to his first romance, *Erec et Enide*, and simply as 'Crestiens' in later romances.

The earlier signature is singular but the fit with Chrétien de Troyes's corpus and subsequent fame is convincing. And yet, within the abundant richness of the romancer's critical bibliography, his astounding work of translation and rewriting has garnered relatively little attention. Haidu's systematic close reading, buttressed by a deep knowledge of Chrétien's works and great familiarity with the effects and patterns of Old French versification, repeatedly points out how *Philomena* anticipates his romances, yet differs in significant ways from them: here pointing out shared features (empathy for the dispossessed, a taste for clever female subordinates, irony as stylistic device and narrative strategy, the use of monologue splitting the speaker in two, epilogue as mocking mirror, etc.), there noting a radical change from nuance to declaration (regarding authorial identity and the narrative's final, emphatically deontological stance). Haidu thus confirms the inclusion of *Philomena* among Chrétien's works, even as he reveals unanticipated vistas for new exploration.

When Peter died on 9 February 2017, his book manuscript was unpublished. With his typically ironic sense of humor, he gave me 'the onerous task, if I was willing' of publishing it. As I shall explain in greater detail below, what follows this introduction is not the entire project. *The 'Philomena' of Chrétien the Jew: The Semiotics of Evil* retains those parts that prepare and frame his brilliant analysis of *Philomena* — the beating heart of an intensely passionate study, 'the original undertaking of this book' (as he described it in the manuscript), first crystallized as

---

4   Chrétien de Troyes, *Cligès*, ll. 6–7 (in *Romans*, ed. by Charles Méla and Olivier Collet, Livre de Poche (Paris: Librairie Générale Française, 1994), p. 291). Chrétien's wit already appears in the use of *muance*: the word used to translate Ovid's metamorphosis is the technical term used for birds in the process of losing and regrowing their feathers. Molting might also describe how Ovid's work undergoes change and renewal as Chrétien's sharpened quill rewrites it.

5   In the general introduction to Chrétien de Troyes, *Romans*, ed. by Méla and Collet, p. 13, Jean-Marie Fritz assigns Chrétien's Ovidian translations to 1160–1170. In Chrétien de Troyes, *Œuvres complètes*, Bibliothèque de la Pléiade (Paris: Gallimard, 1994), p. xlvii, Daniel Poirion places *Philomena* between 1165 and 1175, during the period when an anonymous author translated *Narcisse* from Ovid's *Metamorphoses*.

6   Chrétien de Troyes, *Philomena*, l. 734 (in *Pyrame et Thisbé, Narcisse, Philomena*, ed. by Emmanuèle Baumgartner (Paris: Gallimard, 2000), p. 208) (the diacritic mark preserves the octosyllabic count). This is the edition Peter used for his book. In *Philomena*, ed. by Cornélis de Boer (Paris: Paul Geuthner, 1909), the standard edition included in collections of Chrétien de Troyes's *Romans*, the name appears as 'Crestiiens li Gois'. While Haidu's usage varies between the two spellings, I have followed the Pléiade edition, making 'Crestiens li gois' the standard form used here, except when 'Crestïens' appears in a quotation as such.

a lecture given at the University of Rochester on 9 November 2007 (the anniversary of Kristallnacht, it should be noted).

Admiration for Peter's accomplishment, as much as gratitude for his friendship, impelled me to take on the 'task', the honor, of editing and publishing his final gift of scholarship. If, as Elena Ferrante claims, all we need to know about the author is enclosed in the text, then the mystery of Chrétien that matters is, or can be, fully revealed in *Philomena*, just as Peter Haidu the author is recoverable in his close reading of it. But then again, Ferrante's claim may be both true and not quite true. There may be something left out, something more about an author's identity, as Peter's conjecture about 'Chrétien the Jew' proposes, something that requires further exploration of his text in relation to the co-text of personal as well as collective history. Here then is an introduction not only to Peter's last book but to the man who lived through some of the most dramatic events of the twentieth century in European and American history.

The Personal

Path-breaking is something of a habit in Peter Haidu's career as medievalist. His first book, *Aesthetic Distance in Chrétien de Troyes: Irony and Comedy in 'Cligès' and 'Perceval'* (1968), revolutionized the study of Chrétien, shifting the focus to the literary and rhetorical aspects of the romancer's art and framing the concept of aesthetic distance as a tool for medieval studies. Haidu himself describes this 'entry into medieval studies' as 'a willed historical extension of the irony of modernity in the form of medieval grammar and rhetoric' (see the Introduction). His second book, *Lion-Queue-Coupée: l'écart symbolique chez Chrétien de Troyes* (1972), whose witty title highlights a compellingly enigmatic moment in *Yvain*, took aim at misplaced applications of allegorical interpretation, thus offering a refutation of Robertsonian excess, while introducing an unusual, cutting-edge approach to semiotics. Many of Haidu's influential articles elaborated a semiotics that integrated literary theory and the co-text of history. The attention to violence brought to bear on the horrors of *Philomena*, particularly force in its political dimension, can already be seen in *The Subject of Violence: The Song of Roland and the Birth of the State* (1993), which introduced a radically new way of reading *La Chanson de Roland* as an open-ended text. Finally, his study of medieval subjectivity's formative role for modern statehood, *The Subject Medieval/Modern: Text and Governance in the Middle Ages* (2004), built on and broadened the issues and works included in his literary, historical, and political purview.[7] Haidu's innovative monographs, his numerous, often incisive articles on topical issues in medieval studies (including romance and semiotics, repetition and narrative structure, alterity and medieval subjectivity), span the period of critical blossoming that marked the second half of the twentieth century. In the landscape of American criticism, forty years of remarkable publications that continue to exert their influence on students and scholars of

---

7   In the course of writing his book on *Philomena*, Haidu was simultaneously planning another book focused on the communal movement in France.

medieval French literature have arguably made Peter Haidu the most significant French medievalist of his generation.

In the Introduction, Haidu himself describes his professional trajectory from an initial encounter with medieval poetry through his long conversation with the works of Chrétien de Troyes. It is not a stretch to see this work on *Philomena* as a summa of his career as medievalist, literary theorist, and even historian of the Middle Ages. His wide and deep knowledge of Chrétien and modern theory, reaching into philosophy, politics, and cultural history, offers the base upon which he grounds and constructs his method of choice, as he explains it: close reading of the texts in question.

What needs to be further highlighted here are two life experiences beyond Haidu's professional career that furnish, I believe, a key to understanding how he conceives his startling interpretation linking Chrétien's identity and *Philomena*'s import. First, the crux of Haidu's own identity as a Jew. Born in Paris in 1931, the son of Hungarian immigrants, secular, assimilated Jews who chose the country of 'égalité, fraternité et liberté' as their home of choice, Haidu's young life was abruptly uprooted by World War II and the Holocaust. His father Paul enlisted in the French Foreign Legion at the outbreak of the war and subsequently died in a German prisoner of war camp. Once she learned of his death, Haidu's mother Henia buried his memory and 'silenced an important discourse' between mother and son.[8] The multiple connections between silence and speech — speech that is silenced but also silence that speaks — will play an important role in Haidu's reading of *Philomena*.

In 1940, without telling nine-year-old Peter that they were Jewish (presumably to protect him from inadvertently revealing their identity and so putting their lives at risk), Henia moved with her son into unoccupied France and then on to Morocco. Hospitalized for malaria in Casablanca but fearing internship in a camp, Henia escaped with him once again by boarding a ship for New York where Haidu's grandparents were already established (his grandfather Arpad had been Administrator of Agriculture in Hungary's short-lived Communist government).

Haidu took his father's enlistment and disappearance personally and never forgave his mother for not telling him that he was Jewish. What was at risk for the boy remembered by his adult self? Without knowing it, he could have died for being Jewish; he could have died without knowing why.[9] Haidu's belated discovery of his Jewish identity combined with limited knowledge and practice of Judaism led him to make sure his daughter and son received a Jewish education. Later, Haidu himself became more personally engaged, finding in Yom Kippur particular meaning. Problematic, sometimes hidden, Jewish identity remained 'such an important thing in his life'.[10]

---

8   Rachel Haidu, Haidu's daughter, personal interview, 10 May 2017.
9   Noah Haidu, Haidu's son, personal interview, 5 July 2019. My discussions with Noah and his older sister Rachel inform much of the personal account supplied here.
10 The quotation is from Noah Haidu. According to Haidu's daughter, he was thrilled when she wanted a Bat Mitzvah and always fasted on Yom Kippur.

Rachel Haidu suggested to me that her father's intellectual engagement with Judaism began in 1990 when Saul Friedlander invited him to participate in a conference at UCLA and contribute to the resulting volume, *Probing the Limits of Representation: Nazism and the 'Final Solution'*.[11] As will be seen in the chapters to follow, Haidu conducted extensive research into the massacres of Jews during the First Crusade and Jewish life within the twelfth-century renaissance, especially the constraints imposed on Jewish converts, in order to anchor his conjecture regarding Chrétien as the son or grandson of forced converts from the 'Holocaust of 1096'. Haidu's own experience of the twentieth-century Holocaust channels his view of 1096 and its consequences, both emotionally and intellectually.[12] As he will affirm, the scale of the killing was different, but the motive and objectives of the killers were the same. Add Haidu's name to the list of those suffering from the Holocaust, as he sums up trauma's effects so movingly in Part I: 'Trauma is not the cover of a coffin, but a burden a subject carries in a backpack on a trail, or the springboard of an imagination. Both. Ask Benjamin. Kafka. Celan. *Crestïens li gois*'.[13]

The second key element informing Haidu's study of *Philomena* concerns the nature of his political engagements. They can be traced through a number of significant experiences: going to high school in Los Angeles (after a period of extreme isolation in New York) and getting a sense of what he and Susan Sontag considered the valley's fascist climate; passion for the civil rights movement; and

11   During the course of our exchanges about the Chrétien book, Haidu sent me his 'The Dialectics of Unspeakability: Language, Silence, and the Narratives of Desubjectification', in *Probing the Limits of Representation: Nazism and the 'Final Solution'*, ed. by Saul Friedlander (Cambridge, MA: Harvard University Press, 1992), pp. 277–99. On 16 February 2016, he wrote about his experience in working on the article: 'When Saul Friedlander first got to UCLA, I was running a rather interesting critical theory operation with the help of Joe Riddel & Vince Pecora. Saul, with the Historikerstreit in mind, organized a conference on the limits of representation, & invited me to contribute a paper. This was embarrassing. I was only dimly aware of the terms of the German debate, but all too deeply aware of the stakes. On the other hand, it was an invitation I could not turn down. The problem was finding something to latch on to that I felt capable of dealing with. I found it. A text. A text, probably a series of texts, speeches by Heinrich Himmler to his top generals, discourses I could parse & analyze. It was the most excruciatingly painful work of my life, & took several months'. According to Rachel Haidu, this moment of intellectual engagement was also the moment when her father finally accepted himself as a Jew. He himself saw it as the moment when he began to read Walter Benjamin with increased seriousness, 'even in German, ever since' (email dated 22 February 2016).
12   His acknowledgment of that link is hidden away, with typically ironic understatement, in a footnote: 'My own perception of certain things about the Middle Ages, things that had lain hidden and only perceptible in part, is entirely attributable to the combination of a capacity for intellectual labor with the de-subjectifications of the Second World War' (see the Introduction below, n. 10). It should also be noted that much earlier Haidu pursued the link between his personal history and the formation of statehood, medieval and modern, from Philip II to the twentieth century, in an article published under the auspices of UCLA's Program in Comparative Literature: Peter Haidu, '1194/1941/1994: Five Bucks and the Suitcases of State', *Suitcase: A Journal of Transcultural Traffic*, 1.1–2 (1995), 28–35.
13   Just before that quotation, Haidu comments on Dominick LaCapra's notion of writing history as equivalent to trauma: 'trauma becomes a condition of active life for survivor populations, surviving *their* traumas as best *we* can, normalizing the condition of being a traumatized survivor' (my emphasis). Note the shift from third to first person.

direct involvement as a faculty liaison in the Columbia student uprising in 1968.[14] In a posthumously-published essay, 'The Columbia Stir Fry', Haidu described that critical moment of taking an active part in a political movement.[15] Afterward, distressed by the growing violence, he moved away from direct participation but continued throughout his career to stand up to academic fascism wherever he saw it. As he concluded in assessing the Columbia struggle, '*Luta continua*' (p. 106). And just as he lived through the upheavals of the 1960s and detested the undermining of justice to the end of his life, so he risked the 'willful anachronism' of connecting fascism to medieval textuality and medieval history. Just so, he delved fervently into the question of tyranny and injustice represented in Chrétien's *Philomena*.[16]

On the occasion of his son's bar mitzvah in 1986, as Haidu described the demands on Jewish survivors to seek righteousness and sustain a righteous anger against injustice, he drew a direct line between being Jewish and standing up for what's right.[17] The link he established then between history, identity, and politics anticipates many of the themes pursued later in this book. In my view, Haidu's own experience of World War II led him to a fusion of sensibilities with *Crestiens li gois* that fuels his understanding of the Jewish massacres along the Rhineland as one of the contexts from which to read *Philomena* as an act of personal, political, and philosophical engagement. It also fuels the anger and passion that characterize both Haidu's style and his study of how Chrétien rewrites Ovid's tale. When the contemporary French author Édouard Louis explains what anger meant for him, he makes explicit what is at stake in *The Semiotics of Evil*:

> There is no truth without anger. [...] anger is a key to understand our world(s), [...] it's maybe even the most scientific tool human beings invented. [...] Only if you are angry you understand that this violence is not normal. Anger is what allows you to take a step back and to understand the social structure you are stuck in.[18]

Of course, anger alone does not account for the character of Haidu's writing as it seeks to do justice to the power of Chrétien's 'translation', a linguistic and cultural transposition designed for his twelfth-century public, a *muance* calibrated to plumb the depths of horror represented in Philomena's story.

---

14   Mentored by a teacher who anchored a group of liberal, intellectual students, Sontag and Haidu remained friends long after they worked together on the school newspaper.
15   Peter Haidu, 'The Columbia Stir Fry', in *A Time to Stir: Columbia '68*, ed. by Paul Cronin (New York: Columbia University Press, 2018), pp. 99–106.
16   See the discussion below in Part II, especially Excursus II and Episode 3.
17   Noah Haidu sent me a copy of his father's speech dated 8 March 1986 (the day after Peter Haidu's own birthday).
18   Édouard Louis, in Matt Seaton, 'Édouard Louis on Fiction and Reality, Reinventing the Self, and Writing Out of Anger', *NYR Daily*, 9 February 2019 <http://email.nybooks.com/t/y-26F0F10A68357A5D> [accessed 15 September 2019]. I would like to thank Matt Seaton, editor of the *NYR Daily* (electronic newsletters from the *New York Review of Books*), for providing the url to his interview with Louis.

The Style and Method

Anyone who has read previous work by Peter Haidu knows that reading his prose often presents an intellectual challenge. That will no doubt prove to be the case here as well, but I think there is a definite difference in this final book, so closely tied, as I have suggested, to the personal. This is both a scholarly analysis of and a poetic response to *Philomena*. The approach is at once academic (in the best sense of that word: exact, systematic, thorough) and strongly emotional; the study is linear in its analytic rigor and non-linear in its poetic, almost lyric, repetitions and digressions. (It might be noted that Haidu wanted to be a poet but then decided that his skills and talents led in another direction.) The reader is constantly made aware of the writer's presence through the how and what of his writing. Haidu writes prose but it often reads like poetry, here elegiac, elsewhere bitter with sarcasm, while the spice of ironic wit (as in Chrétien's own virtuosic octosyllables) often winks knowingly at the reader. The writing is colloquial at times: consider Haidu's use of free indirect discourse to report or paraphrase Chrétien's narration, or the way he translates the Old French to give the 'modern' sense of his verse as a writer participating in the twelfth-century renaissance, a new giant on the shoulders of giants, to give the proverbial maxim a twist. The translations cling to Chrétien's French as closely as possible: if that occasionally produces an oddness in the English ordering of words, the effect serves as a reminder of how skillfully Chrétien plays with the construction of his verses, moving words and phrases to fit into the pattern of rhyming couplets and take advantage of those special places highlighted at the beginning and end of his octosyllables. Haidu doesn't hesitate to indulge in the crudest language when he deems it appropriate to characterize Tereus's vilainous desire and evil actions. These changes of register set up a strong contrast to the theoretically sophisticated and technical vocabulary from literary theory, philosophy, politics, etc., that keeps the reader intellectually alert. All the while, Haidu is clearly enjoying the pleasures of the text through repetition and emphasis.

The in-your-face vigor of his style accords with the many quarrels he raises with critics, critical approaches, and institutions (courtly love, certain kinds of feminist criticism, Lacan, the modern academy, the state, capitalism, etc.). Haidu's polemics are doggedly pursued, his political consciousness informed by a materialist, historicist perspective that pits him against particular currents and figures he views as obstructive or misleading in the domains of politics, philosophy, history and historiography, literary theory and criticism, while aligning him with others (Agamben, Derrida, Badiou *et alii* vs Aristotle, Benjamin, Balibar, Sartre). Among his literary peeves, a question of vocabulary looms large: how to designate the long narratives most scholars call 'romances', a term Haidu rejects as trivializing. As he explains in an unedited version of his introduction:

> 'Romance', for all but a few scholars, precludes any possibility of serious thought or critique: 'romance' designates adventure stories that are mysterious, fanciful, dreamy, fantastic, romantic, sentimental, escapist … adjectives that exclude the possibility of serious, analytic or critical social thought. Yet that is the traditional designation for the works of Chrétien de Troyes. I have taken of late to naming them 'novels in verse'.

Haidu's preference for the term 'novel' thus highlights Chrétien's works as thought-provoking fiction, linked to a literary tradition that the twelfth-century author set on its course from Cervantes to the modern novel. Though Haidu's argument is persuasive, the term 'romance' is not easily dismissed: even he used it in the titles he gave to earlier versions of this book.

The serious purpose associated with Chrétien's work motivates the dialectical close reading that is Haidu's most basic mode as literary critic. Indeed, his dedication to close and attentive reading of text is as important as the turns toward theory and the co-text of history, medieval and modern, French and Jewish. The link between rhetoric, aesthetic effect, and the political and historical dimensions of culture remains foremost. This combined methodology can be seen in the chapters that prepare his reading of *Philomena*, as in the contrapuntal structure of textual commentary and excursus that characterizes Part II squarely centered on Chrétien's Ovidian tale. As he indicates in the Introduction, Haidu offers the reader a dialectical reading where philology, history, and theory meet. Close reading thus becomes in his hand 'an act of aesthetic respect and political retrieval'. Unfettered by disciplinary boundaries, it is 'holistic, totalizing and historically contextualizing', in 'service to an author and to a notion of civilization'.[19] Such is Peter Haidu's creed as literary scholar and critic.

The Issues

An overview of the most important critical problems that Haidu pursues across the chapters included here will help prepare the reader for the way issues arise, intersect, and connect, surfacing and resurfacing as he weaves together the multiple threads of his argument. Consider first the view of history that sustains Haidu's vision and guides his reading throughout. He introduces two key figures to define the workings of history: on the one hand, Aristotle's notion of potentiality, on the other, Walter Benjamin's idea of history as an angel looking backward, blown by the wind of time. The two are complementary, one moving forward to the future from the past, the other turning back from the future present to the past.

The conjunction of future, present, and past articulated through such a vision leads Haidu to speak, as I indicated earlier, of 'willful anachronism' when he identifies fascism in medieval experience. It reappears when he uses modern terms and concepts like 'trauma' to describe Chrétien's dispossessed identity or Philomena's invention of 'new signs' as semiotics. Haidu even suggests that there may be a dimension of the universal in human sciences that traverses time (universalism in relation to the question of history and culture is itself one of the key recurrent themes, on which more below):

> The aptness of both theoretical forms of modern semiotics, Peirce and Greimas, to the twelfth-century writer's narrative invention leads to speculation about the question of transcendence and universalism in the human sciences. The minimal claim to be made is that advanced modern forms of semiotics are

19 See the Introduction.

textually present *in* narrative *nuce* in the twelfth century, even if not theorized. (Part II)

In 'Mind the Gap: Modern and Medieval "Religious" Vocabularies', Peter Biller explores the same issue Haidu raises with his acknowledgment of 'willful anachronism'.[20] Biller's analysis of how the words and concepts we use compare with those available to medieval people begins and ends with Marc Bloch's reflections on 'Nomenclature' in *Apologie pour l'histoire, ou métier d'historien* (1949), translated as *The Historian's Craft*. As Biller phrases it in his own title, historians following Bloch's example need not limit themselves to the terminology of the past, but should 'mind the gap', that is, respect the sense of an apology, signified by Bloch's main title, which encouraged 'meditation on historians and language' (p. 222). That is indeed what Haidu has done.

To push the notion further, we might understand that 'willful anachronism' applies not just to an individual term or concept such as 'trauma'; it expresses most significantly the conjunctions situated at the heart of Haidu's project.[21] The 'Holocaust of 1096' is another willful anachronism, named by an act of historical and political engagement so that the eleventh-century and the twentieth-century Holocausts look forward and back at each other, exemplifying Aristotle's notion of potentiality and Benjamin's angel of history. So too, Philomena and Rachel of Mainz (whose story of sacrifice is told in the Hebrew chronicles of the Jewish massacres) hold up mirrors to each other, thanks to Haidu's conjecture on Chrétien as the unconverted convert. With a Benjaminian flash of retrospective understanding, past and future connect: the slaughter of Jews during the First Crusade is recognized as the Holocaust of 1096, a potential embedded in history, not inevitable, but nevertheless realized in the magnified Holocaust of World War II.[22]

Frédéric Pajak, a Swiss-French writer and artist, may help us penetrate a bit deeper into Benjamin's role here. Pajak explains his fascination with 'the German Jewish philosopher and cultural critic who witnessed Europe being consumed by fascism':[23]

> The past has two faces: the past of the victors and the past of the vanquished, erased from history. But, history can only exist if the present repairs the trauma of the past. The injustice done to the victims of history must be repaired, even

---

20 Peter Biller, 'Mind the Gap: Modern and Medieval "Religious" Vocabularies', in *The Making of Medieval History*, ed. by G. A. Loud and Martial Staub (Woodbridge: York Medieval Press, 2017), pp. 207–22. Cf. more recently, Peter E. Gordon, 'Why Historical Analogy Matters', *NYR Daily* <https://www.nybooks.com/daily/2020/01/07/why-historical-analogy-matters/> [accessed 1 January 2020].
21 Compare Haidu's use of trauma as 'willful anachronism' with Susan Einbinder's effort in *After the Black Death: Plague and Commemoration Among Iberian Jews*, The Middle Ages Series (Philadelphia: University of Pennsylvania Press, 2018) to contextualize and historicize contemporary theory's use of trauma as a universal human response.
22 In an unedited version of Part I, Haidu speculates for a page, wondering if the kind of critique found in Albert of Aachen's account of the slaughter might have prevented the Final Solution, if it had been more generally shared.
23 Gal Beckerman, 'The Agony of Walter Benjamin' (review of Frédéric Pajak's *Uncertain Manifesto*), *New York Times Book Review*, 25 April 2019 <https://www.nytimes.com/2019/04/26/books/review/frederic-pajak-uncertain-manifesto.html?searchResultPosition=1> [accessed 14 August 2019].

and especially if, as Benjamin wrote, 'it is more difficult to honor the memory of the nameless than that of the known'.[24]

Carrying the burden of trauma, recognizing, if not repairing, the traumas of the past, and honoring the memory of the victims of history, named and unnamed, these are essential features of Haidu's project. Certainly his own fascination with Benjamin's vision can be glimpsed in the book's earliest title, as in the epigraph on the title page that introduces his final version:

> The true image of the past shoots by in a lightning bolt. The past can be retained only in an image which shoots up and vanishes forever in the very moment it offers itself to knowledge. 'Truth has no legs to flee us' ... designates the exact spot in the historicist conception of history into which historical materialism drives its wedge.[25]

Materialist thinkers — Aristotle, Marx, Benjamin, Balibar — are Haidu's models; his opponents, Idealists from Plato to Kant to Badiou (Badiou, however, remains a critical interlocutor, as Haidu's subtitle 'with and against' demonstrates). Aristotle's definition of potentiality offers the possibility of change and choice, not for the prototypical acorn but for the human actors in history. And that means potential can be deferred, even negated, or the negation negated, if later enactments actualize it. Thus a desubjectified *Crestien li gois*, two generations after 1096, the child of Jewish converts, translating Ovid's *Philomena* in order to critique rape, mutilation, and infanticide, in order to meditate on violence, tyranny, and injustice, may illustrate the notion of deferred actualization. Trauma — not a medieval term but nevertheless a medieval experience — is always the story of a belated experience, counter-mourning for unclaimed experience, as Sigmund Freud, Cathy Carruth, and Dominick LaCapra theorized what Haidu lived (see Part I).

Haidu further connects potentiality deferred and later actualized to a process of reading, his mode of reading as dialectical engagement:

> The fact that potentiality is not materially or teleologically determinative, the fact that potentiality is not determinative in any sense whatever, but depends on later enactments for its actualizations, brings the question of reading to the fore. The text is not determinative of its readings: it lies on the page as a set of potentialities only. How these potentialities are actualized turns out to be quite unpredictable. (Introduction)

Hence literary history's failure to read *Philomena* as Haidu does; hence the crucial role of his combined personal and professional experience contributing a Benjaminian flash of understanding to reveal belatedly the potential inscribed in Chrétien's translation.

In the dialogue between past and future that potentiality represents, Haidu also locates an important dialogue with Alain Badiou and his notion of the 'Event'. In his Introduction, Haidu first cites Peter Hallward's succinct definition of Badiou's Event, 'located by its site at the edge of the void in a [political] situation.'

---

24 Frédéric Pajak, email to Gal Beckerman, included in the latter's review.
25 Identified as 'After Walter Benjamin', the epigraph is now placed at the beginning of his Introduction below, appropriately subtitled 'History, Potentiality, and Dialectical Reading'.

He then returns to the Event as both concept and historical example (the genius Chrétien de Troyes, the Jewish massacres of the First Crusade, the Holocaust) to introduce further characteristics that expand the definition. The Event is 'radically inexplicable' (Introduction), an unexpected transformation, a surprise 'that brings into existence a new and maximal existential intensity'; it is a historical event and yet ahistorical inasmuch as 'it cannot be said to be caused by what precedes' (Part 1). Haidu and Badiou significantly part company in conceptualizing the future produced by an Event. For Badiou who 'identifies himself as a professional philosopher and a Platonist defending a materialist cause' (Part 1), any future revolution moves necessarily in a Christian, salvific direction. For Haidu, there is no guarantee that revolution leads to a positive future. Indeed, 'the fissure that loosens the radical event into history can turn to disaster as well as to emancipatory revolution' (Part 1). Yet Badiou's 'Event and its futurity' still retains Haidu's interest:

> It is perhaps not the necessary form of all coming-to-consciousness, but certainly implication in an Event determines both retrospective and forward-looking conceptions of history. For Badiou's optimistic idealism, the Event is presumed 'good', and the on-going connection to consciousness is termed 'fidelity'. But for one whose Event is not a good, for one whose Event comes not from the birthing of a 'good' but the nauseous eruption of criminal, barbarous monstrosity, for one whose Event is abyssal disaster, the dimension of continuity, the relation to the temporality is not fidelity but trauma. (Part 1)

In conceptualizing his notion of history and the conjunction of past and future, Haidu has one more interlocutor of note: the tradition of Jewish historiography, not only evident in his discussion of Jeremy Cohen's and Robert Chazan's work on the Hebrew chronicles, but also in his references to two major currents in the representation of Jewish history. One is typically called 'lachrymose' history (identified, for example, with Salo Baron), 'which makes Jews victims of a devastating teleology' (Appendix); the other is characterized by Haidu (without naming names) as 'optimistic, rosy-tinted forgetfulness, intensifyingly successful in a post-Holocaust Academy' (Part 1). Haidu opts for dialectics — a third approach encompassing the good and the bad of Jewish history — but dialectics 'shorn of the cast-iron certainties of both philosophical Idealism (Hegel) and orthodox materialism ("vulgar Marxism"): a non-teleological understanding of contradictories at work in the concrete body of history' (Appendix).

Key among the Events Haidu will analyze in this book is the appearance of the writer Chrétien de Troyes, 'the first vernacular genius' — unexpected, radically inexplicable, yet 'a force in European civilization' (Introduction). Inasmuch as Haidu's conjecture regarding Chrétien's identity constitutes the starting-point for his interpretation of *Philomena*, the analysis flows from two very particular characteristics recognized in 'a convert bearing an unconverted self':[26] his dual subjectivity as Christian and Jew; his sensibility uniquely attuned to dispossession

---

26 In the first version of the Introduction sent to me, Haidu summarized his view of *Perceval* as confirming the notion of Chrétien as 'a convert bearing an unconverted self'.

and the suffering caused by violence.[27] If the writer's subjectivity is 'coterminous with his texts' (Part I), Chrétien's double consciousness opened a space for literary invention and social critique, generalized his own dispossession to represent that of others.[28] But Haidu notes a difference between Chrétien de Troyes and the youthful writer *Crestien li gois*: whereas the author of five romances covers over his identity as a convert, only revealing himself through traces, textual indirections, the earlier writerly persona plays on his hybrid identity through the signature placed at the midpoint of *Philomena*. Parting company with previous translations of the enigmatic 'gois' (enigmatic at least for modern readers), Haidu reads the name as 'Christian the goy': a witty, ironic, paradoxical 'bilingual denomination of redundancy' (Part I) that eludes the parents' choice of 'discrete covert concealment' (Part I) appropriate for converts living in the uncomfortable milieu of twelfth-century France.[29]

The signature, an act in language, reminds us that, except for the rarity of the name 'Christianus', there is no evidence for the conjecture, first suggested by Urban Tigner Holmes, that Chrétien was a Jewish convert. It is language that anchors Haidu's conjecture and Chrétien's identity. Through language *Crestien li gois* makes 'radical poetic invention out of total abjection', like Rimbaud's *lettre du voyant*, 'a manifesto for inventing a new language — *nouviax signes*' (Part I), carried out by Chrétien de Troyes in the later romances. And of course, language, the invention of semiosis, and the interplay of speech and silence, constitute major issues in Haidu's analysis.

---

27   Chrétien's empathy may not be a universal reaction, but consider in this respect both medieval and modern Jewish examples that support or align with his particular sensibility. Ivan G. Marcus describes how medieval French Jewry, unlike the German Pietists, understood themselves as participating in the exile of Jews throughout the diaspora, thus sharing a general sense of community: 'Rashi writes about all of Jewry as *keneset Yisraʾel*, a generic expression of Jewish identity, not a regional one' ('Why Did Medieval Northern French Jewry (Ṣarfat) Disappear?', in *Jews, Christians, and Muslims in Medieval and Early Modern Times: A Festschrift in Honor of Mark R. Cohen*, ed. by Arnold E. Franklin and others (Leiden: Brill, 2014), pp. 99–117 (p. 114)). In the mid-twentieth century, Simone Weil demonstrated an acute sensibility in identifying with the suffering of others (dedicating her life to the disadvantaged, joining the Republican fight in the Spanish Civil War, identifying with workers, eating only what she thought equal or even less than what was available to people in German-occupied France). As Parul Sehgal puts it in her review of *The Weil Conjectures*, Karen Olsson's book on the Weil twins: 'Her genius was for the moral imagination, for empathy so extreme it flirted with self-erasure' ('Two Brilliant Siblings and the Curious Consolations of Math' (review of *The Weil Conjectures* by Karen Olsson), *The New York Times Book Review*, 17 July 2019 <https://www.nytimes.com/2019/07/17/books/review-weil-conjectures-math-karen-olsson.html> [accessed 23 January 2020]).

28   Echoing Haidu's view of the duality experienced by a convert living in a Christian society, David Milch suggests that 'the "seeming doubleness" of Jewish life makes Jews perfect for the entertainment biz' (Adam Sternbergh, 'David Milch Headlines Most Uncomfortable Panel Discussion Ever at "New Yorker" Fest', <https://www.vulture.com/2007/10/three_things_you_would_have.html> [accessed 21 August 2019]). Chrétien was indeed in the 'entertainment biz' for an aristocratic courtly public and knew how to create a variety of comic effects with characters, situations, plots, and octosyllables.

29   See the general picture of life for converts painted below, as well as the specific examples of Hermann *quondam Judeus* and Petrus Alfonsi (Part I). Rutebeuf's 'Charlot li Juif' might have offered an interesting literary example from a later period.

Philomena's rape and mutilation reduce her to silence but, like the author/translator, she must communicate her story. Haidu's attention to one of the many innovations in Chrétien's translation, when Tereus cuts out only half of Philomena's tongue, prepares us for the tension between speaking and not speaking. If 'the condition of writing disaster' places 'an implacable imposition on the subject', the necessity to remain silent and avoid the risk of repetition and further persecution is equally compelling, hence the 'imperative of silent speech' and Haidu's evocation of the Benjaminian angel blown backward by the violence of history (Part II). The paradox of silence that speaks is caught in *Crestiens li gois*, the name that reveals and conceals the author's hybrid identity. Chrétien's genius, formed by trauma, will generalize the convert's social marginality to multiple categories of the dispossessed — women, the poor, peasants, widows, and orphans — by first translating the horror of Philomena through the optic provided by Rachel of Mainz. Trapped in the Bishop's palace, cornered by Crusaders ready to slaughter men, women, and children, Rachel committed an act of *Kiddush Hashem*, 'sanctifying the name' by killing her four children, lest they be polluted by the Crusaders' swords or forced to convert.[30]

In Haidu's view, Philomena's rape provides a parallel to the catastrophe of 1096: both destroy a world; both engage political and historical questions of tyranny and injustice. These are Events in Badiou's terms, redefined by Haidu. When he speaks of 'the genocide of 1096', Haidu bases his claim on the stated intentions of Crusaders as found in the Christian account of Albert of Aachen and the Hebrew chronicles. When he describes Rachel's act of *Kiddush Hashem* as a powerful statement, an act that refuses powerlessness at the hands of Christian knights, Haidu's direct reading of the Hebrew chronicles suggests admiration of Rachel's agency, which creates a striking tension with his reading through *Crestiens li gois*'s *Philomena*. There he insists on the author/narrator's emphatic rejection and critique of infanticide — the horrific revenge Procne and Philomena take on Tereus by killing his son and serving him to his father as dinner, the son's innocence and the mother's unjustified act underlined by Chrétien's departure from his Ovidian model.[31] Chrétien's uncharacteristically unnuanced, unmitigated condemnation is based on what Haidu identifies as 'an absolute universal [...] a declarative deontological statement that is clear and univocal' (Part II). It stands as a universal human truth established by the convert's experience as Jew-not Jew, Christian-not Christian, the son who survived, located in the space of dispossession.

Here we have arrived at the final issue I would like to highlight in this introduction: the question of the universal that runs throughout Haidu's book. It is as much present in various guises as it is problematized. Associated with a series

---

30 Ivan G. Marcus emphasizes the Temple cult and the Akedah as traditional models used to justify the untraditional acts of suicide and homicide: *Kiddush Hashem* thus becomes a means of protecting holy things from contamination by the Crusaders ('From Politics to Martyrdom: Shifting Paradigms in the Hebrew Narratives of the 1096 Crusade Riots', *Prooftexts*, 2.1 (January 1982), 40–52).

31 I would like to thank Dr. Larysa Smirnova for highlighting the paradox of Haidu's double reading, encompassing endorsement and repudiation in the refracted mirroring between Rachel's act and the sisters' revenge.

of individual topics as they arise from *Philomena* (e.g. mourning, irony, semiotics), universality is most troubling when key concepts are deconstructed, their face value undermined by the text: *amour*, love revealed as desire for sex; justice as 'an ideologically charged universal' (Part II), uncovered as violence inflicted by the stronger; the Other reverting back to 'us' as the possibility of cultural relativism and alterity collapse. The problem of universalism is centrally addressed in the Conclusion as a debate between Alain Badiou's and Etienne Balibar's definitions, which Haidu finally resolves by way of Naomi Schor's reading of Jean-Paul Sartre's 'singular universal'. How can we understand the centrality of the universal to Haidu's argument and the logic behind his complex itinerary through the Conclusion?

His persistence in pursuing the question stems initially from the fundamental conjecture underpinning the book. As a convert, Chrétien's relationship with universalism reflects a social subtraction: forced into the Christian universal, he is desubjectivized. His hybrid identity forces him in turn to construct 'a fictional universe whose representations comported universalist values from which analytic critique of his own society was possible' (Conclusion). Hence *Crestien li gois*'s access to universalism through mythologizing fictions and Chrétien de Troyes's use of Arthurian fiction as an alternative universe.

At another level, we should recognize Haidu's own need to find a definition that works politically, historically, and philosophically for himself as reader and critic, an understanding that satisfies his own double consciousness as a Jew whose history crosses the catastrophes of the twentieth century and who has much to critique in the world around him. He too looks for a definition outside the confines of *katholikos*, the Christian claim to the universal, hence his rejection of Badiou's univocal universalism tainted by messianic idealism. Haidu's exposition pauses briefly on Badiou's generic, seeing in it a possibility of a politically acceptable universality. But his adherence goes most emphatically in the direction of Balibar's materialist approach, moving from universalism to universalization as a process that integrates historical change and foregrounds its political impetus:

> What strikes me in Balibar's exposition is the dual movement towards naturalization and historicization of the universal. The refutative nature of universalist discourse indicates that it arises in a natural reaction to growing, unjust impositions become intolerable to those who are forced to endure them by violence: that is, the dispossessed. The universal, grounded in human nature, thus becomes the name of a historical process — it would be preferable to speak of universalization, rather than a static universal — driven by the necessity of refuting and repulsing established powers experienced as tyrannous. (Conclusion)

But Haidu's search for a satisfying sense of the universal does not end with Balibar's universalization impelled by the violence of dispossession. Sartre's concrete 'singular universal' adds another dimension to connect back to Chrétien and *Philomena*. The 'singular universal' is 'what transforms the contingent, aleatory, insignificant singularity of the individual into a meaningful and concrete universal', to which he adds a qualification: the singularities constructing the universal 'must be singularities in

concert, singularities activated by collective values and enthusiasm, that (dis)allow engagement with other similar singularities in collectivity' (Conclusion).

And so Haidu, driving in the wedge of historical materialism, can identify and claim the two universalist values, two universal truths inscribed in *Philomena* by way of Rachel of Mainz and the Holocaust of 1096: (1) mothers should not kill their children, and (2) justice should prevail over the horrors of tyranny and dispossession.[32] Through the singular universal, *Crestien li gois* translates his own story into the story of all those who are the victims of violence, desubjectification, dispossession. Through the singular universal of his experience and the Benjaminian flashback, Haidu reads the potentiality written into Chrétien's Ovidian translation.

The Editing

From February through August 2016, I read and commented extensively on the manuscript Haidu sent me. It initially included all the material published here plus chapters on *Erec et Enide* and *Yvain*. At one point, in response to my comments, he decided to write a new chapter on *Perceval* rather than treat it summarily in the Conclusion.[33] At that point Haidu reorganized the book into three parts (*Philomena* alone in Part II, the romances grouped together in Part III). Our emails back and forth ran a lively dialogue, as Haidu continued to work on the book despite his worsening health (unknown to me at the time). I first learned about his illness a year later when he answered my query about the effort to publish his manuscript: he would not know the outcome, he was dying.[34]

In the process of making a final revision for submission, Haidu engaged Professor Daniel O'Sullivan to help him edit and reduce the manuscript.[35] Despite some cutting, the total size of 'Chrétien de Troyes — a Jew? — Writes Rape, Poverty, Exploitation and Messianism: Dispossession in Twelfth Century Romance' remained substantial. I did not see the version submitted for publication until after Haidu's death, when I was able to obtain a copy of the manuscript thanks to

---

32 It is perhaps in the dialogue between these two universals that we can understand Haidu's admiration for Rachel of Mainz's act of just resistance and his horror before a mother who kills her children (or denies them knowledge of their identity and past, as did Perceval's mother, as did Henia Haidu).

33 In an email dated 1 August 2016, Haidu wrote: 'What has really changed is what you read as the conclusion. A question you raised about Gauvain forced me to go back over both my text & Chrétien's — very much against my desire. As a result, there's a new chapter on Perceval, & and a new Conclusion to the book beside'.

34 Haidu's final email to me is dated 2 February 2017. If misspellings speak eloquently of his illness, his wit shows through with its usual verve: 'There's no news on the book, no would I be also contribute to the final work: Rachel is moving me to Rochester in a few days. Pity, to be dying now that life is getting disgustingly interesting again. With lying and clumsy, thorougholy corrupt assholes like Trumpfery & Banning, showing what pjerks they are — & maybe adding a few feathers to one's collection might befun!' Peter died in New York City a week later.

35 Haidu admired O'Sullivan's editing of the Festschrift published on the occasion of my retirement, *Shaping Courtliness in Medieval France: Essays in Honor of Matilda Tomaryn Bruckner*, ed. by Daniel E. O'Sullivan and Laurie Shepard (Cambridge: Brewer, 2013). As indicated by the emails O'Sullivan exchanged with Haidu and then shared with me after his death, our feedback on style and content often coincided.

Professor Sarah Kay and Editorial Director Caroline Palmer of Gallica.[36] As a result, I had access to two somewhat different versions of the book. In editing it for this publication, I have negotiated between them for reasons I explain below.

The overall purpose of my editing has been to clarify the logic and concentrate on highlighting the order and presentation of Haidu's argument. I regularized the use of translations and the Old French text, straightened out and reduced repetitions, without, I hope, altering the character of Haidu's style. I consolidated a number of his critiques, dispersed and inserted repeatedly, so that they would not encumber and distract from the main points. Divisions and subtitles have been regularized, footnotes brought up to standard, and a bibliography provided.[37] I have added a certain number of footnotes and identified them as those of the editor to distinguish them from those Haidu wrote. Part I originally had four sections: in order to maintain the flow of the argument, I moved the fourth to an Appendix ('Counting Jews in Medieval History' and 'An Incomplete List of Events in the Twelfth Century Concerning Jews and Jewish Converts').

Given the unworkable size of the manuscript, I eliminated Part III on the romances in order to keep the book's focus on Haidu's close reading of *Philomena*, the original project and its strongest, most compelling analysis. Hence certain omissions in the Introduction and Conclusion, although in the latter I retained comments on the romances to give the reader a sense of how Haidu extended his reading of dispossession into Chrétien's later works as illustrated, for example, by Enide's poverty and the giant peasant encountered by Calogrenant in *Yvain*. It is with some regret that I was not able to retain the chapter on *Perceval*, since it is the one romance in which the Jewish question resurfaces. In his reading, Haidu comes back to his Jewish conjecture: he interprets the wild boy Perceval as a figure for the author's unconverted self; reads the prologue and the Hermit episode via Maimonides on charity, and moves from Chrétien's evocation of Saint Paul to Badiou and the foundation of universalism as ethics; suggests that the romance's two parts intertwining the Perceval and Gauvain narratives relate to each other through rupture and continuity just as Judaism and Christianity relate to each other; and finds in the Arthurian disaster described by Perceval's mother resonance with the disaster of 1096. 'As with *Philomena*, Jewish history offers a potential contextual register of meaning that enriches the significance of the text'.

My regret for the omission of the *Perceval* chapter is all the stronger, given that it is the one romance Haidu and I read quite differently. We had especially divergent views on mothers and sons, and on the relationship between the two heroes. In the course of our exchanges, we discussed why and how he took issue with the approach in my book, *Chrétien Continued: A Study of the 'Conte du graal' and its Verse Continuations* (2009), which situates the unfinished *Perceval* in the dialogue with its

---

36 I would like to thank Sarah Kay for suggesting Legenda Research Monographs in French Studies as a potential publisher and for helping me present the proposal to its General Editor, Diana Knight. My thanks also go to Professor Virginie Greene for reading the *Philomena* chapter at an early stage in the editing process and for encouraging me to pursue publication.

37 Dr Smirnova played a crucial role in checking and improving Haidu's footnotes and in constructing the index and the bibliography of works cited. I owe her a debt of thanks.

continuations, as most medieval readers would have encountered it in the extant manuscripts. Haidu's readings of *Perceval*, from his first book to his last, focused on Chrétien's unfinished text and gave little attention to Gauvain who remained, in his view, a secondary character as in the earlier romances. Unfortunately, Haidu had neither the strength nor the opportunity to develop the potential of an analysis added belatedly to his project.[38]

In addition to the Appendix, I introduced one other major reorganization by creating a third excursus in the *Philomena* chapter to include material that appeared in the first version Haidu sent me but was eliminated in the last revision for the sake of slimming down the manuscript for publication. 'Excursus III: Alterity, Cultural Relativism, and Universalism' allowed me to use the digressive structure Haidu had already established in the chapter for extended discussions of important supporting concepts, materials, etc., and include his analyses of the relationship between cultural relativism and universalism. Since this theme plays such an important role in the overall structure of the book, I believe the discussion of alterity as used in modern theory and criticism, as well as the study of how cultural relativism appears in the text of *Philomena* to undermine the difference between the 'barbarian' Other and Chrétien's French public, makes a significant contribution to the book. This change also required me to reorganize some of the discussions in 'Law, Revenge, and Justice' to make the presentation clear and coherent.

I would like to close this introduction by thanking the editors of Legenda for taking on this unusual posthumous publication and the specialist reader, Professsor Simon Gaunt, whose report encouraged them to do so. Gaunt's assessment of the potential impact of the work serves here as a fitting tribute to Peter Haidu — medievalist, survivor, historian, and critic — who has done so much to uncover and explore the semiotics of evil:

> The true originality of *The* Philomena *of Chrétien the Jew* lies in how [Haidu] teases out the implications of its author being a convert by seeking to identify how the text is haunted by traumatic events from recent Jewish history in Northern France, and in particular by the pogroms of 1096, the records of which include at least one account of infanticide. While [...] this does entail some speculation, it also leads to an extremely original and provocative reading of *Philomena* as motivated by trauma provoked by evil in ways entirely unanticipated by the Ovidian tale on which it draws, and this may have far broader implications for understanding the input of Jewish culture into pre-courtly and early courtly literature in French than anyone has previously realised.

Though Haidu's conjecture on the double consciousness of *Crestien li gois* remains outside the realm of proof, the possible ramifications of discovering what may lie behind his unexpected *nuance* make this study of *Philomena* indispensable reading for understanding the Event that shapes a twelfth-century author's Ovidian twist, indispensable for understanding the Event that is Chrétien de Troyes.

---

38 Haidu recognized the limits of his late work on the *Conte du graal*: 'Already dealt with extensively — and to some degree superficially — in my 1968 dissertation, the *Perceval*'s religious ambiguity is explored here a bit more, though not its introduction of something else perhaps not recuperable by any institutionalized religion: mystery' (from an unedited version of his Introduction).

PREFACE

Peter Haidu

A strand of European literature, from Geoffrey Chaucer to Walter Benjamin and beyond, fuses subjectivity with the aesthetic coherence of fragmented holism, a witty self-reflexivity that betokens a critical attitude toward the social totality, and a sense of ultimate redemption, even in the face of impending disaster — a sense, a hope that sometimes glimmers as little more than grasping at straws. That strand of modernity was wound, and unwound in the work of Chrétien de Troyes, during the second half of the twelfth century, when modern European literature was knit by a Jew, a holocaust survivor of the pogrom of 1096: such is the thesis of this book — or rather, its conjecture.

Throughout his narrative work, though clothed in social decorum which posited an idealization of comportment associated with a court civilization, including a normalization of stable marriage as the conclusion to passionate love, Chrétien de Troyes wove a continuous attention to the claim of the dispossessed, as instanced by women, the poor, the *vilains*, exploited commoners who are recurrent figures in his narratives.[1] This book suggests that this continuous concern — unique perhaps among his contemporaries? — instances a singular subjectivity: that of a descendant of forced Jewish converts of 1096. That in fact, Chrétien de Troyes's continuous attention to poverty and dispossession, as well as to gender inequality as instanced by the importance of women in his narratives (more than mere objects of desire or rewards for males' achievements), concretizes a Jew's universalization of his own, subjective dispossession.

The suggestion of this book then is that a major strand of European literature descends from the Holocaust — the holocaust of 1096 — lodged as a potential in the heart of European civilization. The effort to identify it as inscribed in the work of Chrétien de Troyes, the offspring of Jews forced to convert to Christianity as the first stage of the First Crusade, who inscribed that identity and expanded it via a subtractive cultural reduction to a unique generic universalism, can only proceed by an unholy admixture of serious respect for the writer's text, its embroilments with history, and the complex theoretical and philosophical heritage which is that of consciousness at the present moment (as arguable as that is). Martianus Cappella's *De nuptiis* must be rewritten as an adulterine triangulation of philology, history, and theory — each taken at full value. It should come as no surprise that such admixture

---

1 As Norbert Elias saw on the eve of World War II: *Über den Prozeß der Zivilisation: soziogenetische und psychogenetische Untersuchungen*, 2 vols (Basel: Haus zum Falken, 1939); *The Civilizing Process*, trans. by Edmund Jephcott, 2 vols (Oxford: Blackwell, 1969–1982).

produces a literature that is simultaneously polyvalent, formally self-reflexive, and utterly delightful.

★   ★   ★   ★   ★

A word about the organization of this book. It falls into two parts. The first deals with matters both theoretical and historical, materials around the nexus of the author's identity. The matter is complex and recondite: I have not managed to simplify it.

The second part is an extensive commentary of *Philomena*. Long presented as student juvenilia, it has never received the attention it deserves as the first work of the writer of genius who initiated Europe's unceasing vernacular quest for the modern. That it is a youthful work is unquestionable. It is not yet the work of Chrétien de Troyes's maturity, but — particularly if the conjecture of his Jewish heritage is allowed to figure in the reading — it is a powerful and a passionate work in witness of dispossession. More: it is a universalizing protest against dispossession.

The Conclusion concentrates on this embattled question of universalism, which is ultimately implicated in the struggle for survival of any minority identity. The closing movement thus aims to reinforce the thesis of the book as a whole: that the forced convert's Jewish heritage took form as a politically determined subtractive universalism, a fate of Jewish diasporic identity to be repeated in history, not as a necessary determination, but as an option sometimes chosen by the chosen people, a historical potentiality that is both a burden and a privilege.

INTRODUCTION

History, Potentiality, and Dialectical Reading

> The true image of the past shoots by in a lightning bolt.
> The past can be retained only in an image which shoots up and vanishes forever in the very moment it offers itself to knowledge. 'Truth has no legs to flee us' … designates the exact spot in the historicist conception of history into which historical materialism drives its wedge.
>
> *after* Walter Benjamin

Chrétien de Troyes witnesses the beginning of a momentous transformation. Indeed, he participates in that transformation in a fundamental way. Chrétien himself is transformed along the way.

The transformation is that of Europe from a predominantly agricultural civilization, subjugated to the control of a local, self-denominated 'noble' aristocracy whose material extractions were exercised through mounted instruments of violence (called 'knights') in a largely pastoral and forested landscape dotted with a network of occasional towns and cities, into a predominantly urban and industrial civilization, necessarily supported by an increasingly diminished farming background, subjected to the domination of increasingly centralized systems of governance.[1] The process, intensified as of the eleventh century, will last until the nineteenth, and continues into the present. It anticipates Max Weber's nineteenth-century definition of the state as possessing the monopoly of violence.

Chrétien's witness, anchored in the feudal system of agricultural control, registers specific moments of this transformation. He is contemporary to the reign of the principality, an early, more compact form of the state (a statelet if you will). Champagne and Flanders were outstanding examples of this political form, as were Normandy (which conquered the western islands and made England a colony) and the Ile-de-France, in which wealth confiscated from its own Jews financed military aggressions which imposed its dominance on neighboring principalities and other neighboring powers to lay the bases of what would become the state and the nation of France.

Chrétien's own contribution to this political development was multiple. It was an Event, a historical Event 'located by its site at the edge of the void in a [political]

---

1 That process may itself be viewed as integral to a yet larger, continental metamorphosis: R. I. Moore, 'The Transformation of Europe as a Eurasian Phenomenon', in *Eurasian Transformations, Tenth to Thirteenth Centuries*, ed. by Johann P. Arnason and Björn Wittrock (Leiden: Brill, 2011), pp. 77–98.

situation'.² In the domain of literary art and culture, Chrétien has repeatedly been said to have founded European literature in some 'modern' sense. More particularly, his texts mark not only an aesthetic beginning, but a spectacular moment in the ideological subjectivation of the class segment of the warrior knights, namely their potential for service and devotion to the weakest of society: women. Chrétien de Troyes shows battling chivalric knights of unquestionable heroism such as Erec, Gauvain, Alexander, Cligès, Lancelot, Yvain, Perceval, and Gauvain, as willing and competent servitors of deserving noble women, repeatedly subjecting their natural bloodthirsty violence and greed to service to a Lady, a superior lord, and, as important, a set of deontological rules. That latter — the notion of submission to a set of rules, even if implicit — would give rise to several types of behavioral rule books in the following century, codifying the examples found in Chrétien's narratives. His extraordinary skill lay in making this ideological subjugation of violent knights appear desirable and elegant as a cultural project to the brutes concerned, even as his narratives allowed for slivers of cultural critique to manifest themselves. Besides his unquestionable talent and literary inventiveness, Chrétien de Troyes also marked the appearance of the first vernacular genius as a force in European civilization. That too was an Event.

As with any genius, this Event is radically inexplicable. The word 'genius' denotes something that escapes logical or historical understanding. Yet, historical context does allow some understanding of the material problematics the genius addressed. The conjecture this book advances is that 'Chrétien de Troyes' was the name of one descendant of the forced Jewish converts of 1096, Jews who survived the first Christian genocidal holocaust on European soil at the beginning of the First Crusade. In *Philomena*, Chrétien's Jewishness, largely repressed by the force of history, found a path to a form of generic universalism largely ignored by modern literary history.

Chrétien's literary creation — including a certain notion of 'literature' itself, allying art's creation with the dispossessed of political oppression — evolved within a specific historical context, political and economic. While the aesthetic of his works is far from the mimetic realism that defines serious social commentary in modernity, attentive reading of his texts — close reading — allows for recovery of their attitudes towards the material realities of the period: realities which grounded both social life and political organization. Close and attentive reading is simultaneously an act of aesthetic respect and political retrieval.

---

2   Peter Hallward, *Badiou: A Subject to Truth* (Minneapolis: University of Minnesota Press, 2003), p. 37, n. 25. Editor's note: more on Badiou and the notion of the Event below and in Part 1, especially section (iii), 'Episode 2: Re-subjectifiction, Semiotics, and Class Transcendence'.

On Potentiality in History

Aside the punctual act of respect due a poet and novelist of the late twelfth century, something else is at stake: the recovery of history, neither as corpuscular repository nor teleological damnation, but a seed-bed of potentialities which nourish its futures — potentialities, it must be said immediately, both for evil and for good. 'Potentiality' is a major philosophical invention of Aristotle, whose incisive utility in the interpretation of history has been obscured by two combined currents of thought: the historicist ideology, widely shared among historians, and the Idealist tradition in the academic discipline of philosophy, particularly among Europeans, like Jacques Derrida and Giorgio Agamben. Their marketing, capitalism in the academy, has displaced more materialist thinkers such as Etienne Balibar, A. J. Greimas, and Jacques Rancière, whose attention to concrete materiality is repugnant to the moralistic Idealism of the American counter-revolution.[3] Potentiality as thought working within history avoids two enticing historiographical traps: historicism's cookie-cutter castrations of temporality, justified by an ideology of positive specificity in the fetishism of the archive (dominant in the historical profession), and the neo-Kantian reduction of historical temporality to the historian's rear-view mirror.

Walter Benjamin, cornered in temporarily unoccupied France by Nazi Germany's unfurling military assault, part of its extended crusade against Jews, Judaism, and other alterities, refused the scission of materialist history from the Idealist tradition that had given birth to Marxism. Materialist history and messianism remained conjoined for Benjamin.[4] His ultimate reflections on history are crucial for contemporary historical understanding.[5]

Nevertheless, it is Aristotle's formulation in the *Metaphysics*, Book Theta, sometimes complex and obscure, that placed potentiality on the theoretical agenda. In doing so, Aristotle took a certain risk: that of the deformation of his ideas by the Platonic Idealists he specifically criticized. Aristotle was perfectly aware of the

---

3 Balibar, it should be noted, is one of the few thinkers to have recognized the necessity of incorporating the linguistic critique of (post-)structuralism as intellectual mediation within a larger, more general critique of political economy. Derrida and Agamben, especially, deployed techniques that must be viewed with caution, given that both are thinkers who contributed forcefully to indexing epistemological cruxes. Nevertheless, both are post-Heideggerians whose rewritings of materialist thought over-ride its alterity and deform its theoretical content, most notoriously when addressing the works of Karl Marx and Walter Benjamin (Derrida, above all in *Force de loi* and *Spectres de Marx*; Agamben's entire corpus feeding off Benjamin and Foucault). Neither Derrida nor Agamben, it must be stressed, is without merit. Neither recognized the limitations of his own thought, however. As a result, both seem treacherously totalitarian.

4 That peculiar fusion has undoubtedly helped the marketing of Benjamin in America, where, as was pointed out some time ago, he functions as iconic cover for left-wing academic political impotence. See Otto Karl Werckmeister, *Icons of the Left: Benjamin and Eisenstein, Picasso and Kafka after the Fall of Communism* (Chicago: University of Chicago Press, 1999).

5 Walter Benjamin, 'On the Concept of History', in *Selected Writings*, ed. by Howard Eiland and Michael W. Jennings, 4 vols (Cambridge, MA, & London: Belknap Press, Harvard University Press, 2004–2006), IV, 389–400. The last version of this essay written by Benjamin (and hence the authoritative text) is probably the French text: 'Sur le concept d'histoire', in *Écrits français*, ed. by Jean-Maurice Monnoyer (Paris: Gallimard, 1991), pp. 425–55.

ideological toes his theory trampled. He designated his antagonists scornfully as those of the 'Megaritic school' who, arguing for Ideas eternal and unchanging as the sole location of the actuality of being, denied the existence of potentiality.

The world of imperishable Ideas — Plato's ideational world, repeatedly invoked by Alain Badiou — has no room for historical change. The only change Plato's system allows is degradation: as the Ideas in the empyrean realm where true being resides are incorporated in the material, sub-lunar world, they cannot but be degraded by their materialization. Perhaps that inherited non-place accounts for Badiou's difficulties in dealing philosophically with actually existing revolutions. Change, sub-lunar change, is the specific problem of Book Theta. Plato's system of ideas, devoted to a world of eternal, imperishable Ideas, is unable to twist itself to explain change in the world of carnal materiality.

Modernity relies on simplified notions of causality: reducing Aristotle's quaternary causal system, it selects the efficient cause as the one element that makes a thing what it is. By discarding material, formal and final causes, modern thought disregards the full potential of Aristotle's complex system. As a result formalism and teleology are ritualistically derided. In addition, Aristotle considered the question of potentiality on the sub-lunar plane of temporality within the binary of potentiality and actuality: actuality occurs as the fulfillment of potentiality. One might also hazard the thought that any actuality within the sub-lunar world is the effect of a prior potentiality. The simplest version of potentiality and fulfillment in the vocabulary of modern thought is the example of the acorn and the oak: the seed's very existence is the potential it bears of the full-grown tree. Aristotle does not use that example: he avoids it for a good reason. It is inadequate to explain changes in what we call the mental, social, and historical worlds.

Change is the material topic of Book Theta. What interests Aristotle is finding a conceptual vocabulary to address change in beings that have ideas (not Ideas), and that regularly face the necessity or possibility of making choices. The complexity of Aristotle's thought devolves from the effort of constructing such conceptualization in the mental space occupied by Platonic Ideas.

Among the choices available to the thinking, sentient agent is the possibility of not fulfilling a particular potentiality. Agamben reduces the political and historical problematic of choice to the rhetorical form of the paradox: potentiality can manifest itself by non-existence. He is right to recognize the paradox: Aristotle already presents that possibility as a paradox. But Agamben's argument is tendentious insofar as it leads to a 'mystical' Aristotle, a result that dismisses the material problematic he addresses.[6]

Potentiality inheres in the world understood by historical materialism: change inheres in things, the *res* designated either as material objects, things and animals, or as necessarily interwoven with them. It is of particular importance to the animals endowed with what translations of Aristotle call the 'soul', a word with spiritualistic connotations. The 'soul' in Aristotle is better understood as 'that which animates

---

6 Giorgio Agamben, *Potentialities*, trans. by Daniel Heller-Roazen (Stanford, CA: Stanford University Press, 1999).

animals', including the human animal, with one additional consideration that sets those animals apart: choice.

One kind of potentiality inheres in the material object that is a seed, the material object that will grow into a tree: an acorn into an oak. This is the conventional example of the process of potentiality actualizing itself. Aristotle, however, is intent on the one thing that Agamben has understood quite thoroughly: the paradox that potentiality demonstrates itself not only in the seed's coming to fruition, its 'self-actualization', but also in something unavailable to the acorn. Given adequate conditions of water, heat, and soil, the acorn cannot but grow into the oak that is its completion, the fulfillment of its potential. Choice does not interfere in the fulfillment of the acorn's potentiality. The acorn cannot decide to turn around and not grow. Given appropriate conditions, the acorn is forced by its nature to grow into the oak. That is natural teleology: the determination of fulfillment by natural process. Teleology exists in 'nature'. The question is whether such teleology operates in the affairs of human animals, and particularly in their social history.[7]

That evolution of potentiality, its fulfillment in the appropriate actuality, is available only to those animate beings whose 'soul' allows them to fully exercise what is referred to as 'freedom of choice'. The exercise of that possibility, by human animals, for example, can result not only in the production of the 'natural', positive fulfillment of potentiality. It can equally well manifest itself in the decision to not write the poem, to not build the house, to not boil the pot of tea-water, to not burn the oil — material examples used by Aristotle.

The paradox is that, for certain kinds of beings, carnal, material, animate beings, potentiality fulfills itself not only in an actual, positive production, but in absence. Its actuality is then non-fulfillment of the particular potentiality, even as it fully fulfills potentialities' own potentiality of privative production. The paradox is privation as actualization of potentiality. One potentiality of potentiality is self-negation — but that is only *one* potential of potentiality, not its totality or its summation.

Potentiality and its actualization are pointless except in dealing with material beings, and most fully pertinent to those material beings (like humanimals) who possess and exercise the dual function of thought/choice. The Aristotelian meditation on change *ici-bas* recognizes that, in a world of humanimals, the exercise of choice can sometimes, perhaps often, produce effects that are contrary to the actualization of fulfillment of the potentiality in question. In the social dimension, where the subject is collective, frequent phenomena are the loss and disappearance

---

7   Teleology was adopted by religiously-inspired universal history in the Christian Middle Ages. The modern belief in 'progress', Marxist and liberal alike, devolves from that theology, and represents an extremely difficult problematic, unsuited to simple-minded dismissals. Teleology has been a recurrent issue for practicing historians: see Chris Wickham, *Framing the Early Middle Ages, Europe and the Mediterranean, 400–800* (Oxford: Oxford University Press, 2005), *The Inheritance of Rome: Illuminating the Dark Ages 400–1000* (New York: Viking, 2009), and *Sleepwalking into a New World: The Emergence of Italian City Communes in the Twelfth Century* (Princeton, NJ: Princeton University Press, 2015); as well as *Historical Teleologies in the Modern World*, ed. by Henning Trüper, Dipesh Chakrabarty, and Sanjay Subrahmanyam (London: Bloomsbury, 2015).

of unfulfilled potentials, and the deferred fulfillment of potentiality. The temporal dimension introduces a gap between the introduction of the potential, its deposit in ideational form in the body politic, where it may subsist, half hidden, and ferment for a while or for a long time, possibly changing form, before its actualization. Particular paradoxical negations may be decided otherwise in the potential's futurity. Indeed, observation of contemporary social evolution suggests that the introduction of such potentials for change incite virulent antibodies that may defer actualization for substantial stretches of history. Thus, the vision of a fraternal democratic revolution of equaliberty, introduced long ago, continues to lead the double life of negated potentiality and fermenting potential.[8] So, alas, does the potentiality of utter enslavement of the productive forces of society. And so does the potentiality of altericide.[9]

It is the unexpected recognition of such historical twists and deferrals that may occasion the Benjaminian flash of retrospective understanding. The subject — for particular, local, circumstantial historical reasons — may grasp the valence of futurity in a particular non-fulfillment whose pertinence was not previously understood. Needless to say, ideological reasons most often attend such efforts at the burial of deferred potentials. But breaking through the dissembling wall of ideology is not at all impossible: all it takes is a social upheaval, a world war or two, a genocide here or there, to upset established ideological apple-carts, and constitute the ideological liberation of desubjectification.[10]

It is this kind of deferral, of cultural and ideological lag, that helps account for a number of puzzling phenomena in the European Middle Ages: the appearance of a child of Jewish converts two generations after the holocaust of 1096 in the Rhineland, in the region geographically just above Troyes, in the historical personage known as Chrétien de Troyes (from whose verse novels much of the history of European literature flows in unending deferred actualization); the appearance, within the thought occurring in the Christian Middle Ages, of theories of anti-authoritarian political self-determination, to the point of tyrannicide; and finally the appearance of political experimentation, sometimes requiring the active, willful decision to employ violence, with new communal modes of resistance, revolution, and self-determination, that would find their fulfillment only centuries later, in the collective decisions to employ violence in the creation of self-determining polities called 'communes' (including the communist potentiality traduced and betrayed in Stalinism, as well as the present-day betrayal of democracy in America). History comports multiple ruptures and continuities of the present's twisting infidelities with its constitutive pasts.

---

8   Etienne Balibar, *La Proposition de l'égaliberté: essais politiques 1989–2009* (Paris: Presses universitaires de France, 2010).
9   Dominique Quessada, *Court traité d'altéricide* (Paris: Verticales, Gallimard, 2007).
10 Haidu, 'The Dialectics of Unspeakability'. My own perception of certain things about the Middle Ages, things that had lain hidden and only perceptible in part, is entirely attributable to the combination of a capacity for intellectual labor with the desubjectifications of the Second World War.

On Dialectical Reading

Finally, the fact that potentiality is not materially or teleologically determinative, the fact that potentiality is not determinative in any sense whatever, but depends on later enactments for its actualizations, brings the question of reading to the fore. The text is not determinative of its readings: it lies on the page as a set of potentialities only. How these potentialities are actualized turns out to be quite unpredictable.

Ordinary experience suggests several different kinds of reading. Adolescence normalizes reading as a substitute for actual life, at least among certain adolescents: I certainly was one of those, for a period of time. Reading can also be an apprenticeship for writing, both as technical skill and personal configuration. Reading can be the experience of another world, one of aesthetic beauty. Or it can be the experience of another culture, a cultural alterity. In other words, reading is not a single experience. Reading exists in different forms and is constructed variously at different moments and in different circumstances.

Reality is not *in* the texts, nor do medieval texts 'represent' reality, as Erich Auerbach, following one nineteenth-century model, assumed all literary texts did or should.[11] But all literary texts are produced in a given reality, linguistic, literary, cultural, social, and historical, even as all great literary texts aim at transcending their given contexts of origin. There is no single, correct medieval readerly position for the modern reader to assume. 'Medieval' does designate a past set of realities objectively external to the modern reader, who is not, however, merely an epistemological prisoner in his or her house of language, or caught in an exclusive web of theory.

The modern reader engages in an on-going dialectical engagement with the medieval text, bringing to that encounter what he or she can of acquired skills and knowledge, of ethical and political commitment — if it is an encounter. At its best, that engagement attempts to recognize the specificity of the author's text, the author's historical situatedness, and the author's effort in the text to transcend that historical situatedness. All good readings are dialectical readings, and they are variable.

In this case, the encounter has lasted a long time, half a century or so. The present text is merely the latest of a series of conversations with the texts of Chrétien de Troyes that began during the late 1950s in privileged graduate seminars with Lawton P. G. Peckham and William T. H. Jackson at Columbia University, rigorous and intellectually generous professors both, to whom Kurt Lewent brought a salutary additional dose of European philology — the Old Philology, of course — encounters that continued through the usual series of professional publications. The present work continues that on-going conversation.

My own introduction to medieval poetry had been through the works of Ezra Pound, read enthusiastically in high school, before the issue of Pound's Fascism came to the fore: his own poems, translation, criticism, even a book which problematized

---

11 Erich Auerbach, *Mimesis*, trans. by Willard R. Trask (Princeton, NJ: Princeton University Press, 1953). On this topic, see Peter Haidu, 'A Perfume of Reality? Desublimating the Courtly', in *Shaping Courtliness in Medieval France*, ed. by O'Sullivan and Shepard, pp. 25–45.

reading itself (the *ABC of Reading*) were primary. Around Pound, in my mind, clustered not only the work of other poets like Marianne Moore and William Carlos Williams, as well as mysterious forces named Hart Crane and Gerard Manley Hopkins, and one who was pure delight: Dame Edith Sitwell. Around the poets clustered the American New Criticism, which prepared the way for the *Nouvelle Critique* of French Structuralism — déjà vu all over again, discovered only after my graduate work. The discovery of a medieval rhetoric of irony in Chrétien de Troyes, which marked my entry into medieval studies in 1968, was a willed historical extension of the irony of modernity in the form of medieval grammar and rhetoric. Its very possibility suggests a relative formal universal, within Western European civilization at least.

In preparing to write a doctoral thesis on Chrétien de Troyes, I naturally read all the texts assigned to my author. That included his early work *Philomena*. It was horrifying. Worse, nothing in my mental universe, as then furnished by extensive independent reading and the discipline of literary history, nothing prepared me to deal with *Philomena*. I read it, horrified, put it down, and shoved it aside. Nothing in the next several decades required me to turn my attention to it.

Only when I retired in 2003 and installed myself to live in Paris, quite outside disciplinary and professional frameworks, did I return to *Philomena*. That was when the kind of reading recorded here became possible. It hearkens back to a kind of commentary practiced in my dissertation, which itself echoed a far earlier commentator: the fourth-century commentator Servius on Virgil, without whom our understanding of the *Aeneid* would be far poorer. It is hardly a naive, untutored reading. It is, however, a reading no longer bound by disciplinary norms. It is a reading that, quite consciously, sets those disciplinary norms in question on the basis of close reading that is holistic, totalizing, and historically contextualizing. That reading could be strengthened by a familiarity with a varied sense of Jewish culture and intellectual life in the twelfth century which I do not command at first hand in Hebrew. To some degree, even this ignorance may follow Chrétien's lead.

The discussion of *Philomena* seeks to elicit the subjectivity implicit in the text itself, rather than imposing on it either a pre-supposed Jewish identity or, as has been done frequently enough, a doctrine of 'courtly love'. The essential thing is that Chrétien's texts are always poetry, that — as Alain Badiou asserts — poetry is a site of thinking, a truth procedure prior to philosophy or theology, and that Chrétien's works are original explorations of human experience in a real historical world, even if they are necessarily coded in historical conventions and vocabularies of their times. Throughout, the mode of discourse followed as a model is that discovered in graduate school, commentary, and most fully exemplified by Servius on Vergil. While I cannot hope to furnish the amount of original historical information as did my model, the notion of service to an author, as well as to a notion of civilization, is very much the same.

PART I

Identity and History

(i) Christian the Goy

In the spring of 1096, responding to Pope Urban II's call for a military expedition against the East at Clermont-Ferrand the preceding fall (what would come to be known as the First Crusade), a wide variety of persons began to mass in the staging area of the Rhineland, including an international group of mid-level feudal powers, magnates like Thomas of Marle and Clarembold of Vendeuil, who recognized the local leadership of one of their own, Emicho of Floheim.[1] These feudal warriors of mounted violence rousted local burghers and peasants to a hunt for Jews, over a period of weeks scouring towns, cities, valleys, and mountains to make the Rhineland *Judenfrei*, whether by savage massacre, forced conversion, or both (accounts vary). In some cases, Jews denied their persecutors victory by re-inventing *Kiddush Hashem* ('Sanctification of the Name'): individual or collective suicide. The forced conversions would later be lifted, in spite of doctrinal problems.

The outline of the basic facts is not in dispute. Details are lacking, and interpretations conflict, but the basic outline of the Event is clear. Large disagreements exist among serious historians about its importance and its interpretation, from the numbers of victims to the impact on the culture and consciousness of the survivors. This polyvalence is a prime example of how history and historiography intertwine, and explains the rather peculiar shape of this chapter, including the presentation of historical facts along with discussions of historiographical issues.[2]

Chrétien: Writer, Subject, and Identity

Chrétien de Troyes's works and influence are well known: he himself is not. What we think we know about him comes entirely from his works. There is no

---

[1] The literature on Urban's call to crusade is enormous and well-known; on the class of magnates, see Conor Kostick, *The Social Structure of the First Crusade* (Leiden: Brill, 2008); on Emicho, Kenneth Stow, 'Conversion, Apostasy, and Apprehensiveness: Emicho of Floheim and the Fear of Jews in the Twelfth Century', *Speculum*, 76.4 (2001), 911–33. Editor's note: see also Benjamin Z. Kedar, 'Emicho of Flonheim and the Apocalyptic Motif in the 1096 Massacre: Between Paul Alphandéry and Alphonse Dupront', in *Conflict and Religious Conversation in Latin Christendom: Studies in Honour of Ora Limor*, ed. by Israel Jacob Yuval and Ram Ben-Shalom (Turnhout: Brepols, 2014), pp. 87–97.
[2] Editor's note: In addition to what follows below, see the Appendix for further discussion of historiographical issues and an 'Incomplete List of Events in the Twelfth Century that Would Have Concerned Jews and Jewish Converts'.

independent historical documentation on this author, his social status, or his life. His identity is entirely questionable.

For reasons both theoretical and political, one should be wary of the hypertrophic identitarianism rampant in Anglo-Saxon theory, which all too readily confuses identity with the question of the subject. There is good historical reason for the American obsession with identity: it derives from the nation's original sin, its founding in slavery, a fact historical and material which continues to corrupt the nation's politics. Nevertheless, in spite of this wariness, identity is central to the present inquiry into medieval texts and their author. Identity sometimes forces certain questions upon the subject. Such forcing occurs under the subject's necessary transcendence of identity.[3] The subject is what acts. In the case of a writer, the subject's immediately defining acts are his texts. The writer's subjectivity as writer is coterminous with his texts, particularly in the absence of documentation regarding either his identity or his personal, 'subjective' life, an absence characteristic of early medieval writers.

In the modern aesthetic regime, the artwork is accompanied by an identifiable author.[4] This 'identifiability' is exactly what inexists for the twelfth-century vernacular artist. For commoners like the *jongleurs*, oral poets of the epic, lyric inventors like Bernart of Ventadour or Jaufré Rudel, or the narrative poets who launch the novel in France like the authors of the *Thèbes* and the *Eneas* along with Chrétien de Troyes, no attachment to the identitarian grid of society is really possible. In spite of the elucubrations of modern scholarship, it is difficult to credit the equation of *auctor* with *auctoritas* in any sense other than a general socio-political admiration for aesthetic achievement of a universal order. Their authority, insofar as they have any, derives from admiration for the poetic power of their words. The poetic achievement of their work attracts whatever authority is granted them by society.

Chrétien's identity reduces to the body of his work. Moderns tout medieval anonymity, but Chrétien always 'signs' his work. Except, of course, that he doesn't. A signature, in the literal sense, is defined by the signator's physical contact with the traces that remain on paper or parchment.[5] We never possess an authentic signature of this author, only representations of signatures. These representations, the contrary of authentic signatures, are numerous and cohesive enough that if a name is identity, Chrétien's got it. I will continue to use the word 'sign' in this secondary sense, derivative and contrary: nowhere do we possess Chrétien de Troyes's actual signature, only literary simulacra that establish a literary identity.

---

3   For 'the subject', see the 'Introduction', in Peter Haidu, *Subject Medieval/Modern: Text and Governance in the Middle Ages* (Stanford, CA: Stanford University Press, 2004). The notion of 'subject position' (not identical to that of 'subject') was originally sketched out in Ernesto Laclau and Chantal Mouffe, *Hegemony and Socialist Strategy: Towards a Radical Democratic Politics*, trans. by Winston Moore and Paul Cammack (London: Verso, 1985); Laclau returned to it in *Emancipations* (London: Verso, 1996). For discussion of specular identity in medieval texts, see Donald Maddox, *Fictions of Identity in Chrétien de Troyes* (Cambridge: Cambridge University Press, 2006). But the notion of identity, crucial to contemporary theory and politics in both the United States and France, where it is largely suppressed, is in fact profoundly ambiguous.

4   Sven Lütticken, '*Personafication*', *New Left Review*, 96 (November-December 2015), 101–28.

5   See Béatrice Fraenkel, *La Signature: genèse d'un signe* (Paris: Gallimard, 1992).

Chrétien signs *Erec et Enide* as 'Chrétien de Troyes'. The Troyes from which the author signs his work is not a fictive construct irrelevant to the political and economic lives of the people of his time.[6] Troyes was the political capital of the principality of Champagne, a thriving, intensely politicized mini-state with a cycle of continuing international trade fairs drawing goods and merchants from all Europe including Russia and the Near East. Troyes, in the twelfth century, was also the lively center of European Jewish studies, its yeshiva founded in the eleventh century by Rashi, acronym for *Rabbenu Shlomo Yitzhaki*, Rabbi Solomon ben Isaac (1040–c. 1105).[7] Among other things, Rashi was famous for the *responsa* he issued: binding rules adjudicating issues of practical living in a hostile environment, based in the study of Hebrew, Torah, and Talmud. Rashi's eminence in Bible and Talmudic commentary was unmatched in his own time. His grandsons continued the tradition as the leading Tosafists of their generation. Students came from all over Europe to study with Rashi and his descendants, as contemporary Latinate students flocked to the schools of Paris that became the Sorbonne.

After *Erec et Enide*, our author signs his later works — *Cligès, Lancelot, Yvain,* and *Perceval* — simply as 'Chrétien', signaling that he was becoming better known and more secure in his place, whatever that was. The compiler of the fourteenth-century *Ovide moralisé* will refer to the author of *Philomena* as 'Chrétien', a name universally understood in the world of letters. Chrétien's verse novels, all written in sprightly, rhymed octosyllabics, are fairly long, between six and seven thousand lines each, except for the *Perceval*, incomplete at over nine thousand lines. In the narrative system of the time, these figure as long narratives, as against the *lai*, which could be as short as a couple of hundred lines, but occasionally went over one thousand. The contrast is that between the novel and the short story. The different lengths also implied structural and aesthetic differences, of course. Chrétien also wrote love lyrics, and translations from Ovid.

Chrétien's first surviving work is *Philomena*.[8] The poem translates one of Ovid's

---

6   'Troyes' was not Homer's Troy, as Roger Dragonetti once maintained in *La Vie de la lettre au moyen âge: le Conte du graal* (Paris: Seuil, 1980), p. 20. Dragonetti excluded history from the text in order to define its 'littérarité', the self-reflexivity of the text. That form of self-reflexivity is a factitious construct which excludes political and economic history.

7   On medieval Champagne, the classic works are Michel Bur, *La Formation du comté de Champagne, v.950–v.1150*, Mémoires des Annales de l'Est, 54 (Nancy: Université de Nancy II, 1977), and Robert Henri Bautier, 'Les Foires de Champagne: recherches sur une évolution historique', in *La Foire*, Recueils de la Société Jean Bodin, 5 (Brussels: Librairie Encyclopédique, 1953), 97–145. On the Jewish community of Troyes, see Emily Taitz, *The Jews of Medieval France: The Community of Champagne* (Westport, CT: Greenwood Press, 1994); *Church, State, and Jew in the Middle Ages*, ed. by Robert Chazan (West Orange, NJ: Behrman House, 1980), and Robert Chazan, *The Jews of Medieval Western Christendom, 1000–1500* (Cambridge: Cambridge University Press, 2006); as well as the literature on Rashi and descendants, especially Irving A. Agus, *Urban Civilization in Pre-Crusade Europe*, 2 vols (New York: Yeshiva University Press, 1965). Editor's note: see also Simon Schwarzfuchs, *Rachi de Troyes* (Paris: Albin Michel, 2005); and more detailed materials in *Rashi et la culture juive en France du Nord au moyen âge*, ed. by Gilbert Dahan, Gérard Nahon, and Elie Nicolas (Paris & Louvain: Peeters, 1997).

8   An excellent synthesis of scholarly criticism, which fuses what can be saved of a sorry critical tradition while adding important original insights, is Roberta L. Krueger, '*Philomena*: Brutal

Metamorphoses. Here, the author's signature is odd. Instead of either 'Chrétien' or 'Chrétien de Troyes', he names himself 'Crestiens li gois'. This has long puzzled scholars. It raises all sorts of questions. The poem is relatively short: it numbers 1,468 lines. That odd name occurs at line 734. Do the math: the author names himself at exactly the mid-point of his text. He places himself precisely at the center of the poem. Is the poem somehow *about* our twelfth-century 'Crestiens'? The centered signature poses the question: is *Philomena*, somehow or other, granting multiple transformations, a self-narration?

And what does *Crestiens li gois* mean? The word *gois* is not common in Old French: you won't find the word in Greimas's standard dictionary of Old French.[9] One grammatical clue: Old French retains a simplified version of Latin declensions. Usually, it's the accusative that survives. Final *-s* is the nominative, the case of the subject. So what do you get as the normal form if you subtract the nominative *-s*? What you get is unexpected. You get something of a surprise, even a paradox. You get, as self-designated *auteur* of *Philomena*, 'Christian the Goy'.

The author's self-designation as *Crestiens li gois* is a complicated and witty linguistic manoeuver that does several things simultaneously, reaching beyond the somber tone of *Philomena* toward Chrétien's later manner. It is a particularly disarming move which invokes a radically new linguistic and political situation, in which a convert both acknowledges his complicated status and steals a march on his interlocutors in a duel of serious charms. The manoeuver will be explored more specifically as the semiotic rhetoric of a witty, ingenious Jewish convert. Its *explication de texte*, however, requires some social and historical contextualizing.

Converts in the Twelfth Century

In 1096, as European Jews became the first victims of the First Crusade, they faced a radical alternative. Jews could stretch their necks to the sword or endure forced conversion, at least sometimes.[10] The preservation of life has always been

---

Transitions and Courtly Transformations in Chrétien's Old French Translation', in *A Companion to Chrétien de Troyes*, ed. by Norris J. Lacy and Joan Tasker Grimbert (Cambridge: Brewer, 2005), pp. 87–102. The standard critical edition of *Philomena* is that of Cornélis de Boer; the text used here is *Pyrame et Thisbé, Narcisse, Philomena*, ed. by Baumgartner.

9   A. J. Greimas, *Dictionnaire de l'ancien français* (Paris: Larousse, 1968). Godefroy's older dictionary does have an entry *goi*, with the meaning of 'pruning hook'. An anomalous reading was that of Raphael Levy who read, not 'li gois' but 'li goz', meaning 'little dog', reinterpreted as 'dwarf', and concluded that Chrétien de Troyes was a dwarf: 'Old French Goz and Crestiens Li Gois', *PMLA*, 46.2 (June 1931), 312–20, and again in 'Etat présent des études sur l'attribution de *Philomena*', *Lettres Romanes*, 5.1 (1951), 46–52.

10   The alternative was explored in texts called, with terrible inadequacy, the 'Hebrew chronicles', available in English since 1977: *The Jews and the Crusaders: The Hebrew Chronicles of the First and Second Crusades*, ed. and trans. by Shlomo Eidelberg (Madison: University of Wisconsin Press, 1977), and in Robert Chazan, *European Jewry and the First Crusade* (Berkeley: University of California Press, 1987). Whether this alternative really existed has been questioned: David Malkiel, 'Destruction or Conversion: Intention and Reaction, Crusaders and Jews, in 1096', *Jewish History*, 15 (2001), 257–80. Perhaps different groups of Crusaders followed different protocols in massacring Jews in particular pogroms.

praiseworthy in Judaism. In 1096, some Jews accepted death meekly. Some converted. Some re-invented heroic ideological warfare. These alternatives will be revisited. For now, we examine the situation, later in the twelfth century, of those who converted.

For those who accepted forced conversion, some would be freed from their forced conversion after political and legal wrangling at the highest levels of governance: the question pitted empire against the integrity of church doctrine. Others would remain in the status of converts. For those in the latter category, for those who endured as converts, that meant accepting unrelenting Christian surveillance lest they relapse into their former error. Those who accepted release from forced conversion and returned to their original status would once again endure campaigns of pressure on Jews to convert to Christianity in order to allow a happy, final, totalizing, universal, ultra-messianic apocalypse. Potential apostatic relapse might replace the former pressure to convert. Being either Jew or convert was not a comfortable position during the twelfth-century renaissance.

Both Jews and Christians viewed the convert with suspicion and resentment. Most converts, however, did not wash their linen in public. As one classic article on the topic pointed out in the 1980s, information on real-life converts is generally scant. 'Jewish apostasy in medieval Christian Europe' long remained 'a relatively uncharted phenomenon'. Apostasy or conversion 'endangered the sanctity of the most hallowed relationships in the [Jewish] community — between parent and child, husband and wife, rabbi and disciple'. Primary sources are scanty; rabbinic *responsa* tend to deal with individual cases only. 'Apostates themselves only occasionally made lasting marks on the society and culture of Latin Christendom [...] many must have remained on the margins of medieval society.'[11]

There was good reason for this informational scarcity. Converts did not want publicity. One scholar has noted the convert's strategy with great acuity, particularly when conversion had led to the assumption of religious orders:

> One should take into account the possibility that a convert, always under suspicion, might well wish to avoid the consequences of appearing to have remained a Jew in monk's clothing. Caught in attacks of anti-Semitism, Jewish converts [...] have sought to defend themselves by minimizing the residue of their pre-Christian commitment and maximizing, in stereotypes familiar to their attackers, the degree of their assimilation.[12]

A few exceptional cases do stand out. One was that of Judah, the young Jewish moneylender, renamed 'Hermann' upon conversion, long taken as the author of an authentic individual account of personal conversion, an *Opusculum* that dates between the First and the Second Crusades. The history of modern scholarship on this text is of some interest. In 1987 Judah/Hermann was one of a small handful of individuals whose texts exemplified the situation of the individual medieval convert

---

11   Jeremy Cohen, 'The Mentality of the Medieval Jewish Apostate: Peter Alfonsi, Hermann of Cologne, and Pablo Christiani', in *Jewish Apostasy in the Modern World*, ed. by Todd M. Endelman (London: Holmes & Meyer, 1987), pp. 20–47 (p. 22).
12   Karl Morrison, *Conversion and Text* (Charlottesville: University of Virginia Press, 1992), p. 40.

or apostate. Given many areas of uncertainty, Judah still could figure as the scion of an upper-middle-class Jewish family looking for stability and security in a hostile and insecure world, where courtesy, kindness, and gentleness worked wonders.[13] Even fifteen or so years later, Judah/Hermann, as an individual, could help fill in a picture of a remarkably fluid social and intellectual world where social conversation seemed not all that distant from religious conversion.[14]

Another major discussion of conversion, under the banner of hermeneutics, had the great virtue of recognizing that conversion implied a before and an after. Conversion is not only a positive event, a turning toward, it is also a negative event, a turning away from, a turn away from a past which may not be easy and total, and which may indeed overshadow the understanding of the new. 'The text might have a prehistory that the author did not acknowledge'.[15] The scholar might seek out that complexity in order to grasp the significance of the whole. Indeed, one wonders if Karl Morrison, in 1992 in his first page on Judah ha Levi's text, did not have in view the kind of interpretation — 'a fabrication [...] a pious fraud made by Christian hands' (p. 39) — that would make its appearance two decades later, where conversion's ambiguous status as a before-and-after event was erased in favor of a pure, de-temporalized, document considered the work of a religious community.

The great medievalist William Chester Jordan could ask as late as 2001: 'What sort of person, finally, was Judah?' and reach back to Jeremy Cohen's research for an answer: a 'child [...] searching for security and meaning in life as his adolescence drew to a close [...] a groping adolescent'.[16] Jordan, a historian doing poetic analysis, demonstrated in his thoughtful, historically informed interpretation of Judah's dream vision that there was no conflict between taking Judah's *Opusculum* as a literary text *and* simultaneously as the personal statement of an individual subject.[17]

Since 2003, however, discussion of the *Opusculum* has been dominated by Jean-Claude Schmitt's brilliant work, radically revising the terms of discussion.[18] At close to four hundred pages, Schmitt's tome presents as a masterwork of cultural history which frequently exceeds its nominal topic: the twenty-page *Opusculum*, usually attributed to Judah/Hermann *quondam Judeus*, a convert to the Premonstratensian abbey of Cappenberg. As important as Schmitt's book unquestionably is, however, it is highly debatable. Only two or three points can be addressed here.

One initial point is that the book continues Schmitt's long dispute with the

---

13   Cohen, 'The Mentality of the Medieval Jewish Apostate'.
14   Jay Rubenstein, *Guibert de Nogent: Portrait of a Medieval Mind* (London: Routledge, 2002), pp. 118–20.
15   Morrison, *Conversion and Text*, p. 45.
16   William Chester Jordan, 'Adolescence and Conversion in the Middle Ages', in *Jews and Christians in Twelfth-century Europe*, ed. by Michael A. Signer and John van Engen (Notre Dame, IN: University of Notre Dame Press, 2001), pp. 77–93 (p. 87), citing Cohen, 'The Mentality of the Medieval Jewish Apostate'.
17   In interpreting the dream vision, Jordan understands Emperor Henry V giving Judah a white horse as a symbol of voluntary conversion ('Adolescence and Conversion in the Middle Ages', pp. 84–85).
18   Jean-Claude Schmitt, *La Conversion d'Hermann le Juif: autobiographie, histoire et fiction* (Paris: Seuil, 2003), also includes a French translation in place of the English translation offered by Karl Morrison.

notion of the medieval origins of the modern notion of the 'individual', a highly complex issue.[19] While Schmitt earlier found the connection problematic, here he denies it radically. Indeed, the fundamental argument of the book is to deny authorship of the *Opusculum* to Judah/Hermann, and reassign it to the monastic community of Cappenberg: the individual author has been obliterated by the community. All that is left is a text that, according to Schmitt, aligns perfectly with institutional ideology, with no leftovers, no gaps, no spaces, no wrinkles, nothing missing. Individual authorship has been disappeared and reassigned to the monastic community.

At first, Schmitt insists on the complex name that substituted for the Jewish Judah, or, as he writes, 'Judas'. Hermann *quondam Judeus was* a complex signifier that insisted on the hybrid nature of the person named by the society naming the person. But in the longer run, Schmitt is intent on proving that the thing named, the individual person, the signified, did not exist. At least, Schmitt makes it impossible to think that he did exist, in effect eradicating another bothersome Jew.

A second point is that Schmitt denies autobiography 'in the modern sense' not only to Judah/Hermann, but to the Middle Ages. Schmitt imports a term from the original title of Guibert de Nogent's self-writing. Autobiography does not exist in the Middle Ages, he says, only a 'narration monodique' which he limits to confession, consecrated as the bond of a subject and God. This declaration has wide-ranging effects, in effect, castrating Peter Abelard's intent to write his version of his life for an unnamed friend and reassigning it a confessional purpose. Even major sections of Guibert's own text (the historical sections, like the description of the commune in Laon, or the slaughter of Jews in Rouen, and the salvation of one young Jew by two acts of Christian charity) wind up being problematized. Have they no *historical* existence, outside their participation in Guibert's confession? Do we want to accept the negation of his text's value as historical witness to events in Laon and Rouen?

No medieval self-discourse outside the confessional: this incision, tantamount to a willed excision of history, becomes grievous when it is suggested that the Jew is incapable of a kind of abyssal introspection available only to the Christian: the Jew 'ne saurait [...] ouvrir entièrement son âme, connaître les abîmes de la conscience réservée à l'introspection chrétienne'. Hermann cannot be an individual or a singular 'author'. Rather than a person, he is a *persona*, a mask, a double visage, 'au sens moderne que nous donnons à ces mots' (p. 88).[20] The individual person was swallowed by the monastic community: what was once a person becomes nothing but an ideological function (what an Althusserian might call an 'ideologeme') to be discarded.

Yet, if at times, Schmitt seems to have let himself be sucked into a deferred maelstrom of structuralist self-reflexivity exclusive of all reference to non-textual

---

19 Major contributors to the discussion have been Colin Morris, Robert Hanning, and Carolyn Walker Bynum, as well as Schmitt: see Peter Haidu, 'Althusser Anonymous in the Middle Ages', *Exemplaria*, 7 (1995), 5–74, and *The Subject Medieval/Modern*, pp. 3–4, 96, 115, 216, 279.
20 Schmitt, *La Conversion d'Hermann le Juif*, pp. 87, 88.

reality, at other times he is pulled, by the very historical nature of the text, in exactly the opposite direction, to consider issues well beyond 'the text itself'. As a follower of Genette, Todorov, and Bremond, Schmitt insists on the necessity of focusing on the narrative structures of the text; yet he is also led to assert — for no reason discernible 'within' the text itself — that *'Le génocide ne date pas du Moyen Age'*.[21]

The immediate context modifies the assertion, which is simultaneously true (albeit in a ridiculous sense) and profoundly false. The assertion occurs in a paragraph that notes several things. Forced baptisms existed in the Middle Ages. Medieval Jews suffered expulsions repeatedly ('expulsions à répétition') as of the thirteenth century (they actually began in the twelfth). He then asserts that 'never did a medieval sovereign order the mass death [of Jews]' ('jamais un souverain médiéval n'a ordonné leur mort en masse'). But, of course, the state did not exist at Judah's time: sovereignty did not have the same effective meaning. Genocide was only defined and declared a crime by international decree in 1948, when the General Assembly of the United Nations adopted the Convention on the Prevention and Punishment of the Crime of Genocide.[22] Schmitt is right, technically: legally speaking, the crime of genocide did not exist in the Middle Ages. Hence, *'Le génocide ne date pas du Moyen Age'*.

On the other hand, it is the kind of 'being right' that renders 'being right' meaningless. While no document exists demonstrating that either a medieval sovereign or a medieval pope ordered the mass slaughter of Jews, the same can be said of Adolf Hitler. That no written document subsists demonstrating that Adolf Hitler or Heinrich Himmler signed off on a direct written order for the Final Solution is a staple of Holocaust Studies. No one concludes that its absence absolves the Third Reich of moral, political, or legal responsibility for the massacres. It takes a little more to wipe the question of genocide off the table than the demand for a document signed by a sovereign head of state. The silence regarding the crime was a studied strategy.

When juxtaposed to the brute facts on the ground, that legalism is a pyrrhic victory of cultural warfare. On the ground, on the territories that would retroactively come to be known as France and Germany, feudal magnates from France and Germany, gathering for what would come to be known as the 'First Crusade' — its baptism as the 'First Crusade' was also retroactive — led local farmers and burghers in repeated, intense scourings of towns and territories where Jews were known to reside. They rounded up all the Jews they could find, forcing neighbors to identify Jewish residences. They faced each and every Jew they could roust out of their houses and out of the woods and in the archbishopric, where the Jews had taken collective refuge under the archbishop's protection, with the absolute choice of death or forced conversion. Of those who did not accept forced conversion to Christianity, they sliced every single Jewish neck — male, female, child of any sex — with their good, well-sharpened Christian swords, and tossed the corpses out the windows into ever-growing piles in the courtyard.

21   Ibid., p. 94.
22   But note that retroactivity was a legal principle involved in the Nuremberg trials themselves.

Oddly enough, Schmitt makes no mention of the Hebrew chronicles where these events are recounted in gruesome detail, texts which should be required reading in any introduction to medieval civilization, any introduction to Western civilization, or indeed, in any introduction to Christianity. Many Christian intellectuals of the Middle Ages, intellectuals and historians like Albert of Aachen, Ekkehart of Aura, Otto of Friesing, recoiled in horror at the Event. The mass slaughter of Jews under Christian protection, the forced conversion of Jews at sword's edge, these were radical perversions of Christianity, as Schmitt's discussion of *Freiwillikeit* shows he understands full well. Modern intellectuals have all too often lost the bond with their medieval forbears, and have retreated into administrative academic corners of ethnicity, imagining that the historiographical issues of the Rhineland in 1096 or the ethical issues of York in 1190 concern only some imagined 'Jewish community' and can safely be relegated to a sub-discipline of Jewish Studies.[23]

Nevertheless, the fact on the ground is that Christian knights on the way to the Crusades slaughtered every single Jew they could lay their hands on, excepting only those who accepted forced conversion. Lacking both Zyklon-B and orders from a sovereign other than a despicable Emicho of Flonheim, Thomas of Marle, Clarembold of Vendeuil, they attempted genocide with the burghers at hand. Like Hitler, they did not quite succeed, but that was not for lack of trying.

At the level of praxis, the European Middle Ages initiated genocide in 1096. The dimensions of the genocides are not comparable numerically, but the principle was identical: killing the Jew, making Europe *Judenfrei*, ridding Europe of Jews and Judaism. After the spring of 1096, thanks to those feudal magnates and the ideology that loosened their hate on those Jews, genocide lodged as a potentiality at the heart of Europe, sovereignty or not, numerical comparability or not. The Holocaust was not teleologically determined as a result. The Holocaust might have been avoided, but genocide lay at the heart of Europe as a potential since 1096.[24]

Schmitt is far too sensitive a reader, far too moral a thinker, and far too culturally-aware a cultural historian, to have the wool pulled over his eyes by his own intently willed interpretation. The medieval name given Judah says a great deal. Hermann *quondam Judeus*: from Jew, Judah became a Christian, a *conversus* who had been baptized, then became a canon, and finally a priest in the order of the Premonstratensian monks at Cappenberg who made him abbot. Throughout his life as a Christian, he remained a convert. His former identity tagged along in his name. As Schmitt concludes his book, such is the ultimate law of conversion for beings, words, places, and things: 'Et pourtant, il reste un "converti". Telle est la loi ultime

---

23   David Nirenberg, 'The Rhineland Massacre of Jews in the First Crusade: Memories. Medieval and Modern', in *Medieval Concepts of the Past: Ritual, Memory, Historiography*, ed. by Gerd Althoff, Johannes Fried, and Patrick J. Geary (Cambridge: Cambridge University Press, Germanic Historical Institute, 2002), pp. 279–309; Hannah Johnson, 'Massacre and Memory: Ethics and Method in Recent Scholarship on Jewish Martyrdom', in *Christians and Jews in Angevin England*, ed. by Sarah Rees Jones and Sethina Watson (York: York Medieval Press, Boydell & Brewer: 2013), 261–77.

24   The philosophical discussion of potentiality has to return to Aristotle's difficulties to avoid Agamben's Heideggerian contaminations. Editor's note: see the discussion of potentiality in the Introduction.

de la conversion des êtres, des mots, des lieux et des choses [...]. La conversion transforme, elle n'abolit pas'.²⁵ Conversion transforms, it does not abolish. Does one detect some note of puzzlement in this final remark, addressed not only to the life of one convert, or indeed at Jewish converts in general, but at Christianity itself?

In fact, the name-tag affixed to Judah, 'Hermann *quondam Judeus*', specifies quite exactly the problem with the theory of supersession as represented by the Old and New Testaments, the issue implicit in Schmitt's book, which is the issue of Christianity itself: its continued dependence for its self-definition on the Judaism it claims to replace. It can be stated, in a kind of post-structuralist spectrality, as a formula: X — *quondam* — [W = anti-X]. The equation would be a thinned-out allegoreme for the living and intense relation of interdependence between Judaism and Christianity, where 'W' is simultaneously antecedent to X, the origin of X, its permanent antagonist, and its permanent guest. This is the relationship Jews tolerated thanks to a discipline developed over centuries of exile, and which popes and feudal warriors found intolerable. Their relation of interdependence was absolutely necessary to the existence of Christianity as a religious belief system, and to Judaism for mere physical survival, as Augustine recognized. The understanding of that complex contract is what was severed by the mass massacres of 1096 and their sequela.

A striking contrast to the problematics marked by the hybrid name Hermann *quondam Judeus* is provided by another convert, who made conversion pay in spades in terms of secular self-aggrandizement: the roughly contemporary Petrus Alfonsi, a Jewish convert from Andalucia. Born Moses, a brilliant intellectual versed in Hebrew, as well as Arabic and Christian sciences, with sovereign disdain for mere *grammatica* and a deep attachment to astronomy, his primary social status was as court physician to King Alfonso I, and he may also have served as physician to Henry I of England. Petrus Alfonsi is best known as the author of a work oddly titled the *Disciplina clericalis*, a collection of Mediterranean folk tales, reinterpreted in remarkable and unexpected manners, addressing a world of narrative alterity from a universalist interpretive perspective not identified with either Jewish or Christian modes of interpretive techniques: it seems to bespeak a universal interpretant.²⁶ A bespoke universalism is characteristic not only of a certain group of converts in the face of contradictory religious ideologies, but of Jewish émigrés forced into a second-degree nomadism by later political upheavals.

Alas, this brilliant intellectual, Petrus Alfonsi, not only converted from Judaism to Christianity, he also turned his undoubted intellectual talents aggressively against his own people of origin, using a universalizing rationality in a *Dialogus Petri et Moysi Iudei* to initiate a savage polemical movement *adversus Judeos*. If Rashi and Maimonides urged Jewish communities to receive converts warmly, both thinkers probably referred to the victims of forced conversion like those of 1096, not performers of hate like Petrus Alfonsi. He used an existing class difference

---

25 Schmitt, *La Conversion d'Hermann le Juif*, p. 240.
26 The change in narrative perspective might be compared to the fate of Celtic narrative material later in the century.

within Jewish communities throughout Europe — that of the rabbinical elite and its study of Talmud — as a wedge to label contemporary Jewry corrupt and evil, in contrast to an assertedly rational Christianity, faithful by contrast to the sacred biblical text. Petrus Alfonsi's attack on Judaism thus preceded by a generation the more famous attack *adversus Judeos* of Peter the Venerable. His was ultimately more damaging, perhaps, but Petrus Alfonsi's was an attack from the inside, with intimate knowledge of the Jewish texts and the theology they bore. Petrus Alfonsi was the Trojan Horse within the House of Judaism, the treacherous Jew who sold out to a rapidly expanding, oppressively hegemonic power.[27] He may have been the original source of much Christian anti-Semitism. As such, Petrus Alfonsi represented exactly what a hybrid and universalist Jewish convert would have wanted to avoid.

Crestiens li gois, as will be seen, proposed quite a different alternative, unique and non-reproducible: a poetic program of radical poetic invention out of total abjection, a metamorphosis inserted into Ovid's metamorphosis to transcend the moral barbarism which is the young poet's world in *Philomena*. Within an aesthetic world of conventionalism, *Crestiens li gois*, somewhat like Rimbaud in the *lettre du voyant*, published a manifesto calling for the invention of a new language, 'nouviax signes', a programmatic manifesto which Chrétien de Troyes would carry out.

Christian the Goy

Both Judah/Hermann *quondam Judeus* and Petrus Alfonsi achieved exactly what Chrétien de Troyes avoided: personal identity as a convert. More specifically, Chrétien de Troyes avoided identity as a Jew, or a convert, or a descendent of converts. He was never labeled *quondam*. To some degree, this lack of identity was implicit in the choice of writing in the vernacular: lack of biographical information, as we have seen, was normal for vernacular authors not of elite status. Chrétien's self-awareness as a writer, announced in his prologues, might have countered the tendency towards avoidance of identity. But that strategy had not yet been completely adopted in composing *Philomena*. Hence the word-play in which he slips in a side-wards allusion to his identity, never to be repeated, in the exact center of the poem.

In the very center of *Philomena*, there is Chrétien's self-naming as 'Christian the Goy': 'Ce conte Crestïens li gois' (l. 734). *Goy*, of course, is Hebrew for the non-Jew. *Goy* goes back to the Bible, to what Christians call 'the Old Testament', where it occurs a number of times, meaning something like 'the nations', as opposed to Jews.[28] As such, it was current in the Middle Ages. The expression *goy* (*goyim*), had some currency among at least some Christians. Bernard Gui instructs the inquisitor, questioning potential apostates, to find out whether they pray against the *goyim* and

---

27 On Alfonsi, see John Tolan, *Petrus Alfonsi and his Medieval Readers* (Florida: University Press of Florida, 1993), and Wikipedia, 'Petrus Alphonsi' <https://en.wikipedia.org/wiki/Petrus_Alphonsi> [accessed 21 January 2020].
28 Structurally speaking then, *goy* in Hebrew is an analogue to *barbaroi* in Greek for 'the other', with the potential for turning into 'the Other'.

clerics: 'quomodo Judei orant contra goym et contra clerum Romane ecclesie'.[29]

Now, 'Christian the Goy' is logically redundant: a Christian is *goy* by definition. *Crestiens li gois* is using his own name to play with language in a manner that will return later in his career with *Erec et Enide* and *Cligès*. But what *cultural* sense does 'Christian the Goy' make in mid-twelfth-century France? What cultural sense does the statement make in a *social* context? The redundancy is doubly assertive: it asserts 'X' + 'XX' — except that 'X' is Old French and 'XX' is a term in Hebrew! *Crestiens li gois* is a bilingual denomination of redundancy. *Crestiens li gois* is assertive of Christian *not* being a Jew. It sounds like an assertion against a contrary expectation, something like the interjection '*Si!*' in modern French, which introduces an affirmative asserted against an anticipated negative. Under what circumstances would it make sense to identify oneself — if one's name is 'Christian' — as '*not* a Jew'? *Crestiens li gois* sounds like an assertion made in the face of the expectation of 'Christian the Jew', an oxymoron that fits perfectly Chrétien's taste for paradox and irony.

Culturally, it makes sense for one social category: a convert named 'Christian'. Was this 'Christian of Troyes' a Jewish convert? The assertion by this 'Christian of Troyes' that he really *was* a Christian, that he should be named 'Christian the Goy', would have made sense against a socio-cultural expectation of being tagged 'Chrétien *quondam Judeus*', as was the convert formerly called Judah, known as Hermann since his conversion, but especially as Hermann *quondam Judeus*. It would have made sense, in a certain socio-cultural context, and within a certain socio-linguistic context. Furthermore, it is an assertion made with a taste for wit and paradox not unknown for this author.

In *Crestiens li gois*, 'Chrétien' is assumed as a given: a given name, determined for the child by its parents, a social and political calculation made by parents as appropriate for the child of converts. If 'Chrétien' is selected for a convert to suppress difference under totality, *Crestiens li gois* is more an individual tactic that counters an expected 'Chrétien *quondam Judeus*' in the style of 'Hermann *quondam Judeus*', a formula applied to converts in general. It recognizes Chrétien as a convert, yet asserts his difference within that class: a *goy* is a convert who asserts not being a *quondam Judeus*, whether seriously or playfully, but does so in a Hebrew linguistic import, the pre-conversion language, nestled within Old French and Medieval Latin, as Jews nestled within feudally-dominated Christian towns and farmlands. The assertion implies an audience capable of recognizing the identitarian play of a 'Christian' expected to be a 'Jew' who asserts himself against expectation to be a Hebrew 'Goy' in Old French. The display of this linguistic playfulness around 1160 may imply a mixed and tolerant audience, whose socio-linguistic expectation is some variant of *Crestiens li Juif*, or *Crestiens quondam Judeus*, hearing instead *Crestiens li gois*.

---

29 Bernard Gui, *Manuel de l'inquisiteur*, ed. and trans. by G. Mollat and G. Drioux, 2 vols (Paris: Les Belles Lettres, 2007), II, 12. Bernard Gui's sources go back to the early thirteenth century.

Epistemological Remarks

The idea that Chrétien de Troyes may have been either a Jew or a convert from Judaism is not new. It was voiced, early in my career, to support an interpretation of Chrétien's *Perceval* as a religious allegory, a literary interpretation rightly rejected by the profession.[30] The idea of Chrétien as a Jewish convert to Christianity was a subsidiary argument regarding the author's possible identity; it is rarely considered today. Articles and books on the theme of '"Who" or "What" is [a] Chrétien de Troyes?' regularly disregard it.[31]

To repeat myself, there is no generally accepted documentary evidence regarding this writer's identity, one way or the other. Most scholars take their cue from the name, inserting it into the ideological clichés that all individuals of note were Christians, and that the name 'Chrétien' was ordinary in medieval Europe. Shortly after the Second World War, it occurred to a stiff, graceless old philologist to actually inquire as to the frequency with which 'Chrétien' or 'Christianus' might be encountered in medieval documents of twelfth-century Champagne. Far from the pullulation of 'Christians' expected, Urban Tigner Holmes discovered quite the contrary: 'There is no Chrétien anywhere here', and drew the obvious conclusion: 'When we do not encounter the name Christianus as a frequent baptismal name in the vicinity of Troyes in the latter half of the twelfth century, we cannot continue to say sweepingly that Chrétien was a common name'.[32] Holmes consulted another historian, John Benton, who confirmed that *Christianus* as a name was rare among the documents of the archive of the Counts of Champagne. Holmes cautiously concluded his chapter on 'Chrétien in Champagne': 'the name Chrétien and its feminine equivalent do not appear with any frequency'.[33]

When the name *does* appear, as in the case of the author 'Chrétien de Troyes', it might well represent calculated forethought in response to a specific social situation: a calculated choice by the parents for the child of converted Jews. When 'Chrétien' appears as a name, as in 'Chrétien de Troyes', Chrétien's parents chose *not* to call him 'Judah', 'Moses', 'Jeremiah', or 'Isidore'. They named him 'Chrétien' as an assertion of Christian identity, because they were themselves converted Jews

---

30 Urban Tigner Holmes, Jr., and Sister M. Amelia Klenke, *Chrétien, Troyes, and the Grail* (Chapel Hill: University of North Carolina Press, 1959). Holmes had already published the basic idea a decade earlier: 'A New Interpretation of Chrétien's *Conte del Graal*', University of North Carolina Studies in the Romance Languages and Literatures, 7 (Chapel Hill: University of North Carolina Press, 1948). The idea was picked up by Daniel Poirion in his introduction to the Pléiade edition of Chrétien de Troyes, without attribution (Chrétien de Troyes, *Œuvres complètes*, ed. and trans. by Poirion, p. xii).
31 On Chrétien's (non-)identity, see: Stephen Steele, 'Qu'est-ce qu'un Chrétien de Troyes?', *Florilegium*, 12 (1993), 99–106; Sarah Kay, 'Who was Chrétien de Troyes?', *Arthurian Literature*, 15 (1997), 1–35; incidental remarks of interest in Michelle R. Warren, 'Memory Out of Line: Hebrew Etymology in the *Roman de Brut* and *Merlin*', *MLN*, 118.4 (2003), 989–1014 (p. 1002); and more recently, the opening chapter of Zrinka Stahuljak and others, *Thinking Through Chrétien de Troyes* (Cambridge: Boydell & Brewer: 2011).
32 Holmes and Klenke, *Chrétien, Troyes, and the Grail*, p. 55.
33 Ibid., pp. 56, 61. Some cases have been signaled: they are so evanescent their very number is in doubt, and they are quickly disposed of by Joseph J. Duggan, *The Romances of Chrétien de Troyes* (New Haven, CT: Yale University Press, 2001), pp. 4–5.

and wanted to assert their son's Christian identity in his name, lest he be tagged with an X *quondam Judeus* tail. An assertion their unpredictable, perhaps youthfully incautious son toyed with in naming himself *Crestiens li gois*.

Holmes's book dates from 1959. His research has lain fallow since. From the perspective of empirical science, the possibility of Chrétien de Troyes as a Jewish convert can only be voiced as a speculative conjecture. It cannot be termed a 'hypothesis', a term of science which implies a narrative of testing to prove or disprove any given hypothesis. At the present moment (2016), the discovery of evidence to either confirm or disqualify the conjecture seems unlikely: it is equally un-provable and un-*dis*-provable.

What will appear in the ensuing discussion are occasional textual details, surprising within the cultural framework of the twelfth century. More telling is a larger question which conjoins the imagination and history: what could possibly have driven a young imagination to work on a narrative of such horrifying human evil as is displayed in *Philomena*, when the historical cultural moment seemed oriented in a far different direction, a direction in which Chrétien de Troyes himself would participate, indeed which he famously led, that of a generally triumphant and joyful cultural renascence?

What will not appear in the ensuing discussion is what could be described as a 'compelling' case, based on empirical evidence, that Chrétien de Troyes's texts reveal him writing as a Jew. Moderns do not appreciate the implications of persecution for the art of writing.[34] The much-celebrated moment of 'renascence' was doubled by ferocious and increasing persecutions of unbelievers, so-called 'heretics', and Jews. Living as a child or grandchild of converts, surviving as a spectacularly successful vernacular fiction-writer in Christianity's twelfth century, would require absolute suppression of personal identity and individual difference, its sublimation into the conventional artifices of textual alterity. Only moments of unguarded detail that wander accidentally into the texts, or elements of delicate structuration, or odd moments of unexpected fictionalization, can alert retrospective reading to the universalizing identifications that have sometimes led Jews forward in history, to reveal the hand of the writing Jew writing at the beginning of European literature. Oppressive persecution attended its birth, as described in *Philomena*'s beginning, for the wedding of Procne and Tereus.

Philomena transcribes horror into translation. Chrétien's later writings, in what is misleadingly called 'romance', continue a pact initiated in *Philomena* with others who suffer dispossession in the world. It is a secular universalization, forced to turn toward religion most ambiguously at the end, and which proceeds by textual indirections such as the multiple forms of irony, or indeed broader forms of comedy, short of the direct polemical confrontations of modernity: no manifestos appear in Chrétien's texts, nor do they provide ready fodder for manifestos. They proceed by wit, charm, and indirection, which does not ignore the pact with the dispossessed.

---

34 The topic was explored for discursive medieval Jewish writers by Leo Strauss in *Persecution and the Art of Writing* (Glencoe, IL: The Free Press, 1952). A contemporary bibliography would start by referring to Michel Foucault and the work of historians such as R. I. Moore, Dominique Iogna-Prat, as well as Gilbert Dahan, Anna Sapir Abulafia, and David Nirenberg.

The convert's world of the twelfth century would have been a formidably different place from what might be imagined today. It was, in some sense, the twelfth century inverted, with increasingly restrictive economic and political conditions. Forced conversions, leading to conditions of life where subjects were under constant surveillance, are rather different from the voluntary, spiritual conversions common in both medieval and modern worlds. Conversion, in *Chrétien li Gois*'s world, was not that far removed from the sword. It needs to be examined in historical context. That context is further complicated by a historiographical dispute of some moment that must be acknowledged.

(ii) A Twelfth Century *à rebours?* The Convert's World

The twelfth century we know since 1927, the date of Charles Homer Haskins's masterpiece, *The Renaissance of the Twelfth Century*, is that of a Europe in full cultural upswing, a rebirth of letters and knowledge accompanying economic growth and the political recentralization that will yield state-formation and the building of modern national entities.[35] Nothing in these pages negates that representation, except to note — after generations of profound historiographical revisions, commentaries, and explorations — that it is an incomplete representation of the twelfth century. The works of major historians in multiple languages and in multiple disciplines have much complicated our view of the twelfth century. If the world Haskins represented, that of the regnant cultural elite of clerical, Latinate Christianity, was indeed enjoying a remarkable upswing, at the very same time, much was going on not addressed by the notion of a cultural and intellectual renaissance.

More recent representations of the period paint a picture of society forming itself around a persecutorial kernel hunting out different forms of otherness, prime among which were the Jews. This different image of eleventh- and twelfth-century Europe was soon followed by an extended, detailed analysis of Cluny, the capital of a monastic empire, as the center of a theology of order based on exclusion, specifically as developed in the writing of Cluny's abbot, Peter called the Venerable.[36] Worse, Peter used his position of religious power to dehumanize Christianity's Others: 'Peter the Venerable did not only debate the enemies of Christ. He demonized them'.[37] Reading Peter the Venerable's excoriation of Jews, another historian, cognizant of his own position in history, comments: 'How can a modern historian, a contemporary of the Holocaust, not be gripped by retrospective fear in hearing the Abbot of Cluny berate the Jews and ask himself if they truly belong to the human race?'[38]

---

35 Charles Homer Haskins, *The Renaissance of the Twelfth Century* (Cambridge, MA: Harvard University Press, 1927).
36 R. I. Moore, *The Formation of a Persecuting Society: Power and Deviance in Western Europe, 950–1250* (Oxford: Basil Blackwell, 1987), and *The War on Heresy: Faith and Power in Medieval Europe* (Cambridge, MA: Harvard University Press, 2012).
37 Moore, *The War on Heresy*, p. 148.
38 Dominique Iogna-Prat, *Ordonner et exclure: Cluny et la société chrétienne face à l'hérésie, au judaïsme et à l'islam, 1000–1150* (Paris: Aubier, 1998), p. 273. Needless to say, such studies of medieval foretastes

It should be noted that different 'takes' on medieval realities, as contradictory as they may be, are justified to some extent. Made of continuous, conflictual, and contradictory change, medieval reality was not a stable unity, in spite of generations of being taught as such. The challenge to pedagogy is to find the appropriate terms to track the changing transformations of medieval conflictuality.

Replicating the persecution of alterities within European societies were analogous aggressions against external Others. The Crusades are the best known. Contemporary historians deconstruct the West's continued propagandistic representation of the savage attacks on largely uncomprehending others, attacks modern historians (hiding their own ideological performance under the veil of historicism) have represented as touristic journeys and 'acts of love', thus reproducing the language of the documents. Beyond the Crusades, Europe engaged in intense, active colonization which required not only the conquest of territory but the eradication of cultural diversity.[39]

Within the very same geo-political space, however, other ethnicities, another ethnicity — that of the Jews — underwent a different history altogether. To some degree, Jews actively participated in the 'renaissance', and in the urban, economic, and political surge which undergirded it. Indeed, the Jews of medieval Europe were likely one of the engines of its economic and intellectual rebirth. Yet, in the same time-space continuum, the Jews were progressively excluded from participating in the 'renaissance'. Politically, Jews were hounded, kidnapped, blackmailed, and murdered by official instances of governance, especially in the French monarchy after the accession of Philip, tagged 'Augustus'. To some degree, the Jewish experience might be thought a twelfth-century renaissance *à rebours*. Thanks to Philip II, Jews in the French *polis* went into a tailspin. Indeed, Jews were one of the specific targets of 'the persecuting society' identified by Robert Moore.

That downspin was not a 'natural' social phenomenon. It was directly caused by the hegemonic Christian society in its two major incarnations: political and religious. This countercyclical historical phenomenon is perfectly well-known, but has largely been hidden from general view by the dominant pedagogy. In fact, that inverted history has been suppressed by being shoved into a corner, the corner baptized 'Jewish Studies' where disciplinary knowledge has grown, protected from hegemonic censorship but often ignored by the generality of history.[40] In that

---

of modern totalitarianisms were countered by denials and affirmations of the more liberal, more tolerant aspects of the period: see, for example, Cary J. Nederman, *Worlds of Difference: European Discourses of Toleration, c. 1100–c. 1550* (University Park: Pennsylvania State University Press, 2000); *Tolerance and Intolerance: Social Conflict in the Age of the Crusades*, ed. by Michael Gervers and James M. Powell (Syracuse, NY: Syracuse University Press, 2001).

39   Robert Bartlett, *The Making of Europe: Conquest, Colonization and Cultural Change, 950–1350* (Princeton, NJ: Princeton University Press, 1993), and Julia M. H. Smith, *Europe after Rome: A New Cultural History 500–1000* (Oxford: Oxford University Press, 2005).

40   The present text derives from a lecture delivered on 9 November 2007, under the title 'Jews and Christians, Massacres and Universalism in the Twelfth Century Renaissance: The Ventriloquism of Chrétien de Troyes' *Philomena*'. At the kind invitation of Professor Thomas Hahn, it took place at the University of Rochester under the auspices of a Humanities Project, 'The Medieval West: Contemporary Views'. With a well-known medieval studies program, this private north-eastern

corner, extraordinary critical scholarship has been produced. It has produced as well an inverted scholastic debate between the tearful, self-pitying view of Jewish history (Salo Baron's 'lachrymose' interpretation) and a remarkable, endlessly optimistic, rosy-tinted forgetfulness, intensifyingly successful in a post-Holocaust Academy.

1096 The Event: Albert of Aachen

For converts and non-converts alike, the Jewish twelfth century starts four years before the new century, with the bloodbaths of 1096, the opening acts of the First Crusade. As is usually the case, issues of historiography are intimately connected with medieval history.[41] The most telling documents regarding the Jewish pogroms are the so-called Hebrew chronicles. Anything but 'chronicles', they are monuments of indomitable ideological resistance in the face of overwhelming, irrational hate and power.

For strategic, rhetorical reasons, I choose to follow, initially, a Christian writer, Albert of Aachen, one of a number of Christian writers of the period who, unlike modern Christian propagandists of the Crusade movement, viewed the actions of their fellow Christians with horror and moral revulsion. Albert of Aachen was an honest and thoughtful historian, whose text, based on personal interviews with participants conducted shortly after the events, is worthy of literary attention.[42] Like any good historian, he cares both for concrete detail and the overall significance of his narrative. While he plunges the reader quickly into the extraordinary mix of elite social dignitaries, unruly rabble, and a handful of despicable feudal magnates who initiated the Crusade, Albert (a serious Christian) also has in mind the fact that Christianity itself is at stake in the Event, particularly because of the horrifying pogroms visited upon the Jewish populations by the crusading mass, most particularly in the Rhineland, not far from his own homeland. Albert of Aachen's own moral judgment of this disgraceful Event at the beginning of his *Historia* is unquestionable. He recounts the massacres of Jews in the Rhineland of 1096 with a brevity that does not elude complexity and moral judgment. It requires attentive reading, however. It requires close reading, the kind of literary reading that is fast

---

research university is just a cut below the Ivy League, to which I personally owed a great deal of my career advancement, though it has a particular record in regards to Jewish studies: see Dan A. Oren, *Joining the Club: A History of Jews and Yale* (New Haven, CT: Yale University Press, 1985). Years earlier in 'Jewish Studies and the Medieval Historian', *Exemplaria*, 12.1 (2000), 7–20, William Chester Jordan had celebrated the dawn of the new millennium: now, by contrast to earlier periods, 'the position of the Jews seems to be at the very core of studies of medieval, and, to some degree, modern European state-building and national identity formation' (p. 15). At the level of historical information, my lecture rehearsed well-known facts of the massacres of 1096 and their aftermath. Afterwards, in the discussion period, an obviously bright graduate student said to me in private conversation: 'You know, I never heard any of this before'. News of the centrality affirmed by Jordan had obviously not reached all corners of academia.

41 Giles Constable, *Crusaders and Crusading in the Twelfth Century* (Burlington, VT: Ashgate, 2008).
42 Albert of Aachen, *Historia Ierosolimitana: History of the Journey to Jerusalem*, ed. and trans. by Susan B. Edgington, Oxford Medieval Texts (Oxford: Oxford University Press, 2007); additional references to this edition are given in the main text.

going out of style. His text's recent re-edition, with translation and accompanying commentary, allows for appraisal of its objectivity, its moral seriousness, as well as its finely-honed literary rhetoric.

In the first words of Albert's *Historia* he states that one 'Peter the Hermit' was the 'primus auctor de via et expeditione ierusalem' [the first 'author' of the journey and the way to Jerusalem]. The word 'crusade' has not yet been invented. Naming Peter the Hermit leader of the Crusade was not intended to appeal to modern democratic values: the historian's view of 'the people' is not flattering. It has not been noted so far that, by assigning 'authorship' for the expedition to Peter, Albert shifts moral responsibility for the dubious enterprise, at the beginning of his narrative, from the Pope's shoulders (and from official Christendom) to the ambiguous figure of a hermit.[43]

Literary scholars like to consider the hermit in romance a religious figure, just as they think medievals unanimous in support of crusading. Indeed, the Middle Ages have frequently been made to figure as a period of cultural and ideological unanimity. In fact, at the time there was a good deal of dubiety regarding the Crusade.[44] Hermits, far from the figures of religious or spiritual authority, were sometimes laymen without training in theology, associated with heterodoxy and heresy, an ambiguity highly useful in textualizing marginality in secular, vernacular narratives. Hermits belonged to marginal worlds of hunters, outlaws, bandits, innkeepers, and anti-cultural rebels whose rebellion took religious form. There was scarcely a community which did not have hermits living at its edge, in rivalry with the secular clergy for spiritual prestige. Without focusing on them in particular, John of Salisbury's discussion of hypocrisy in religion in the *Policraticus* includes hermits.[45]

While in the Berry, Albert of Aachen continues, Peter the Hermit became a persuasive orator. In response to his preaching, 'every sort of people of the Christian faith' (p. 5) joined the Crusade. That catholicity involved lots of different character types. Immediate division occurs in Albert's list of those who joined the movement. First there were the elite, both religious and secular: 'firstly bishops, abbots, clerics, monks, then the most noble laymen, princes of different domains'. No complaint there. But then there were the rest. Albert skips all intermediary layers of society: knights, parish priests, clerics, merchants, artisans, *laboratores*, agriculturalists, etc. — none are mentioned. Maybe none showed, maybe they were of no interest.

---

43   Assigning primary Crusade leadership to Peter the Hermit was far from universal at the time. Another contemporary chronicler, Bernold of St Blasien, specifically declares: 'The lord pope was the foremost author of this expedition' (*Eleventh-century Germany: The Swabian Chronicles*, ed. and trans. by Ian S. Robinson (Manchester: Manchester University Press, 2008), p. 329).

44   See Elizabeth Siberry, *Criticism of Crusading: 1095–1274* (New York: Clarendon Press, 1985); Norman Housley, *Contesting the Crusades* (Oxford: Blackwell, 2006); Martin Aurell, *Des chrétiens contre les croisades (XIIe–XIIIe siècles)* (Paris: Fayard, 2013).

45   On hermits, see Heinrich Fichtenau, *Heretics and Scholars in the High Middle Ages, 1000–1200*, trans. by Denise A. Kaiser (University Park: Pennsylvania State University Press, 1998); R. I. Moore, *The Origins of European Dissent* (Toronto: University of Toronto Press in association with the Medieval Academy of America, 1994); Giles Constable, *The Reformation of the Twelfth Century* (Cambridge: Cambridge University Press, 1996).

Albert drops to the bottom, all the common people, 'totumque vulgus': 'as many sinful as pious men, adulterers, murderers, thieves, perjurers, robbers: that is to say every sort of people of the Christian faith, *indeed even the female sex* [emphasis added]' (*Historia Ierosolimitana*, p. 5).

Albert's 'list' of participants in the Crusade consists only of the extremes of society: top and bottom, socially and morally. His list goes from leaders to dregs. The *vulgus* came from all over, collected from towns and kingdoms all over Europe ('ex diversis regnis et civitatibus in unum collectis', p. 48). They may have burned with the fire of divine love ('divini igne amoris flagrans', as he says), but the fact is that they threw a gigantic orgy, with illegal fucking and immoderate commingling with women and girls who were eager to please or capable of doing so ('assidua delectatio', p. 48).[46] Right from the beginning, and in its very catholicity, there was something worrisome in the personnel of the Crusade — something, you might say, not quite kosher in this mob.

From a beginning determined by the Hermit's preaching, the Crusade had a double fissure, simultaneously social and moral. One was a matter of the personnel attracted by Peter the Hermit: the binary extremes of society described. Another inhered in the social element whose generality is not quite suppressed, but dubiously represented in Albert's description, an element very much in question in society at large at the time, and essentially in question in Pope Urban's call to crusade: the vehicle of violence, the mounted machines of war absolutely necessary to the performance of the Crusade. Their product was to be exported overseas and dumped off-shore by the Crusade.[47]

This chapter introduces the two essential themes: the feudal personnel of the expedition identified by the sign of the cross, the *crucisignati*, repeatedly represented in these early pages by Emicho and his feudal *compères*, and the Jews who would be their victims.[48] It is also the chapter in which Albert of Aachen introduces terms into his discourse which clearly, unmistakably, distance the point of view of the narrator from the event being narrated. More specifically, the historian judges the actions of the historical actors whose history he is telling. Albert of Aachen writes as a morally responsible Christian who disowns at least one aspect or one moment of the Crusade. Indeed, Albert has structured his narrative *Historia Ierosolimitana* so that this morally reprehensible event seizes and grips its opening. Whether he does so in order to get rid of an embarrassment early on and then tell a glorious story, or so that it dominates the entire narrative, I leave to others to decide.

---

46 Editor's note: Haidu's choice of words is occasionally more colorful than Albert's Latin and Edgington's translation: 'sed nequaquam ab illicitis et fornicariis commixtionibus auersis, inmoderata erat commessatio cum mulieribus et puellis, sub eiusdem leuitatis intentione egressis, assidua delectatio, et in omni temeritate sub huius uie occasione gloriatio' ('but as they did not in any way turn from fornication and unlawful relationships there was excessive revelling, continual delight with women and girls who had set out for the very purpose of frivolity, and boasting most rashly about the opportunity offered by this journey') (*Historia Ierosolimitana*, pp. 48 & 49).
47 On this whole question of the mounted machines of violence called 'knights', see Peter Haidu, *The Subject of Violence: The Song of Roland and the Birth of the State* (Bloomington: Indiana University Press, 1993), pp. 44–59, 201–04, and *The Subject Medieval/Modern*, pp. 14–38.
48 It is thus not only the Hebrew chronicles that focus on Emicho.

Massacres: Feudal Internationalisms

When acknowledged in works of history, the massacres of Jews that were the first chapter of the First Crusade tend to be located in the Rhineland. That is where our best information comes from, as reported in the Hebrew chronicles. The fact is, however, that Event, perpetrated by a loosely-defined international class of mid-level feudal magnates,[49] stretched across Europe, even though only fragmentary documentation survives: from Normandy (Guibert de Nogent's account is detailed and precise) to Provence (where the information is less precise) and on to Prague.[50] Indeed, the Event appears to have been European in scope. Inverting Alain Badiou's salvific Christian notion of the Event to take account of horrors like the Holocaust and its prefiguration in 1096, this was a negative Event for the Jews of Europe that fulfilled the Pope's announcement of a military campaign against those who, as non-believers in Christ, could be considered His enemies. While the *ipsissima verbi* of the Pope do not survive, Jews meeting in 1095 in synod in the city of Troyes received reports of the Pope's remarks, considered them, and sent warnings to their co-religionists in Germany to prepare for trouble.[51] A century of what later would be called 'anti-semitic' attacks would begin to unfurl shortly.

The third fissure in the Crusade is not one pointed out by Albert of Aachen: it is later historical experience that illuminates its darkness. The third *faille* is constitutive: it is an absence. An absence of language, quite remarkable, given the importance such terminological matters had in the Middle Ages. An absence of language which has given rise to much historiographical creativity to cover that absence. Medieval society, including the church, depended on a regulation of violence. The Peace and Truce of God was not a denial of violence in society, but a claim to its just regulation: the Crusade claimed to be an extension of that effort.[52] The just regulation of violence depended on a just use of language. Was the journey and expedition to Jerusalem, the first words of Albert's *Historia* ('via et expeditione ierusalem'), the expedition the Pope had called forth (which Albert attributed to Peter the Hermit), was that a war (a *werra?*), was it a battle (a *proelium?*),

---

49 See Thomas N. Bisson, *The Crisis of the Twelfth Century: Power, Lordship, and the Origins of European Government* (Princeton, NJ: Princeton University Press, 2009). On the class structure of the Crusade, see Kostick, *The Social Structure of the First Crusade*.
50 Norman Golb, *The Jews in Medieval Normandy: A Social and Intellectual History* (New York: Cambridge University Press, 1998), pp. 137–70; Taitz, *The Jews of Medieval France*, pp. 119–48. See also Shmuel Shepkaru, *Jewish Martyrs in the Pagan and Christian Worlds* (New York: Cambridge University Press, 2006).
51 Historians seem bothered by the loss of the Pope's 'original' remarks. But speaking extemporaneously is normal in a largely oral society. Urban II would not have been speaking from a prepared text. More serious is another consideration. As an experienced orator who had been trying out his remarks on a veritable campaign tour before Clermont-Ferrand, the Pope would be capable of gauging audience 'pick-up' on his speech, including repeated attacks on enemies of God such as local Jews. Urban II was not an innocent fool.
52 Thomas Head and Richard Landes, *The Peace and Truce of God: Social Violence and Religious Response in France Around the Year 1000* (Ithaca, NY: Cornell University Press, 1992); Haidu, *The Subject Medieval/Modern*, pp. 9–38. The Council at Clermont-Ferrand where Urban II preached the First Crusade was a peace council.

or was it just an *iter*, a sight-seeing trip to the exotic East, as modern propagandists for the Crusades would have you believe, a tourist voyage which, having sought to exterminate Jewish life and culture in the Rhineland and elsewhere in Europe, culminated in unbelievable, repeated, unending Muslim and Jewish slaughters in Jerusalem? The Temple Mount streamed with blood to the killers' ankles, to their horses' knees. Jews were burnt inside their synagogues, Muslims cut to pieces indiscriminately, decapitated, slowly tortured by fire. Unending pillage for profit, secondary slaughter in cold blood, as 'a chilling pre-echo of later genocidal practices'.[53]

Albert of Aachen, having brought together the noble and clerical elite and the rabble collected from towns and kingdoms all over Europe, having told of their great orgy, gets down to the serious business of the *crucisignati*, the fighting men who would enact the mission of the Pope, or of Peter the Hermit. Knowing how it would end, Albert introduces three of those monstrous *crucisignati* in the next few chapters.[54] They are feudal magnates, neither great princes nor mere horse-borne soldiers: Emicho, formerly of Leiningen, now more likely thought to be Count of Floheim; along with a couple of familiar figures, wild, violent robber-barons from France, Thomas of Marle and Clarembold of Vendeuil, both well-known irritants in the hide of Louis VI, according to Abbot Suger. The three together mark the presence of a mid-section of Europe's feudal class: not the great aristocratic rulers of regional principalities, nor lowly individual horse-soldiers who might be hired or discharged individually, for a term, for life, or for a single fief, but substantial, mid-range magnates.

If Albert's Chapter 27 names Emicho as leader of the pogroms in different cities on the Rhine, the preceding chapter also names France, England, Flanders, and 'Lotharingia' as sites of slaughter. The pogroms themselves are termed 'the very cruel massacre of the Jews'. A serious chronicler, but in a medieval sense, not a modern historian, Albert of Aachen uses certain standard rhetorical topoi to make clear his moral views. Was it a judgment of God, he asks, or was it some mental delusion ('aliquo animi errore spiritu crudelitas') when the 'pilgrims' rose in a spirit of cruelty against the Jews scattered in various cities, and inflicted a most cruel slaughter on them ('et crudelissimam in eos exercuerunt necem')? A recent historian seeks to discount the pecuniary interest of the massacring Crusaders, but Albert of Aachen has no hesitation in naming the profit to be made from extorting and murdering Jews, the great sums the Crusaders divided among themselves ('plurimum pecunie illorum inter se diuididentes').[55] Indeed, Albert emphasizes the priceless treasures ('thesaurus infinitos') and incredible amounts of money ('pecuniam inauditam') the Jews deposited with Bishop Ruthard of Mainz for protection (*Historia Ierosolimitana*, p. 50).

---

53 Christopher Tyerman, *God's War: A New History of the Crusades* (Cambridge, MA: Harvard University Press, 2006), pp. 157–58.
54 Albert's 'chapters' are really terse paragraphs.
55 Cf. Jay Rubenstein, *Armies of Heaven: The First Crusade and the Quest for Apocalypse* (New York: Basic Books, 2011), p. 50.

Albert's is a narrative history, with individual actors as subjects. There are moments, however, when his sibilant-filled Latin pulls out stylistic potentials to demonstrate an overwhelming flow that overpowers individual subjects. Emicho and his thousands of troops invade the archbishopric, where hundreds of Jews have taken refuge in good faith. They attacked at daybreak, broke the bolts and the doors at the bishop's residence. They stormed in and slaughtered the Jews they found inside, about seven hundred of them. Albert of Aachen specifies: they slaughtered the women equally ('mulieres pariter trucidauerunt'); young children of whatever age or sex they cut down with their swords. The Jews, Albert writes, seeing the Christian enemy rise against them and their children, sparing none, turned upon themselves. Death is represented as a contagion communicated by Christian savagery to the Jews:

> Iudei uero uidentes Christianos hostes in se suosque paruulos insurgere, et nulli etati parcere, ipsi quoque in se suosque confratres natosque, mulieres, matres et sorores irruerunt, et mutua cede se peremerunt. Matres pueris lactentibus, quod dictu nefas est, guttura ferro secabant, alios transforabant, uolentes pocius sic propriis manibus perire, quam incircumcisorum armis extingui. (*Historia Ierosolimitana*, p. 52)

> The Jews, indeed, seeing how the Christian enemy were rising up against them and their little children and were sparing none of any age, even turned upon themselves and their companions, on children, women, mothers, and sisters, and they all killed each other. Mothers with children at the breast — how horrible to relate — would cut their throats with knives, would stab others, preferring that they should die thus at their hands, rather than be killed by the weapons of the uncircumcised. (*Historia Ierosolimitana*, p. 53)

'How horrible to relate' ('quod dictu nefas est'): Albert as narrator knows the horror of what he is narrating. He takes care to point it out, takes care also to textualize his judgment for the reader, not leaving it merely implicit in the narration. Yet modern historiographers have been unwilling to notice this historiographical distance, analogous to an 'aesthetic distance' noted half a century ago in medieval fiction, and preceding it chronologically. Albert of Aachen is judging the beginning of the Crusade he narrates. Given the poetic intensity of his language, dismissing his witness by saying he 'recoils' from giving an account seems inaccurate.[56]

At this point, Albert of Aachen's account, collected from eye-witnesses on the ground within a few years after the Event, must be complemented by another account, also from eye-witnesses, 'from the inside', as it were: the Hebrew chronicles. They are not without their own theoretical difficulties, however.

---

56 Jeremy Cohen, *Sanctifying the Name of God: Jewish Martyrs and Jewish Memories of the First Crusade* (Philadelphia: University of Pennsylvania Press, 2004), p. 5.

The Hebrew Chronicles

Jeremy Cohen describes exactly the theoretical problem posed by the Hebrew chronicles: 'the historian must recognize and struggle with the complex relationship between event and text'. He then imagines the text of a medieval chronicle presenting 'a pure, unadulterated, or totally objective replica of what transpired' in history. He wants historical chronicles that preserve 'an accurate, play-by-play account of what in fact happened in the Rhineland in 1096'.[57] In other words, the demand is for annulment of 'the complex relationship between event and text' that required recognition and struggle from the historian in the first place.

Demands for totally reliable, precise objective reports on the Christian massacres of Jews in 1096, besides demanding what is scientifically impossible from victims in the process of being murdered, would also render medieval history in general impossible. As is generally understood, all medieval archives are oriented toward the interest of the founder and owner of the archive: none is totally and absolutely objective. Is this not true of archives in general? The standard being invoked for the Hebrew chronicles is superhuman, its destruction of the mere possibility of history almost incidental.

For Cohen, the moment of composition of the Hebrew chronicles chokes off history: 'the most accessible, provable event in question is not reported in the historical record standing before us but *is* the very composition of that record'.[58] The historical text offers itself in history's stead. Cohen may well assert that 'I have encountered no scholarly opinion that the persecutions did not occur or that the Jews of the Rhineland did not martyr themselves in the manner recounted'. Neither has he encountered such revisionism, nor does he formulate such a proposal himself. Yet he withdraws recognition that the Event occurred. He replaces its material historicity with a literary history that proposes, instead of actual historical Jewish resistance to Christian barbarism, a Jewish imitation of Christian martyrology. This may well impress the establishment of literary history, as dominated by an exsanguinated form of 'theory' in the 1980s. It hardly satisfies a poetic sense or a historical sense that addresses 'the complex relationship between event and text' today. The Event occurred, more or less as described in the texts, Cohen agrees, even though some details, which he amply identifies and comments, are not exactly congruent with each other.

Albert of Aachen, at this particular point of his narrative, as a thoughtful Christian hugely embarrassed by the necessary content of his history, omits some concrete details to strip the Event down to its general truth. To compensate for the narrative absence, we will take text from the Mainz Chronicle, also cited by Jeremy Cohen, but analyzed here with a radically different significance. In the present iteration, the same text is presented as the historical representation of Jewish ideological triumph against overwhelming, barbaric Christian violence.

The historical order that exists among the texts of the Hebrew chronicles, established by thoughtful historical criticism, makes sense in terms of their literary

---

57 Ibid., pp. ix, 56, 106.
58 Ibid. p. 8.

characteristics, going from simpler to more complex, from more historical to more literary, with some mix of the two, with the passage of time. The texts have been dated approximatively by Robert Chazan, who has dedicated his life to studying the Event and its documents. The three major texts are the Mainz Anonymous, written within a decade of the events; the composite Solomon bar Simson Chronicle, editing previous work between 1140 and 1148/49, in conjunction with the Second Crusade; and the Eliezer bar Nathan Chronicle, based on the Solomon bar Simson, from the second half of twelfth century.[59]

Chazan is not some dry documentarian, unaware of literary quality, problematics, or passion. He earlier pointed out that the Hebrew chronicles are to be contextualized, not only in the biblical traditions of the Jews, but also in the vernacular evolution of the popular Old French epic known as the *chanson de geste*. Chazan particularly signaled the *Song of Roland*.[60] The word *geste*, in *chansons de geste*, recalls the Latin *res gestae*: things done, i.e. history and historical acts. The epic deals with historical facts, as did the *Song of Roland*, albeit rather freely. Solomon bar Simson's magnificent prose text, juxtaposed against the *Chanson de Roland*, reveals the real, historical achievement of the Jews in 1096, as inscribed in the texts of the Hebrew chronicles: that of transforming the *Song of Roland*'s grammar of quantitative annihilation of the enemy into a syntax of subtraction of victims from the enemy's sword. That is the deconstructive formula for *Kiddush Hashem*, re-invented by Rachel of Mainz and her peers, in utter weaponless deprivation, as the historical ideological praxis of utter destitution of the means of violence against barbarism. That is a historical praxis, a material praxis re-invented on the spot, using a long ideological tradition that Cohen, following Golda Meir, names a 'Masada complex'.

Rachel of Mainz

The Mainz Chronicle tells the story of Rachel of Mainz and is directly pertinent to Chrétien de Troyes's *Philomena*:

> There was a notable lady, Rachel the daughter of R. Isaac ben R. Asher. She said to her companions: I have four children. On them as well have no mercy, lest these uncircumcised come and seize them and they remain in their pseudo-faith. With them as well you must sanctify the holy Name. One of her companions came and took the knife. When she saw the knife, she cried loudly and bitterly. She beat her face, crying and saying: 'Where is your steadfast love, O Lord?' She took Isaac her small son — indeed he was very lovely — and slaughtered him. She ... said to her companions: 'Wait! Do not slaughter Isaac before Aaron.' But the lad Aaron, when he saw that his brother had been slaughtered, cried out: 'Mother, Mother, do not slaughter me!' He then went and hid himself under a bureau. She took her two daughters, Bella and Matrona, and sacrificed them to the Lord God of Hosts, who commanded us not to abandon pure awe of him and remain loyal to him. When the saintly one finished sacrificing her three children before our creator, she then lifted her

---

59   Robert Chazan, *God, Humanity, and History: The Hebrew First-Crusade Narratives* (Berkeley: University of California Press, 2000), pp. 40–49.
60   Chazan, *European Jewry and the First Crusade*, pp. 150–54.

voice and called out to her son: 'Aaron, Aaron, where are you? I shall not have pity or mercy on you either.' She pulled him by the leg from under the bureau, where he had hidden, and sacrificed him before the sublime and exalted God.[61]

Seeing mass slaughter coming upon them in the brilliantly polished, already bloodied swords of the Christian knights, the Jews denied them victory. The Christians would not kill them or their children. Above all, the Christian barbarians would not kidnap their infants to bring them up against a Jewish will as Christians by forced baptisms.[62] The Jews, Jewish mothers represented to the world above all by Rachel of Mainz, re-invented ideological warfare out of total weakness against absolute power.[63] History dirties, it does, and Chrétien will entail that too. But Rachel of Mainz, Rachel did not rest in peace: she fought immediate hate and the power of absolute violence by re-inventing in self-annihilation an ideological triumph over the attacking monsters. She, and others like her, committed mass suicide. Children, women, mothers, sisters. Mothers with children at the breast cut their infants' throats with knives. They stabbed others. 'Rather than be killed with weapons of the uncircumcised.'

Etienne Balibar notes that ideology is an old-fashioned category of thought today, somewhat unfashionable.[64] Not so in the twelfth century. The twelfth century did not invent ideology, of course. Ideology has no history, said Louis Althusser: ideology always exists, even before the invention of the modern state in the eleventh and twelfth centuries. What did occur in the eleventh and twelfth centuries was the willful staging of an open, public ideological scene: Urban's address at a 'Peace Council' in 1095 was an example.[65] Thousands attended, from all walks of life, to attend the Pope's words and be swayed by them or not. Rachel of Mainz countered the Pope's barbaric Christian forces in the only scene of ideological battle at her disposal: the transformation of her own body and her children's bodies into symbolic counters in the ideological final battleground forced on her by Emicho and his ilk. Rather than stretching their necks in meek submission as martyrized victims, they took their own lives as subjects of self-immolation in *Kiddush Hashem*.

Jews would argue passionately about her act. Christian the Goy wrote a text condemning her act. First, her act must be recognized. Her act was not that of a Christian martyr in disguise: it was the act of a Jewess in ideological battle against the violence of Christian barbarism.

★ ★ ★ ★ ★

---

61   Ibid., pp. 238–39. Editor's note: Haidu quotes from the Mainz Anonymous (S), the shorter of the two Hebrew chronicles included in Chazan's Appendix. In the longer version (L), often attributed to Solomon ben Simson, Rachel's story includes phrases that detail and clarify the slaughter of the four children (Chazan, *European Jewry*, pp. 111–13, 258–60).
62   The Jews' fear was perfectly justified. Both Guibert de Nogent and Hermann the Jew tell of Jewish children kidnapped by Christians to be converted into Christians.
63   On this crucial point, see Lena Roos, '*God Wants It!' The Ideology of Martyrdom of the Hebrew Crusade Chronicles and its Jewish and Christian Background* (Uppsala: Uppsala Universitet, 2003).
64   Etienne Balibar, *Saeculum: culture, religion, idéologie* (Paris: Galilée, 2012), p. 65.
65   Haidu, *The Subject Medieval/Modern*, p. 31.

Albert of Aachen picks up the narrative with a brief summary, which acknowledges his elisions:

> After this very cruel massacre of the Jews had taken place — a few escaped, a few had been baptized rather through fear of death than through love of the Christian religion — Count Emicho, Clarembold, Thomas, and all that insufferable mob of men and women continued the journey to Jerusalem with a large amount of booty.[66]

Albert mentions not only Emicho, the local German count, but also the French barons Thomas of Marle and Clarembold of Vendeuil. Albert of Aachen has effectively reminded us of the international dimension of the insufferable feudal *societas* of murderers: the 'intolerabilis societas' of violence that Urban II was desperately trying to export from Europe to the Near East, in an early form of political-economic dumping.[67] The Pope was probably not concerned about sacrificing a few Jews, when he loosed these feudal barbarians on the East. At the worst, he may have thought it might teach the Jews a lesson, giving them a shove they seemed to need toward conversion.

The question has been posed, quite rightly, whether Emicho of Floheim has not been made a whipping-boy by history for the genocidal pogroms of 1096.[68] He unquestionably has the lead role both in the Hebrew chronicles and in Albert of Aachen's narrative. Emicho does appear to have been possessed of a maniacal messiah-complex, legitimated by a tattoo, or perhaps a natural mole. Freud suggests that hatred and a leader are equally effective unifiers of a horde.[69] Emicho's horde of 1096 fused Jew-hatred with a present, living, money-hungry leader, and an apocalyptic vision of a better world — not unlike modernity's later version of the Holocaust.[70] The leadership role was presumably not forced on Emicho: if he has been scapegoated, he volunteered.

Yet other names surface. While documentation is sparse, the Event went well beyond the Rhineland: it was more than the madness of one insensate, money-hungry, low-level count whose personal messiah-complex and tattoo replaced a conscience. The pogroms were most likely led by a group of European nobles.[71] How representative was that group is the question.

---

66   Albert of Aachen, *Historia Ierosolimitana*, p. 52; Haidu's translation.
67   Haidu, *The Subject of Violence*, p. 203.
68   Stow, 'Conversion, Apostasy, and Apprehensiveness'.
69   Sigmund Freud, *Group Psychology and the Analysis of the Ego*, trans. by James Strachey, International Psycho-analytical Library, 6 (New York: Liveright, 1967), p. 32; and Ernesto Laclau, *On Populist Reason* (London: Verso, 2005), p. 60.
70   See Zygmunt Bauman, *Modernité et holocauste*, trans. by Paule Guivarch (Paris: La Fabrique, 2002).
71   Stow speaks of 'Emicho and his fellows' ('Emicho of Flonheim') and also mentions Thomas of Marle and Clarembold of Vendeuil ('Conversion, Apostasy, and Apprehensiveness', p. 916), but not specifically with the Mainz pogrom. Shepkaru seeks to connect the three nobles (Emicho, Thomas, and Clarembold) specifically to 'the massacre of Jews' (*Jewish Martyrs in the Pagan and Christian Worlds*, p. 182).

(iii) 1096: A Holocaust?

1096 was an Event, though not quite exactly as Badiou defines 'Event'.[72] He identifies himself as a professional philosopher and a Platonist defending a materialist cause, even as his notion of the Event is structured by Christian salvationist theology.[73] He elaborates a philosophical theory that defends Ideas, but allows for the possibility of revolution, though only a revolution going in an approved, salvific direction. Like Badiou, I would be tickled pink, or red, at that revolution. However, unlike Badiou, I am beset by the awareness that the fissure which loosens the radical event into history can turn to disaster as well as to emancipatory revolution. Fascism was a 'revolution' no less than October 1917.

What is labeled 'Event' in these pages was such a disaster. Philosophers like Badiou and Agamben, Heidegger's distinguished progeny, are Idealists in more than one manner: their genealogy, like Heidegger's, is Husserlian: anti-materialist and anti-historical. The idealist disconnect from materiality — from slavery, serfdom, guns, from outrageous surplus value extraction — produces the kind of idealism that can lead intellectuals and masses over the edge and into the abyss. No revolutionary thought can do without the impulse of idealism, but no revolutionary thought can claim acceptability today if it avoids the Janus-faced coin of history: disaster is the reverse side of revolution.

Badiou calls 'Event' a transformation that brings into existence a new and maximal existential intensity. Such an Event is a surprise: it absolutizes something previously inexistent.[74] As an utter revelation, inexistent and unthought before the event itself, it cannot be said to be caused by what precedes. In that sense, it is ahistorical. The event comes into being at the site of an existing situation's defining lack; it overturns a situation at the site of a previously existing fault.[75]

The great truth this thought of revolution signals is that revolution is always a surprise: were it not, had it been expected, its possibility would have been snuffed out by existing political power. The revolutionary subject and existing power always play a strategic cat-and-mouse game, to detect the faults, the hidden fissures in the landscape of the present situation. If long-term processes that define the necessity for revolution (repression of material, existential, and political needs) are undeniable, there is always something utterly amazing when the structure yields, opens, and the event actually occurs.

The same structure of long-term underlay and punctual surprise characterizes the approach and arrival of disaster. Formally, the distinction between the desired revolution and its Fascist or Stalinist parody inexists. Only their content and futurity differ. That is what makes the problem of judgment so crucial. Who would entrust what remains of history to be delivered to utter idealists? Nevertheless,

---

72 On Badiou's 'Event', see first Alain Badiou, *Saint Paul: la fondation de l'universalisme* (Paris: Presses universitaires de France, 1997), and then texts cited below.
73 Irving Goh, *The Reject, Community, Politics, and Religion After the Subject* (New York: Fordham University Press, 2014).
74 Alain Badiou, *Logiques des mondes* (Paris: Seuil, 1988), p. 608.
75 Alain Badiou, *Petit manuel d'inesthétique* (Paris: Seuil, 1998), p. 203.

Badiou's notion of the Event and its futurity is to be salvaged. It is perhaps not the necessary form of all coming-to-consciousness, but certainly implication in an Event determines both retrospective and forward-looking conceptions of history. For Badiou's optimistic idealism, the Event is presumed 'good', and the on-going connection to consciousness is termed 'fidelity'. But for one whose Event is not good, for one whose Event comes not from the birthing of a 'good' but the nauseous eruption of criminal, barbarous monstrosity, for one whose Event is abyssal disaster, the dimension of continuity, the relation to the temporality is not fidelity but trauma.

Trauma

Trauma can be a testing-ground for historicism as reactionary ideology: the ridiculous notion that the past is to be discussed only in terms the past used of itself. In the case of the Middle Ages, that would mean using exclusively the prejudicial and profoundly self-interested ideological terms of the clerical land-owning elite that possessed the monopoly of scripture, such as the Pope summoning up Christian violence in terms fit for a travel brochure. The term 'trauma' in its current use was not current in the Middle Ages.

Developments in understanding trauma have tracked major disruptions in world peace. Used originally as a medical term for bodily injury, 'trauma' developed as a term for psychic injury primarily in the wake of the 'war neuroses' of World War I as analyzed by Sigmund Freud in *Beyond the Pleasure Principle* (1920), as well as *Moses and Monotheism* (1939). I am not aware of medieval recognitions of the medical conditions in question. It is an area of reality the modern historian will choose to recognize or not, depending on his or her historiographical ideology.

After World War II, another major advance came with retrospective efforts to grasp the horrors of the Holocaust. A major contribution was Cathy Carruth's brilliant work, *Unclaimed Experience*, which normalized philosophemes of deferral, repetition, and return in theorizing trauma, accounting among other things for different abilities to recognize trauma, even when it occurs within oneself. Trauma remains a wound that cries out in the attempt to speak of a reality or a truth otherwise unavailable, an experience not fully assimilated as it occurs, a crisis that 'simultaneously defies and demands our witness'.[76]

Trauma narrated is thus always the story of a belated experience. It is not fantasy, it is not an escape from reality, from death, or from the referential force of language or narrative: trauma narrated, however indirectly, 'attests to its endless impact on a life'. That impact requires a 'double telling, the oscillation between a *crisis of death* and the correlative *crisis of life*'.[77] For survivors of the Holocaust, trauma could not but be wrapped into mourning, overt or sequestered. The dead demand their due, and receive it, always, but sometimes in complicated manoeuvers of indirection.

---

76 Cathy Carruth, *Unclaimed Experience: Trauma, Narrative and History* (Baltimore, MD: Johns Hopkins University Press, 1996), p. 5.
77 Ibid., pp. 5–7.

Rituals of mourning normalize grief and mourning, but sometimes instituted rituals do not work. Sometimes forms of 'countermourning' need to be invented.[78]

The slaughter of entire communities left behind complex and contradictory movements of fearful martyrdom and vengeful fury among traumatized survivors.[79] These remain largely hidden from contemporary Christian scholarship, since they are hidden in special collections of Hebrew language and culture. But a special kind of survivorship would have been that of the convert who, as Morrison suggested, was forced to keep his identity a secret: far from him the joys of split and openly multiplying selves.

Countermourning of an extraordinary kind will be the choice of Chrétien de Troyes in his major texts. Only occasionally, and primarily in the late *Perceval*, do traces of life-long mourning appear such as a survivor inherits. 'Unclaimed experience', to an immigrant, suggests suitcases, claim checks, musty baggage rooms in nineteenth-century train stations, where presenting a claim check is always hazardous: who knows when police or immigration officials might be hiding behind a pillar for that particular claim-check to be presented. A claim, in other words, involves other than the individual experience, other than the individual 'vesicle' that is Freud's utmost reductive image for the individual organism, a purely theoretical image. Trauma as unclaimed experience necessarily ties the individual vesicle into the world of multiple vesicles that aren't independent vesicles at all, but as Freud's *œuvre* insists, interconnected interdependencies and conflictualities both: in other words, caught in history.

Such connections of trauma to history also make it clear that trauma is not to be taken as a totally debilitating condition. If Dominick LaCapra is to be taken seriously, and writing history is roughly equivalent to writing trauma,[80] trauma becomes a condition of active life for survivor populations, surviving their traumas as best we can, normalizing the condition of being a traumatized survivor. Trauma is a subjective furrow in living flesh in which a survivor's life necessarily grows, sometimes inventing surprising forms of mourning and countermourning. Trauma is not the cover of a coffin, but a burden a subject carries in a backpack on a trail, or the springboard of an imagination. Both. Ask Benjamin. Kafka. Celan. *Crestïens li gois*.

To recapitulate: trauma is an experience driven through the individual, as through the social collective as a whole, threatening experience as an integrated, viably articulated social life. Working through trauma does not imply redemption of the past. Trauma, once endured, cannot be fixed. You don't 'get over it'. It 'is a cause that we cannot directly change or heal'.[81] Recognition of the traumatic effect

---

78   The word is taken from Sanja Bahun, *Modernism and Melancholia: Writing as Countermourning* (Oxford: Oxford University Press, 2014).

79   Susan L. Einbinder, *Beautiful Death: Jewish Poetry and Martyrdom in Medieval France* (Princeton, NJ, and Oxford: Princeton University Press, 2002), p. 26.

80   Dominick LaCapra, *Writing History, Writing Trauma* (Baltimore, MD: Johns Hopkins University Press, 2001).

81   Dominick LaCapra, 'Trauma Studies', in *History in Transit: Experience, Identity, Critical Theory* (Ithaca, NY: Cornell University Press, 2004), pp. 106–43 (p. 119).

of 1096 and other events of the twelfth century is not to be buried under accusations of 'lachrymose' history. The point of trauma studies in the present context is to allow an examination of Jewish creativity reacting to 1096.[82]

The twelfth-century Christian Renaissance was simultaneously a period of disastrous Jewish social mutilations under Christian attacks. That certain fruitful exchanges continued to occur does not negate the historical fact that Jewish culture, and the Jewish *socius* as a whole, suffered severely at the same time. More closely examined, the Jewish trauma of the twelfth century is illuminated retrospectively by the temporal structure of the Jewish trauma of the twentieth-century Holocaust.

Resistance and the Hebrew Chronicles

The Jewish twelfth century starts with the bloodbaths of 1096. Violent troops, the ordinary retinue of knights and their *sergens*, rousted up an undefined local rabble inflamed by cruising preachers like Peter the Hermit and the leadership of Emicho, Count of Floheim, an important political power of the Rhineland. Resentment, hatred, and greed: the traditional elements requisite for massacre are present. The Event, recorded in both Jewish and Christian accounts, was traumatic for Jews.[83] It was traumatic in multiple senses. Christian hordes, under Christian leadership, invoking Christian ideology, slaughtered every single living Jew of any age they could find in the Rhineland, along the main river and its tributaries, where Jews had been living next to Christians for centuries. The massacres went on for weeks, until the Rhineland could finally be claimed to be *Judenfrei* by death or conversion.

Not only were Jews massacred by the thousands, a communal life built over centuries, with and among Christian neighbors, in cooperative and sometimes difficult competitive interdependence, was crushed and exterminated in 1096, much to the horror of contemporary Christian witnesses, let it be said. Christianity itself was split by the misuse of the name of the Christian religion in 1096, far more so than modern propagandists allow. Communities were wracked. The fact that survivors returned after the initial slaughter and began repopulating the towns of the previous inhabitation has been cited as evidence — in total miscomprehension of the structure of trauma's belatedness — that the Event was not shocking. Some of those who returned may have survived by hiding from slaughter in the forests. Survivors survived by dint of having been forced to betray their faith and community as Jews.[84] Many witnessed their co-religionists' heroic suicidal *Kiddush*

---

82   Ivan G. Marcus, 'A Jewish-Christian Symbiosis: The Culture of Early Ashkenaz', in *Cultures of the Jews: A New History*, ed. by David Biale (New York: Schocken, 2002), pp. 449–516. Despite its title, the content of this balanced essay provides much evidence against the notion of a peaceable 'symbiosis'.

83   Kenneth R. Stow, *Alienated Minority: The Jews of Medieval Latin Europe* (Cambridge, MA: Harvard University Press, 1992), p. 101.

84   Of the survivors, most by necessity had been forced to convert. Conversion, all too readily treated as a simple switch in positivities, can also involve endless, contradictory criss-crossings and abyssal negativity. Of the converts, some took advantage of the high-level politicking at the level of Empire and Papacy to return to Judaism: they returned to their Rhenish homeland as openly-declared Jews. Others retained their status as converts, seeming Christians. No statistical accounts were made at the time of the numbers in either category.

Hashem, thereby incurring endless guilt. Communities then began the endless, excruciating incorporation of martyrdom in poetry and ritual.[85]

The Event was profoundly shocking, constituting a need to memorialize and commemorate.[86] The disciplinary ideology of modern history may occlude and condemn the medieval fusion of ritual, liturgy, and history.[87] Nevertheless, an annual fast was instituted in the Jewish community of Worms in memory of the massacres.[88] Memorial lists that inscribed the names of the murdered were read out annually at synagogue services throughout Europe. The victims were commemorated in *piyyutim*, lyric elegies which fused memorialization with cultural resistance to the pressures of 'escalating harassment, persecution, and conversion'.[89]

Above all, a complex historical consciousness develops in the Hebrew chronicles, their essential content confirmed by contemporary Christian historians, rewritten throughout the twelfth century in a complex fusion of history, reverential commemoration, and perspectives of difference.[90] The manuscript tradition of these chronicles is small but involves numbers of different authors; the later chronicle by Eliezer bar Nathan survives in multiple manuscripts.[91] In Yerushalmi's words, these chronicles record 'a palpable sense of the terrifying shift in the relations between Jewry and Christendom that had ended in the destruction of entire Jewish communities [... and] astonished awe at this first instance of Jewish mass martyrdom on European soil'.[92]

The development of a collective historical consciousness is demonstrated by one further text. A recapitulative list of persecutions that had occurred between 1171 and 1192 in France, Germany, England, and Austria, is composed at the end of the century.[93] These texts, especially the chronicles, raise major issues: textual,

85 Einbinder, *Beautiful Death*.
86 One modern theorization of trauma, following the model of Maurice Blanchot, paradoxically implies wiping out memory in the act of writing down the Event: Michael Bernard-Donals, 'History and Disaster: Witness, Trauma, and the Problem of Writing the Holocaust', *Clio*, 30.2 (2001), 143–68. The medieval Hebrew chronicles are quite the opposite of Abraham Lewin's diary of the Warsaw ghetto: their literary quality bespeaks dedicated labor at fixing the narrative record of the Event: *memne* rather than *anamnesis*.
87 See Yosef Hayim Yerushalmi's admirable *Zakhor: Jewish History and Jewish Memory* (Seattle: University of Washington Press, 1982/1996), and more recently, Gabrielle Spiegel, 'Memory and History: Liturgical Time and Historical Time', *History and Theory*, 41 (2002), 149–62. Compare Robert Chazan, 'The Timebound and the Timeless: Medieval Jewish Narration of Events', *History and Memory*, 6 (1994), 5–35; repr. as 'Prologue', in *God, Humanity, and History*, pp. 1–17. Chazan is perhaps more willing to countenance the ambiguity of the Hebrew chronicles' fusion of history and commemoration, in the face of the self-definitions of the modern discipline of history.
88 Yerushalmi, *Zakhor*, p. xxvii. He credits a student, David Wachtel, with discovering the Worms fast. The gesture of the commemorative fast would be repeated for the victims of the Blois murders.
89 Einbinder, *Beautiful Death*, p. 18.
90 Robert Chazan's most recent contribution is *God, Humanity, and History*; the topic and scholarship are reviewed by Roos, '*God Wants It!*' (2003) and, with the same title but revised content,'*God Wants It!*' (Turnhout: Brepols, 2006).
91 Chazan, *European Jewry and the First Crusade*; and *God, Humanity, and History*, pp. 100–11.
92 Yerushalmi, *Zakhor*, p. 37.
93 Robert Chazan, 'Ephraim ben Jacob's Compilation of Twelfth-century Persecutions', *The Jewish Quarterly Review*, n.s., 84.4 (April 1994), 397–416.

historiographical, moral, cultural, and theological. Historical writing was not deeply ingrained in twelfth-century Jewish culture.[94] The effort to create a historiography appropriate to the event of 1096 and to its effect on the population is a remarkable achievement, even if it was not destined to anchor professional historical writing in medieval Jewish culture. The debate on the degree to which the texts are to be read as history or literature reflects the self-consciousness and disciplinary ideology of modern historians rather than the concerns of the medieval writers.[95]

The Convert Invents an Ideological Discourse of Alterity

Above all, 1096 was traumatic in splitting Judaism, a collective subject, into different subjects, with different subjectivities, inscribed in different textualities. There was a literature of willed continuity, 'an outpouring of commemorative literature' centered on the martyrology of a 'beautiful death': dense allusive lyric poetry, a literature of believers, whose belief had been intensified in the cauldron of desperation, issued from learned rabbinical circles including, in the second half of the twelfth century, the Tosafists. 'The Jewish poetry of martyrdom formalized an ideal of Jewish resistance to persecution and conversion'.[96] This literature opposed itself directly to the danger of rupture and conversion, the other effect of 1096.

The literature of the converts is far more problematic than the literature of the believers. Some converts could speak openly about having been Jews by making profession of being converts, like Hermann *quondam Judeus* or Petrus Alfonsi. Later in cultural history, Whittaker Chambers would signal the same category: a convert turned informant to the regnant hegemon. Most converts, however, preferred a more covert life, hiding their past identity under the new, dissimulating as much as possible the remnants of Israel either by suppression, or by universalization of the unsuppressible.

The universal was claimed by the Church *catholic*, i.e. universal by name and by definition. Within it, all seemed possible. Without its borders lay an immense domain increasingly subject to domination and conquest, subject to being laid waste as a *gaste forez*. The epoch was not ready for the argument that Israel — or any *ethnos* other than the Catholic — could harbor the universal in its specificity. See the works of R. I. Moore, Dominique Iogna-Prat, Julia Smith, and others. The possibility of the specific universal re-surfaced in the twentieth century, at the cost of the Holocaust.[97]

That limit applied to the domain of veridictory discourse, the domain of prose where the ultimate criterion is truth. Jews, heretics, even Christian theologians like Peter Abelard, felt the weighty brunt of the prosecution of truth when they transgressed the institutional limits of Catholic truth, as subtle and complex as that developed. The Catholic Church was not only the established church: it saw

---

94 Yerushalmi, *Zakhor*, pp. 27–52.
95 Compare Chazan with Marcus, 'From Politics to Martyrdom'.
96 Einbinder, *Beautiful Death*, p. 1.
97 See the Conclusion.

to it that it became the institutionalized Universal Church. Within the domain of veridictory discourse, there was no escape from the Church's hegemony.

Escape from that domain was one mark of Chrétien de Troyes's genius, the ideological mark: the creation of an alternative universe. The importation of obviously unreal, foreign legendary material, marked as unrealistic in its origin, 'fantastical' at the most superficial level, withdrew its narratives from the realm of the veridictory, and allowed for the postulation of an alternative fictive world. Imaginary, idealistic, and critical at different moments, it managed to escape hegemonic censure for half a century or so. Until the early thirteenth century, the enormous advantage of Arthurian fiction was precisely its rupture in continuity from hegemonic domination by the Catholic Church. In the twelfth century, the only alternative access to the universal could be claimed, and was, through the universal medium of legendary or mythological fiction. Hence Chrétien de Troyes, and the role of Arthurian fiction in the grounding of the European novel, after its beginnings with the Tristan story and classical *Thèbes* and *Eneas*. Hence the rising importance of literature in the vernacular.

In Troyes, in the twelfth century, the Jewish community was bilingual. Old French was its 'natural language', the ordinary, everyday language for social exchange. Hebrew was its sacred language, probably not universal. The 'natural language' of Jewish individuals in and around Troyes was Champenois. Hebrew was the language learned in school for ritual purposes. For both the literary traditions of Jewish martyrdom and for the historical Hebrew chronicles, the language used was the sacred language of the forefathers: Hebrew. Throughout both Christian and Jewish cultures, there was generalized pressure towards the use of vernaculars. Other Jews elsewhere had begun to use vernaculars. The great Hebrew poet Judah Halévy chose to write his famous defense of Judaism, the *Kuzari*, in Arabic, around 1140, during Chrétien's youth. Maimonides would do the same throughout his career, even well before *The Guide for the Perplexed*, perhaps contemporaneous with the *Perceval*, around 1190. Both Judah Halévy and Maimonides, of course, lived in a changing, Judeo-Arabic culture, under cultural conditions more favorable to ethnic diversity than those which governed France, especially towards the end of Chrétien de Troyes's life.[98]

Chrétien, if indeed he was the child or grandchild of converts of 1096, chose to continue a life of discrete covert concealment of identity indicated by his parents' choice of his name — such is the conjecture of this book. Chrétien continued a strategy of survival under a regime that had opted for the formation of a persecuting society that targeted his ethnicity. His choice succeeded, up to a point, in allowing for the creation of a body of constitutive European imaginative fiction. That fiction, in its very polyvalence, and in the deniability allowed by its fictive quality, bore the universalism that would characterize subsequent European modernities, beyond the class structure and the ethnic persecutions that sustained it.

---

98 On Judeo-Arabic culture in relation to Judah Halévy, see Raymond P. Scheindlin, *The Song of the Distant Dove* (Oxford: Oxford University Press, 2008), pp. 54–67.

PART II

Philomena and the Semiotics of Evil

Chrétien's version of Ovid's tale from the sixth book of the *Metamorphoses* is neither a simple translation, nor what medieval translations so often turn into, an adaptation. It is a radical re-appropriation of Ovidian narrative materials, in a new language, a new culture, a new history, and a new intellectual framework, and with radically different effects.¹ Its differences from Ovid are major, operating by addition, subtraction, and transformation.² Abandoning both the brilliant, baroque rhetoric of Ovid's hexameters and his untrammeled pleasure in verbal perversity, the medieval text changes the nature of the story. The changes metamorphose the narrative's significance.

(i) (Re)presentation: Narrative

In the context of the 1160s, the decade assigned *Philomena* by the established philological tradition, the corpus of vernacular written works is limited.³ All are written in the same octosyllabic rhymed couplets, the marked linguistic form for vernacular, literary narrative in written French. There is Beroul's early version of the Tristan story of passionate love — carnal, adulterous, equally ungodly and uncourtly, or anti-courtly? — with the central couple mostly helpless in the toils of passion. There are works of secular history by Gaimar, Wace, and Benoît, far more original, perceptive, and critical of their world than an official academic historiography let on until fairly recently.⁴

---

1   Ovid, *Metamorphoses*, book vi, ll. 424–674, (*Metamorphoses*, trans. by Frank Justus Miller, 2 vols, Loeb Classics (London: William Heinemann, 1916), I, 316–34). The comparison of Ovid's and Chrétien's texts was one of the first aspects of the work to receive scholarly attention: Ernst Hoepffner, 'La *Philomena* de Chrétien de Troyes', *Romania*, 57 (1931), 13–74.
2   As Matilda Tomaryn Bruckner vividly puts it, Chrétien cannibalizes Ovid through dismemberment, remembering, and replacement: 'Of Cannibalism and *Cligès*', *Arthuriana*, 18.3 (Fall 2008), 19–32.
3   The dating of individual works of this period is generally fragile and subjective, all too often based on assumptions of representation that date back to the nineteenth century.
4   See Jean Blacker, *The Faces of Time: Portrayal of the Past in Old French and Latin Historical Narrative of the Anglo-Norman Regnum* (Austin: University of Texas Press, 1994); and Monika Otter, *Inventiones: Fiction and Referentiality in Twelfth-century English Historical Writing* (Chapel Hill: University of North Carolina Press, 1996). On Gaimar, see more recently, Kristen Lee Over, *Kingship, Conquest, and Patria: Literary and Cultural Identities in Medieval French and Welsh Arthurian Romance* (New York: Routledge, 2013).

Closest to *Philomena* are the first two of the *romans d'antiquité*, *Thèbes* and *Eneas*, which cultivate a structural ambiguity between classicizing fiction, mythology and contemporary history, as focused by the political constitution of the state. Both histories and the *romans d'antiquité* are related to the cultural politics of Henry II, not as simple propaganda but in complex ways, as Angevin colonial governance expands over England. Their fundamental paradigm is political, even as it explores different forms of love. Their fundamental ambiguity does not mark indecision: they are sophisticated fictions whose classical diegesis establishes critical perspectives with contemporary pertinence. Retelling the past is not mere commemoration.[5] It is a built-in detour on the way to the present's address of itself, sometimes in legitimation, sometimes in critique, but always addressing fundamental issues of the present polis.[6] The representation of medieval fictions, even constructed around images assigned to past epochs, ineluctably touches contemporary ideology, either criticizing or constructing it, and sometimes both.

In this context, Chrétien's first surviving work, in spite of superficial resemblances, is a shock. Above all, *Philomena* precedes the author's full-fledged verse novels. From *Erec et Enide* to the *Perceval*, those works establish, at the initiation of overt vernacular fiction, a dominating peak. In a real sense, *Crestiens li gois*'s *Philomena* precedes the appearance and the achievement of Chrétien de Troyes. What will become standard conventional fare as a result of his work has not yet come into existence. The well-known corpus of longer fictional works quickly designated above are more than honorable fictional efforts: they are superb and courageous ventures into the unknown. They establish the model whose later imitations Cervantes will find it worthwhile to parody. They establish a notion of 'literature' which will be determining for a future Europe.

In the context of actually-existing texts, *Philomena* is, to reverse a phrase of Stendhal's, a metaphysical pistol shot in the political drawing room of a manor hall. The Ovidian 'adaptation' participates in a nascent vernacular literature which hangs its socio-political problematics on the framework of classical materials. It shares that basis in literary history, but resoundingly contradicts the rosy-colored courtly dawn of both its contemporaries and especially the author's later production. Rather than propose an idealizing ideology conjoining love and heroism, power and culture in the classical formulae of the *translatio studii*, *Philomena* asserts mankind's illimitable potential for evil as grounded in its passion for beauty. Its profound modifications of Ovid's text reject the strategy of externalizing barbarity, assigning it to countries and cultures considered a barbarian Other, even though it invokes barbarian

---

5   Eugene Vance, *Mervelous Signals* (Lincoln: University of Nebraska Press, 1986); R. Howard Bloch, *Etymologies and Genealogies* (Chicago: University of Chicago Press, 1983). On history, see Chazan, 'The Timebound and the Timeless'; see also the 'Prologue', in *God, Humanity, and History*; in contrast, Spiegel, 'Memory and History'.

6   The one fundamental dimension the texts seem to avoid is the economic. In fact, the economic slides in, and in Marxist form at that, at unexpected moments: Peter Haidu, 'The Hermit's Pottage: Deconstruction and History in *Yvain*', *Romanic Review*, 74 (1983), 1–15; repr. in *The Sower and the Seed: Essays on Chrétien de Troyes*, ed. by Rupert T. Pickens (Lexington, KY: French Forum, 1983), pp. 127–45.

Thrace. Instead, *Philomena* draws its implications closer to an undefined but more proximate subject, whose relation to the destinator or the recipient (the audience of an oral performance, the reader of a manuscript) is equally discomfiting. The ideological labor it performs incorporates a savage charge against the proximate humanity it perceives and constructs. It does so explosively, with fragmentation effects of indirection. The ineffable, the unsayable also tracks symbolic resistance by oppressed minorities, sketching a cross-class alliance of working women with the savagely victimized royal princess. The work inscribes a critical subjectivity that produces a surprising counter-history.

In language, determining the meaning of a sentence requires understanding the syntax of the whole sentence. The injunction: 'Thou shalt not kill' posits killing, but does not urge it — quite the contrary. Similarly, in a literary text, narrating a rape does not mean glorifying rape. In order to argue against something, that something has to be posited, which requires some manner of representation. Demonstrating the potential for evil does not mean endorsing it: see *Oedipus the King*.

The mode of presentation here is narrative, the key term for the critical analysis of stories of any length, whether in verse or in prose. It denotes the sequence of anthropomorphic actions whose coherence constitutes the story as the skeleton of the textual entity. The dimension of meaning is constructed by the interactions of the narrative kernel, its verbal integument, and the performance of the narrator. At all three levels, the codes in play are social, but their interplay is indeterminate: the dimension of meaning is plurally ambiguous. Narrative, the representation of narrative action, may imply narration, the presentation of the narrative action through certain perspectives, or the establishment of certain sign-posts that mark sites of questioning. Telling a story may be more than embracing wholeheartedly the values of the action.

The narrative kernel of *Philomena* articulates three moments of repulsive horror: Philomena is raped by Tereus; Tereus cuts out Philomena's tongue; Philomena and her sister Procne avenge the rape and mutilation by murdering Ithys, the five-year old son of Tereus and Procne. The poem's narrative syntax breaks into three episodes, with distinct narrative subjects, the subject being the figure that enacts the narrative action. Tereus is the first narrative subject; Philomena, alone yet together with two weavers, the second; Philomena together with her sister Procne, the third.

Chrétien de Troyes will develop a remarkably sophisticated sense of fictional organization, both on the level of totalizing narrative structure and on an intermediary level of episodic structures, whose dialectic interplay guarantees the narrative coherence of his later texts.[7] That sense of narrative complexity is aborning in *Cretiens li gois*'s *Philomena*, without being fully developed. Bipartition was already established in the culture as a narrative norm: the Bible, Virgil's *Aeneid*, the *Song of Roland*, even the *Vie de Saint Alexis*, all exemplified narrative bi-partition. In his major works, Chrétien would adapt bi-partition, and invest it with a particular

---

7   Peter Haidu, 'Narrativity and Language in Some Twelfth-century Romances', in *Approaches to Medieval Romance*, ed. by Peter Haidu, special issue of *Yale French Studies*, 51 (1974), 133–46; 'The Episode as Semiotic Module in Twelfth-century Romance', *Poetics Today*, 4.4 (1983), 655–81.

dynamism.[8] Yet *Philomena* goes out of its way to develop a middle episode within the essential binarism of crime-and-vengeance. That central episode is concerned with a dual problematics: class and gender on the one hand, and representation by signs on the other. Unable to speak, Philomena will create a collective of women, reach out to her sister, and wreak vengeance on her rapist and tormentor that both equals the ideological triumph of Rachel of Mainz and denies its narrative content. Philomena remains the central focus of empathetic attention, but she is not the only focus. Formally, there are three episodes with three different subjects, even as the reader identifies with Philomena throughout:

1. The marriage of Tereus and Procne was accompanied by evil omens. A semiotic syncretism immediately identifies the subject as the villain. The narrative subject of this episode is established in the installation of desire by beauty and its effect, *amour* for Philomena. Tereus implements his desire in a sequence of four segments: obtention of the object, displacement to his own turf in Thrace, an attempted verbal manipulation that fails, and the central narreme: sexual imposition by force, i.e. rape.

2. The rape which victimizes the object of desire simultaneously constitutes her as countersubject. She utters an immediate verbal accusation and a threat of retaliation by public accusation. Tereus prevents that retaliation by incapacitating her ability to communicate: he cuts out her tongue. She invents alternative semiotic practices as means of communication with the assistance of her jailers.

3. This communication — successful — constitutes her sister Procne as a second countersubject. The two sisters implement the revenge which is the sanction of the villain-subject: they cook up Ithys and serve him to Tereus as dinner.
Procne, Philomena, and Tereus undergo aviary metamorphoses to swallow, nightingale, and hoopoe; Philomena, the nightingale, sings 'Kill! Kill! Kill!'

Excursus 1: 'Courtly love' vs the Twelfth Century

An obstacle stands in the way of reading the text. The conjunction of beauty and the word *amour*, even conjoined with rape, has signaled 'courtly love' as an automatic reflex. Yet it has long been understood that 'courtly love' is a dated notion. The expression does not occur in medieval texts. The coinage has a history of its own, a modern history. As part of *our* modern cultural heritage, it poses a problem. Worse, it causes a methodological mess, preventing intelligent, knowledgeable scholars from actually reading the text before them. In the case of *Philomena*, 'courtly love' has robbed us of a major literary text.

As all informed students know, 'courtly love' was a label invented in the late nineteenth century to express discomfort with the adultery of Chrétien de Troyes's *Lancelot*. The phrase was invented by Gaston Paris in his effort to found medieval

---

8 That dynamism depends on the interplay between bi-partition and episodic form, see Haidu, 'Narrativity and Language in Some Twelfth-century Romances'; Donald Maddox, 'Trois sur deux: théories de bipartition et de tripartition des œuvres de Chrétien', *Œuvres et Critiques*, 5 (1980), 91–102.

French philology as a respectable intellectual discipline with a complex relation to its model of German philology, aping the scientificity of the German model while wresting from that model its own French national and cultural autonomy.[9] The new discipline had to assert its autonomy and the originality of its literary texts in a manner acceptable to a predominantly bourgeois nationalism, marked by a triple trauma: the two highly publicized trials in 1857 of Baudelaire's *Fleurs du mal* and especially Flaubert's *Madame Bovary* with the centrality of adultery, and the Franco-Prussian War of 1870. Gaston Paris was a brilliant scholar, extraordinarily learned, endowed with a rare sense of critical coherence, even though his values and judgments were often distant from ours. He was also a practitioner of disciplinary politics of a high order, from whom some of our contemporaries learned the dark art and underground skills of professional politics.

Gaston Paris is to be admired from afar, not imitated. His invention of 'courtly love' functions today as a major impediment to understanding medieval texts.[10] With few exceptions, it has effectively blocked adequate readings of *Philomena*.[11] In the modern cycle of studies, initial reactions immediately assigned the descriptions of the heroine's beauty and the subsequent birth of *amour* in Tereus to 'courtly love'. The text itself became a 'courtly' text. Paradoxically, rape was made to figure as a 'courtly love' phenomenon. Confounding chronology and thematics both, the author's earliest surviving text was subsumed under a label designed for a work from his middle period, a work that is ethically and thematically anomalous within his *œuvre*. *Erec et Enide*, *Cligès*, and *Yvain* all explore love within the married couple. Like them, *Philomena* also assumes faithful heterosexual marriage as a norm. Only *Lancelot* features adulterous love; the rest of his work constructs love as a social phenomenon within marriage. In fact, the overt centrality of amorous marriage is one of the author's major innovations in the northern French novelization of the southern troubadours' *fin'amor*. Even among the troubadours, adultery is a rare feature.[12]

'Courtly love' is not part of medieval literature: it belongs to the historical reception of medieval literature in the nineteenth century, its *Rezeptionsgeschichte*, invented not quite out of whole cloth. This error of literary history was resurrected by the psychoanalyst Jacques Lacan in his *Ethics of Psychoanalysis*. It is difficult to find

---

9   David Hult, 'Gaston Paris and the Invention of Courtly Love', in *Medievalism and the Modernist Temper*, ed. by R. Howard Bloch and Stephen G. Nichols (Baltimore, MD: Johns Hopkins University Press, 1996), pp. 192–224. Hult's essay exemplifies the persistent utility of 'the old philology'.
10   An argument can be made that 'courtly love' was part of a Foucaldian disciplinarization of European society in the nascent state form: see Haidu, *The Subject Medieval/Modern*.
11   See Krueger's excellent article, with important critical perceptions that exceed the synthetic framework of her essay: '*Philomena*'; Colette Storms, 'Le Mal dans *Philomena*', in *Imaginaires du mal*, ed. by Myriam Watthee-Delmotte and Paul-Augustin Deproost (Paris: Cerf and Université catholique de Louvain, 2000), pp. 103–13; and Nancy A. Jones, 'The Daughter's Text and the Thread of Lineage in the Old French *Philomena*', in *Representing Rape in Medieval and Early Modern Literature*, ed. by Elizabeth Robertson and Christine M. Rose (New York: Palgrave, 2001), pp. 161–87, which notes many crucial textual elements.
12   William D. Paden, Jr., and others, 'The Troubadour's Lady: Her Marital Status and Social Rank', *Studies in Philology*, 72.1 (January 1975), 28–50.

evidence that he had ever got closer to reading a single text by Chrétien de Troyes — even the *Lancelot* — than *L'Amour et l'occident* by Denis de Rougemont, first published in 1939, republished in 1956 and 1972. Lacan got his medieval information second- or third-hand.

The title of one feminist article, a few years ago, encouragingly raised the question: 'Courtly Love: Who Needs It?'[13] The rhetorical question implied an expected response: 'No one!' That expectation was dashed by the author's insistence on retaining the notion of 'courtly love' because so much baggage is attached to the notion, even if the notion falsifies both history and literary texts, and impedes reading the texts. Should feminism — or any other emancipatory movement — consciously ground itself in historical constructs known to be false?[14]

Even in the *Lancelot*, the textual construction of love is angled to generate multiple interpretations.[15] The twelfth century's exploration of love was far broader, deeper, and more complex than the purview marked out by 'courtly love'.[16] 'Courtly love' may have marked a major step in the construct; today, it is an impediment to knowledge and to historical understanding. It was designed to address phenomena that today are best understood in terms of the general problematics of human cohesion.[17]

Two thinkers writing in Latin, one a theologian, the other a scholastic of love, suggest the breadth of twelfth-century reflection on love. For Hugh of St Victor (1096–1141), *amor* is first of all a pleasure (*delectatio*) of the heart, which arises from the inherent qualities of the object. That affective pleasure turns into desire when the subject moves towards the object: narrative movement of the subject toward the object transforms pure (aesthetic?) pleasure into desire. In turn, desire fulfilled becomes joy (*gaudium*). These formulations point towards both the *joi* of the troubadours and the *joie* in the *Joie de la cour* of Chrétien's *Erec et Enide*.

Hugh's *amor* is a unitary concept, which divides however into two categories, depending on the object addressed. Mundane love is the love of contingent things, *cupiditas*: an ardent, inordinate desire tantamount to covetousness. Heavenly love is the love for higher things, *caritas*.[18] The subjective experience of love is unitary, even though, as it addresses profoundly different objects, it becomes cupidity and charity. For Hugh of Saint Victor, a generation before *Crestiens li gois,* the subjective

---

13   E. Jane Burns, 'Courtly Love: Who Needs It? Recent Feminist Work in the Medieval French Tradition', *Signs*, 27.1 (Autumn 2001), 23–57.

14   On rereading this rhetorical question, originally intended to be dismissive, it occurs to me that its import is far less clear in the political domain when applied to a notion, equally fictive, such as 'race'.

15   Matilda Tomaryn Bruckner, 'An Interpreter's Dilemma: Why are There So Many Interpretations of Chrétien's *Chevalier de la Charrette*?', *Romance Philology*, 40 (1986), 158–80.

16   See John C. Moore's classic article, 'Love in Twelfth-century France: A Failure in Synthesis', *Traditio*, 24 (1968), 429–43. What Moore called 'failure' with gentleness looks today more like historical exploration and cultural creation.

17   The classic study of 'political' vocabulary is Pierre Michaud-Quentin, *Universitas: expressions du mouvement communautaire dans le moyen âge latin* (Paris: Vrin, 1970).

18   Simo Knuuttila, *Emotions in Ancient and Medieval Philosophy* (Oxford: Oxford University Press, 2006), p. 200.

phenomenon of *amor* is initially a single experience, differentiated by its address of different objects. It is initially a phenomenon of the subject which becomes more precise in its investment of various objects.

Half a century later in the twelfth century, Andreas Capellanus [Andrew the Chaplain] has been taken to represent the scholastic compartmentalization of love. It has to be emphasized, however, that the initial phenomenon is as broad and turbulent as Hugh of Saint Victor's a generation earlier. Secondly, the Chaplain's disciplinarization of love proceeds by social categories. Two titles are assigned to his work: *De arte honeste amandi*, which W. T. H. Jackson, of revered memory, once wryly translated as 'How to Make Love at Court Like a Gentleman'. In spite of my admiration and my debt to a great teacher, I frankly prefer the other title, simply *De amore*, 'Of Love', with no predetermined qualifications. Not that qualifications are unimportant for Andreas. On the contrary, characterizing his work as 'scholastic' seems to me entirely correct: Andreas proceeds like any good scholastic by sequential categorical distinctions.[19] But his distinctions consist of responding to the violent, turbulent nature of love with social categories. *De amore* is inherently paradoxical: disciplining human passion means working against the grain.

Andreas's initial definition clearly delimits his topic as Hugh of St Victor's love for contingent objects. Let me paraphrase and abbreviate the passage on *Amor est passio quaedam innata*:

> Love is a particular inborn passion, which results from seeing *the beauty of the other sex*, and thinking about it uncontrolledly. What it desires most are the embraces of the other, so as to perform *with a common will* what the rules of love require. This passion is inborn in the sense that it does not arise from an external action or event, but uniquely from the thought conceived on the basis of an object seen. *Thus, this inborn passion proceeds from sight and thought.* But not just any thought suffices to engender love: it has to be *immoderate*. Moderate thought does not obsess the mind: that's why it cannot give birth to love.[20]

What is striking here is the breadth of Andreas's initial conception. The *amor* with which he starts is at the antipodes of the codification it produces. Andreas's starting-point is *amor* as a violent, immoderate passion, born in the visual experience of beauty and continued in the ensuing mental turmoil of obsession.[21]

Let Hugh of Saint Victor and Andreas Capellanus — one profoundly religious, the other ambiguously secular for the first two books, and religious in the third, but with a clear separation between the two — mark the breadth of the period's

---

19 Don A. Monson, *Andreas Capellanus, Scholasticism, and the Courtly Tradition* (Washington, DC: Catholic University of America Press, 2005).
20 Andreas Capellanus, *De amore*, in *Amours plurielles: doctrines médiévales du rapport amoureux de Bernard de Clairvaux à Boccace*, ed. by Rudolf Imbach and Inigo Atucha (Paris: Seuil, 2006), pp. 162–69 (my emphasis). *Passio* can readily be translated as 'suffering' (as Monson does), but I prefer retaining the association of *passio* with 'passive', which 'suffering' logically presupposes. The modern use of 'passion' to mean powerful, particularly intense and even overwhelming emotion, tends to a narrativization where the subject of the emotion is impelled, by its very power, into action — thus achieving exactly the opposite meaning of the originally passive semantic content of *passio*.
21 The title of Tracy Adams's *Violent Passions* (New York: Palgrave, 2005) is exactly right on this general point.

exploration of 'love', and establish a theoretical, Latinate context for *amour* in *Philomena*. Hugh of Saint Victor precedes Chrétien de Troyes by a generation; Andreas Capellanus is more or less a contemporary. Since no precise date is available for *De amore*, no precise chronological relationship between Andreas and Chrétien de Troyes's works can be established: either could have 'influenced' the other. Nevertheless, Andreas's discursive analysis delineates exactly the narrative stages of Tereus's 'love' for Philomena: the sight of a beautiful woman; followed by immoderate, obsessive thoughts and desire; and action to satisfy that desire.

The difference from Andreas is equally crucial, however. The sequence of beauty, sight, immoderate thoughts, and desire does not lead, in *Philomena*, to the 'common will' Andreas postulates as essential in his definition of love. *Philomena* demonstrates just how repulsively violent the passion of immoderate love can get, as well as its after-effects. The deviation of *Philomena*'s narrative structure from its abstract formulation in *De amore* partly defines the notion of 'rape': the 'act of love' without the 'common will'. But the sequence of (i) Philomena's portrait of beauty, and (ii) Tereus's response to that beauty as the object of his immoderate and obsessive desire responds perfectly and presents the birth of 'love' in contemporary terms recognizable as Hugh's *cupiditas*: pure, brutal carnal desire.

Indeed, upon rereading, it is rather as if *Crestiens li gois* had written *Philomena* as a rebuttal to the absurdities that literary history would commit in the name of 'courtly love' during the nineteenth and following centuries. If *Philomena* is a youthful work, it is the work of a young, impassioned genius, to be read with the utmost, attentive seriousness, as a narrative meditation on beauty, evil, and class politics. If Chrétien writes rape, it is to condemn it as a political crime, to show women transcending class difference in reaction to rape, and beyond that, to mark the further horrors attendant on unlimited personal vengeance.

That the personal is political (a fundamental rediscovery of twentieth-century feminism) is a minimal conclusion to be drawn from *Philomena*, which makes the feminist point unmistakably: the personal is political. Yet a body of criticism insistently distorted its significance, claiming it normalizes or aestheticizes rape.[22] *Crestiens li gois* posited evil in *Philomena*, as did a certain William Shakespeare, who recycled the story of Philomena in a play titled *Titus Andronicus*, before going on to certain other problem plays such as *Macbeth*, *King Lear*, and *Othello*, texts that also address evil. Medieval texts of narrative fiction address the evil of rape. They posit the evil of rape without endorsing rape. How else can serious fiction or drama address evil?

---

22 E. Jane Burns, *Bodytalk: When Women Speak in Old French Literature* (Philadelphia: University of Pennsylvania Press, 1993); Kathryn Gravdal, *Ravishing Maidens: Writing Rape in Medieval French Literature and Law* (Philadelphia: University of Pennsylvania Press, 1991); Ruth Mazo Karras, *Sexuality in Medieval Europe* (London & New York: Routledge, 2005).

(ii) Episode 1: On Beauty and the Desirability of Evil

As there are three narrative episodes, three narrative subjects enact the primary narrative action of each episode. Philomena is unquestionably the center of human interest throughout, but she is not the narrative subject of the main action of episode 1, which is the rape of Philomena. The rape of Philomena is the act of King Tereus. Tereus is the narrative subject of episode 1. The text starts with a background of political history. After a war in which the Thracian king Tereus supported Pandion, King of Athens, Pandion gave Tereus his elder daughter Procne in marriage. Marriage of a king's daughter is a political act to start with: politics in the text is not the intrusion of a foreign matter.

In Ovid, the story of Philomela allows the poet to stretch his brilliant hexameters around a descent into the horrors of a primary, originary barbarism: the word 'barbarian' recurs repeatedly in his text.[23] *Crestiens li gois* suppresses the word 'barbarian'. Tereus, the subject of the first episode, may well be a Thracian. He is anything but a 'barbarian' in the sense of an uncouth, unmannered, babbling, crude, and vulgar savage. On the contrary, he is a king, he is modern, he is a modern king, wily, coldly calculating how to satisfy his desire, which, in spite of misleading linguistic clues, is simple, brutal, and utterly vulgar. The essential desire that drives the narrative in episode 1 is this: King Tereus is out to fuck Philomena. And the reader knows it: Tereus wants to fuck Philomena.

One may well opt to retain the word 'barbarian' in commentary to describe Tereus's behavior, but then it has to be shorn of all originary reference to any putative earlier stage of civilizational stages of development. Emptied of such temporal reference, it becomes a purely moral and political term, such as may be applied to any modernity whatever, from that of the twelfth century to the modernity of the twenty-first. In that sense, it may be said we are all moral barbarians, or may become such by our actions (on this, more below).

The inception of the text organizes the initial segments of the narrative as contrastive segments of a closed binary contrast, preceded and followed by brief developments that install deconstructions of closure: the immediate installation of a narratorial subjectivity that is split in discussion with itself, including a remarkable example of anthropological relativistic consciousness. The binary contrast being deconstructed consists of a comparison of dark, obscure, presumably 'primitive' forces of destiny, as against a brilliant portrait of contemporary feminine beauty — a contrast not without echoes of similar comparisons in *Cligès*, whose well-known prologue celebrates the transfer of civilization and culture from east to west, and voices the optimistic hope that 'progress' will stay in France forever.

Here, however, *Philomena* very quickly, immediately in fact, imbricates the problematics of politics, self-reflexive subjectivity, and signification, framed in the dual context of ancient Greece and Thrace, with a technique of deconstructive self-questioning. Pandion, courtly King of Athens, center of culture and civilization, right at the start, gives his elder daughter Procne in marriage to a king of Thrace.

---

23 The character named 'Philomena' in the medieval text appears as 'Philomela' in Ovid's *Metamorphoses*.

The evil auguries that pullulate in the opening section will be fully justified by the ensuing narrative. Pandion rejoiced in the marriage which initiates the narrator's self-questioning. A divided narratorial subject engages in rapid-fire dialogue with himself, breaking up sprightly octosyllabic lines into two- or three-part repartees regarding what to call the new groom:

> [...] Pandïons moult liez se fist.
> Moult liez s'en fist? — Voire. — Por quoi?
> Pour ce qu'il la dona a roi.
> — A roi? Mes a tirant felon.
> Tereus ot li tirans non. (ll. 8–12)
>
> [King Pandion was very happy.
> Pandion was happy? — Indeed. — How come?
> — Because he gave her to a king.
> A king? — Nay, rather a felonious tyrant.
> Tereus was the tyrant's name.]²⁴

From its very first lines, *Crestiens li gois* identifies his tale of rape, mutilation, and gruesome vengeance as political. The difference between legitimate governance and illegitimate rule in the Middle Ages was framed as the difference between rule by a king and rule by a tyrant. The difference was difficult to define. The argument is fundamental. The text will return to the theme of tyranny insistently; so will this commentary.

The problematics of rule — legitimate or illegitimate? — always involves terminology. The text signals this involvement by introducing a special notion of signs and significance right after the political dimension. The general problem of representation is associated with its annunciatory or prophetic potential. At the marriage celebrations of Procne and Tereus, none of the ordinaries officiated. No ordinary 'signe de joie' [sign of joy] (l. 19) was present: instead, all night, ugly 'signes' sang, birds prophesizing doom, pain, and suffering (ll. 19–31). All this *senefiance* — a term of semiotic significance in Chrétien de Troyes's literary vocabulary — here designates evil destinies.

As of the first thirty lines or so, the text of *Philomena* ties together some of its major themes, even before the beauty and sexual attractiveness of its heroine are signaled. All of these will be imbricated with her rape, her vengeance, and the monstrousness Tereus brings into the narrative. The narrative began by invoking the glory of a courtly Athens governed by King Pandion; Philomena's rape plunges the world of the narrative into horror.

At line 35, the issue of the doomed marriage between Procne and Tereus is announced:

> La orent entr'aulz .ii. un fil:
> A mal eür l'eüssent il.
> [...]
> Li enfes crut et amanda,
> Si fu molt biax dedans .v. ans,

---

24 Editor's note: all translations are by Peter Haidu unless otherwise noted.

> Ithis ot non. Ce fu deulz grans
> Qu'il ne vesqui plus longuement.
> Je vous dirai assez comment
> De lui avint a la parclose. (ll. 35–36, 42–47)

> [The two had a son,
> at an evil moment it was.
> [...]
> The child grew and learned well,
> within 5 years it was beautiful,
> by name it was Ithys. Too bad
> he did not live longer.
> I'll tell you exactly what
> happened at the end.]

A son was born to the mixed marriage of King Pandion's daughter and the Thracian king, a son named Ithys. His monstrous fate at his mother's hands will be recounted in ugly detail. It may be that it is this issue that is the main point of the text: the ultimate, the most senseless horror of all, at least as senseless as Philomena's rape and mutilation. The birth of Ithys announced as a tertiary after-effect of Pandion's mistake and the ill-fated marriage of Procne and Tereus may be the very reason *Crestiens li gois* chose to retell, or adapt, or appropriate, this particular metamorphosis of Ovid. It allows Chrétien the Goy to tell the story, two generations after 1096, of a boy sacrificed by his own mother.

Just as Philomena's rape will make a world descend into horror, so did the Christian rape of Judaism in 1096, which forced a re-invention of *Kiddush Hashem* that included the sacrifice of children in the name of God. As the Jews of the Rhineland faced the alternative of forced conversion or certain death, in a moment of vengeful symbolic warfare against an overwhelmingly powerful, dominating enemy, they chose to surmount the alternative by self-inflicted death. The horror of Ithys's murder by his mother resoundingly recalls the narrative of Rachel of Mainz, the most dreadful moment of the Solomon bar Simson Chronicle: the sacrifice of a child by its mother.[25] *Philomena* ends with a ringing declaration, absolute in its universalism: mothers shall not kill their children.[26]

The second part of the opening binary pendant will be the brilliant portrait of Philomena herself — the object of desire that initiates the narrative cycle of horror as a cultural construct of beauty, grace, and instruction.[27] It is an error to

---

25   Roughly contemporaneous to Chrétien's early years, the Hebrew chronicle was written shortly before *Philomena*, probably in 1140. See Chazan, *European Jewry and the First Crusade*, pp. 42–43, 111–13.

26   Editor's note: The argument below will return to this insight to confirm the narrator's textual foreboding ('A mal eür') and the possible motive underlying Chrétien's Ovidian choice. According to the *Cligès* prologue, Chrétien also translated Ovid's tale of Pelops, which he identifies as 'le mors de l'espaule' [the bite out of the shoulder] (l. 4). Does the same hidden motivation peek through a second story of child murder, cannibalism, and the gods, this one ending with the child brought back to life though missing the bite already eaten?

27   See the narrative summary of Episode 1: the initial two parts move from Procne and Tereus's marriage to the introduction of Philomena (ll. 1–123; 124–207), followed by four segments that chart

mistake her representation for a standard courtly portrait. It serves both as brilliant counter-part to the dark, obscure forces of evil that people the marriage of Procne and Tereus, and as the basis of the ensuing narrative, by presenting the evil albeit polished subject of episode I with his object of desire, a turning-point that drives the rest of the narrative.

As we have seen, Tereus and Procne return to Thrace and have a child. Five years later, after the birth and the first years of her son Ithys, Procne asks to see her younger sister, Philomena. The diplomatic form of her request, and indeed the character and performance of Tereus as a whole, suggest observation of a couple of high rank: royalty, upper nobility, or very high-class bourgeoisie indeed. Procne would like to see her sister. Her request states her preference to actually go visit Philomena in Athens. If this does not please her husband, however, she suggests that her husband go to Athens and bring back her sister for a visit. Procne treats relations with her husband diplomatically, presenting him with alternative choices of action. Tereus accepts Procne's request to see her sister, opting for the second alternative. He sets sail back to King Pandion's court. Arriving to port at Athens, after an exchange of courtesies, Tereus presents Pandion with Procne's request, quite fairly and straightforwardly.

Installing the Object of Desire: The Portrait of *biautez*

Then, Philomena makes her entrance, dramatically. Coming out of a room in the palace, she enters hair untied and wild, dishevelled, more brilliant than fine gold:

> Atant est d'une chambre issue
> Philomena deschevelee
> Ne sambloit pas nonain velee
> Quar grant mervoille ert a retraire
> Son gent cors et son cler vïaire. (ll. 124–28)

> [Out of a chamber came
> Philomena disheveled,
> Hardly a veilèd nun,
> A marvel to describe
> Her noble shape, her smiling face.]

Hard to describe, perhaps, but the poet will throw himself body and soul at the task. The end effect is clear and unambiguous, even if it returns the self-argumentative narrator back to the fore, as well as the complexity of beauty, love, and evil. Tereus gazes at Philomena:

> Sa grant biauté le cuer li amble,
> Et sa tres bele contenance,
> Pechiez le met en esperance
> De mauvestié et de folie;
> Amours vilainement le lie.
> Vilainement? — Voire, sans faille
> De vilonie se travaille. (ll. 210–16)

Tereus's desire in action (ll. 208–726).

> [Her great beauty takes away his heart,
> And her lovely face,
> Sin gives him hope
> of evil and madness,
> *Amour* seizes him wrongly.
> Wrongly? — Yes, for sure,
> he torments himself for something of guilt.]

The judgment of the text is clear, even if it renders a history that is not clear, simple, and attractive: it is that beauty, learning, skill, and gifts can make a person so accomplished that, as an object of cultural desire, she becomes the occasion of multiple disasters, even representing successive waves of historical barbarisms. It is Philomena's beauty and her grace that arouse a love and a hope it is a villainous sin for Tereus to entertain. We may judge he should have exercised self-control, and it is likely the author would concur, but that is not in the character of a Thracian barbarian or a king, is it?

Neither the wisdom nor the language of Plato, Homer, or Cato would suffice to the challenge of rendering her noble body and bright face. The self-reflexive narrator gives the structural formula of the traditional rhetoric of literary portraits: first the head, then the body. So striking a beauty is Philomena that the topos of her creation problematizes her authorship. God and Nature both had a hand in it. The heroine's physical charms are detailed more fully than would Chrétien de Troyes do in the future: chin and throat, bosom and breasts, were whiter than ermine, her breasts shaped like two small apples; her hands were slim, long, and white, slim too her flanks, long was her waist, and the hips were low. So very well made was the 'surplus' that such a beautiful thing none ever saw: Nature, giving it more thought than of any other thing born, had put in everything she could (ll. 165–69).

So God created Philomena, but Nature made her? Or just her 'surplus', that which discourse, outside the *fabliaux*, does not properly represent? The 'surplus', the physical ineffable, becomes itself a topos, of course: Chrétien de Troyes will use its teasing ambiguity again in the *Perceval*. Does 'sorplus' (l. 165) mean the physical organ of sex, or a vague 'everything else'? The word's meaning rests on contextual physical emphasis. The remainder of Philomena's attractions, another 'surplus', are physical, intellectual, literary, and extensive. She combines the carnal, the scholarly, the literary, the artistic, and the social: she was prized by great barons as companion in hunt and falconry. The narrator even lays the ground for Philomena's later semiotic invention by describing her ability at embroidery. She was such a good worker ('si bone ouvriere', l. 188) there was not her like anywhere: she could have given artistic form to the very fantasy of Hellequin's infernal army flying through the night sky, embroidering rich silk from Baghdad with floral patterns. This typical woman's skill was also an analogy to writing and hovers ambiguously across both realms of meaning. For Philomena was also a writer, an intellectual, and a musician. She knew the great authorities, literary study, and poetry. She accompanied herself on classical instruments (psalterion and lyre) and on popular instruments as well (*gigue* and *rote*).

The portrait of Philomena — perhaps somewhat hyperbolizing — comes to a surprising conclusion. Not only is she beautiful and accomplished, she is so well spoken, that merely by speaking, *she could have run and taught a school all by herself!* The turn of the compliment (ll. 202–04) is both striking and puzzling. It moves from an idealized high culture that happens to include aristocratic entertainments and popular amusements, to an oddly quotidian institutional form, the school. If *escole* is the primary training for the monk or cleric, the turn clashes with the sharp, ideological, sexual division between medieval men and women: in Christian ecclesiastical institutions designed to serve the priesthood, there would have been no room for women teachers. The exceptions, of course, were women like Heloise or Hildegard, brilliant writers and intellectuals both, cloistered both linguistically in Latin and institutionally within clerical institutions for women well out of contact with a totalizing general culture such as Philomena is endowed with. In fact, the text, right from the start, quite specifically distances her from such Christian religious reference: she just didn't look like a veiled nun ('ne sembloit pas nonain velee', l. 126).

The turn 'she could have run and taught a school all by herself' could be considered a hyperbole of 'she was well-spoken'. On the other hand, it could be taken quite literally. Another form of schooling existed than the Christian, where the presence of women was less anomalous: that of Hebrew schools. Some Jewish women were well-educated, especially members of medieval rabbinical families. Female rabbis did not officiate in the twelfth century, but intellectual, well-educated wives and daughters did exist, especially in northern France.[28] Rashi, in eleventh-century Troyes, had three daughters. Two married rabbinic scholars; one learned Torah. Another twelfth-century rabbi taught his daughter; she became expert in Scripture and Talmud: she herself taught Scripture and Talmud. In Germany, somewhat later in the twelfth century, Rabbi Eleazar ben Judah of Worms wrote an extended elegy for his wife in which he describes her many contributions to his school.[29] Rather than present an institutional housing problem — what does one do with an educated woman? — medieval Jewish tradition praised and respected its women, sometimes educated them, and allowed them useful roles in its schools and educational system. Intellectual women in Judaism were a source of pride and admiration in their community, not problematic creatures to be extruded from society, excluded from schools, cloistered and desexualized as nuns. So it is that Philomena is thoroughly versed in the *auctores*, the masters of antiquity, in the art of theoretical writing called *grammatica*, that she knew how to write poetry and prose, as well as playing a variety of musical instruments: so learned was she that of her discourse alone she could have run a school (ll. 194–204).[30]

---

28 L. Rabinowitz, *The Social Life of the Jews of Northern France in the XII–XIVth Centuries*, 2nd edn (New York: Hermon Press, 1972), p. 160.
29 Marcus, 'A Jewish-Christian Symbiosis', pp. 474–78.
30 A comparable and contemporary figure of beauty, talent, education, and knowledge would be Heloise in the Christian Latin world. It is characteristic of that world that her qualities cost Abelard his *couilles* and forced Heloise herself into the Paraclete.

Installing the Subject: Tereus, Desire, and *Amour*

The description of Philomena's beauty is not a mere 'ornament', the empty performance of a given convention, a routine, rhetorically self-indulgent school exercise.[31] The description of physical beauty, learning, and accomplishment, is functional. It does not legitimate, but it naturalizes the sudden birth in Tereus of something the text calls 'amour' (l. 214). This word is normally translated as 'love'. It is not, however, anything like the medieval *fin'amors*, nor its nineteenth-century knock-off, 'courtly love'. In truth, what the text presents is not quite what most of us would want to call 'love'. It is not entirely disconnected however. It is a problem for twenty-first-century interpreters because it was a problem for the twelfth century as well, and because *Crestiens li gois*'s *Philomena* presents it as a problem, a rather profound problem. It is that beauty, an unquestioned value, can inspire evil. It is that men, lusting for beauty, can lust for evil passionately, and fundamentally. Not only men in general, but especially men of power: kings.[32]

The author/narrator insists on these fundamentals. Tereus is inflamed by Philomena's incarnation of all feminine values of beauty and accomplishment, physical and cultural combined. What drives Tereus, however, is an urgency of desire for physical possession. It is not 'love at first sight': it is immediate, intense, obsessive *desire* at first sight, a desire whose lack of moderation turns to madness ('folie', l. 658). Philomena is so beautiful herself, so courtly, elegant, and skilled in all beautiful things, says Tereus to himself, that if he doesn't have her, if he doesn't 'exploit' her ('esploite', l. 454), he'll go mad. He wants her, in a passion of pure, intense physicality. Philomena's beauty and accomplishments are praised, but there is no idealization of the lady as a social superior: relative social rank, status, or cultural difference (he is Thracian, she is Athenian) are disregarded. This *amour* is not only contingent, it is entirely carnal. It is an intense desire for *jouissance*, with no room for affection, respect, admiration, adoration, or anything but physical satisfaction — nothing resembling *fin'amors*, nor anything recognizable as love at all. When Pandion hands over his daughter to Tereus, Tereus has no intention of turning back from his madness and his rage ('sa folie [...] sa rage', l. 707). What Tereus wants, in fact, is to fuck Philomena. The offensive term, with its full load of crude, vulgar, unsublimated aggressivity, is the most appropriate English equivalent for the *amour* defined by the narrative.[33] It is an overwhelming desire for the satisfaction of physical conquest. The use of the word *amour* problematizes it, signifier and signified both.

Nevertheless, that violent carnal desire — 'fucking Philomena' — is articulated in the rhetoric of conventions that will also figure in the stock of literary conventions

---

31 Cf. Michèle Gally, *L'Intelligence de l'amour d'Ovide à Dante: arts d'aimer et poésie au Moyen Age* (Paris: CNRS, 2005), pp. 19–20.
32 The text, as far as I can tell, does not make the point specifically, but it is profoundly anti-Augustinian in asserting a desire for evil as primary. Evil is not merely an absence of good, it is primary.
33 Needless to say, what is in question is neither a 'friendly fuck' nor what modern suburban thought prizes as 'passion'. If 'lust' did not carry the connotation of a clerical judgment that is entirely out of order, it might be appropriate here.

available to writers of the verse novels others call 'romance'. With certain subtractions of physical and social details, the portrait of Philomena's beauty might have appeared in a narrative of love and heroism of Chrétien's maturity or another writer of Chrétien's school. That rhetoric floats the paradoxicality inherent in the conventional representations of love, in the lyric fusion of love and poetry, or in *Cligès* (the author's second verse novel) by the quartet of Alexander and Soredamors, Cligès and Fénice. The great difference is that the description of Philomena's beauty is followed not by the socialization of passionate love in an internalized discipline of sociality, but by its violent, raging physical enactment, effects that have nothing whatever to do with 'making love at court like a gentleman'. The social community, of the court or of more ordinary mortals, does not impose its norms of behavior in *Philomena*.[34] The only 'management' of passion are temporary deferrals impatiently suffered, and somewhat later, the passing attempt to get the victim to consent — not unlike a forced conversion to 'being fucked'. Social codes function only to construct the object of desire on the basis of her beauty: beauty becomes an ideologeme to construct an object of desire. Linguistic convention labels that desire as *amour*. Tereus's carnal desire is similar to Tristan's, but where Beroul's narrator espouses the protagonist's desire and grants him a female object of desire who shares his will and desire for love and sex, Christian the Goy insists on the moral horror that desire, even inspired by ravishing beauty, can incite, if untrammeled by social codes of morality and commonality of wills. Desire for an object of superlative beauty and social grace — 'love' meaning untrammeled desire — can lead to monstrosity.

The *amour* in question is not 'love' in any received sense: it is vehement carnal desire, forced by circumstance to temporize on its satisfaction.[35] *Amour* in *Philomena* designates 'physical-desire-that-is-not-love'.

Cultural Relativism and Desire for Evil

When Philomena makes her dramatic appearance, her great beauty captures Tereus's heart and gaze:

> Amours *vilainement* le lie.
> *Vilainement?* — Voire, sans faille
> De *vilonie* se travaille. (ll. 214–16)
>
> [*Amour* binds him villainously.
> Villainously? — Yes, for sure,
> he torments himself with villainy.][36]

---

34   See Barbara H. Rosenwein, *Anger's Past: The Social Uses of an Emotion in the Middle Ages* (Ithaca, NY: Cornell University Press, 1998), and *Emotional Communities in the Early Middle Ages* (Ithaca, NY: Cornell University Press, 2006).
35   'Carnal desire' can of course imply a complexity of secondary characterizations, including domination, rage, violence, sadism, etc. Which of these is in question is not addressed by the text, nor whether it is a socio-cultural or a psychological given. Nor does the text address the question of whether desire is corporeal or psychic. As the section on the 'narration of evil' will show, what the text does is identify Tereus's desire as evil from the beginning.
36   Editor's note: I have given here a more literal translation than Peter Haidu's earlier quotation in

The negative judgment is clear, yet the text throws in a curious curveball that has been misinterpreted as a simple-minded misinterpretation of classical philosophy. The medieval tyro, making his debut as a juvenile writer, inserts a brief note of hypothetical cultural relativism at this point. It might readily be dismissed as ridiculing simple-minded paganism, a medieval misinterpretation of classical epicureanism. On the other hand, it might reflect the cultural awareness of a young writer brought up to hide the Jewish half of his identity in a hostile Christian world, and the temptation of cultural relativism quite natural in such a situation. Under a certain anthropological dispensation, Tereus's desire might not have been so culpable:

> De vilonie se travaille [Tereus]
> Quant il son cuer veult atorner
> A la serour sa feme aimer.
> Pour ce, s'ele iert sa suer germaine,
> N'estoit mie l'amour vilaine,
> Quar un lor dieu que il avoient,
> Selonc la loi que il tenoient,
> Establi que il feïssent tuit lor volenté et lor deduit.
> Tel loy lor avoit cil escripte
> Que quanque li plaist et delite
> Pooit chascuns faire sans crime.
> Itel loy tenoit paienime. (ll. 216–28)

> [Tereus was working over something criminal
> when he turned his heart toward loving his wife's sister.
> And yet, even though she was his sister-in-law,
> his love was not at all vilainous,
> for one of those gods they had,
> according to the law they held,
> established that they could fulfill all their desire and their delight.
> Such a law the god had written for them
> that each could do as much as pleased and delighted him
> without committing a crime.
> Such was the law held in pagan lands.]

Each one could do as he wanted to pleasure himself, without thereby committing any crime. 'Itel loy tenoit paienime': such was pagan law, such was pagan culture, since in Old French *loy* means both 'law' in the strict legal sense and the mode of living according to law, hence also its culture.

It is unnecessarily uncharitable to assume this is an ignorant foreshortening of classical epicureanism. The passage does ridicule ignorant versions of classical philosophy, in order to suggest the possibility of cultural relativisms which would be natural to the double consciousness of a child of Jewish converts in Christian society. Yet this possibility of a cultural relativism is introduced in absurdist fashion so as not to be credited absolutely: as will be seen from its pragmatic after effects, its ethical outcomes are disastrous. This cultural relativism is raised as a

order to catch the insistent word play with *vilainie*. *Se travailler de* might also be translated as Tereus giving birth to villainy.

theoretical possibility, in order to assert the inherent necessity of a universalism, but a universalism that grounds itself not in the salvific vision of the Event that Badiou for instance inherits from Christianity, but from the possibility resolutely ignored by Badiou's beatific vision, of absolute disaster inscribed by 1096 as material potentiality in European history and materially re-confirmed since by 1939–1945.[37]

Yet if the conjecture that *Crestiens li gois* was a survivor of 1096 is tenable, such relativism holds great dangers: it may be textualized as a hypothetical to be rejected later, when it becomes obvious that *some things simply are not acceptable under any circumstances*.[38]

Obtention of the Object

Let us recall that the narrative subject in episode 1 is a 'tyrant', a manipulator whom the text designates with various terms from the very beginning as evil. His goal is obtention of the radiantly beautiful Philomena whose portrait occurs early in the text. King Tereus obtains the object in a complex series of manoeuvers that include diplomatic negotiations, speculations on the ambiguity of silence, intentionally misleading diplomatic promises, and a formal transmittal of the object, Philomena herself, by Pandion, Philomena's father.

Once Tereus's desire for Philomena has been textually established, Pandion speaks his paternal love for her. Tereus's desire and Pandion's love are juxtaposed. Pandion resembles Lear, and appears foolish, perhaps worse. He is old, nothing pleases him any longer, all his pleasure's in his second daughter, he lives for her alone, he has no sustenance other than her presence and her services to his person. Night and day, evening and morning, no other hand is at my rising, he soliloquizes, nor at my bedding. My sweet daughter loves me so well, she shoes me, she clothes me, her service so pleases me, that were it not for the comforts she brings me, I would long since have died (ll. 363–78; see again ll. 691–703).

Paternal tenderness? Yes, but like the father-king's love in Marie de France's *Deux amants*, on the point of turning incestuous. The phrasing is crucial. It is *on the point of* turning incestuous. That means that the impulse, while there, remains short of narrative enactment. Nothing in the text suggests otherwise. The point of Pandion's incestuous tendency, extensively amplified in his monologue, is precisely that he does *not* act on it. Unlike Tereus, Pandion does not act out desire prohibited by the codes of his *socius*, a universal incest prohibition that is presumably universal because it prohibits a desire equally universal. Men's desires and imaginations may harbor repugnant potentialities: whether they are enacted or not is what concerns traditional ethics. In the structure of this narrative, the textualization of unenacted prohibited desire serves as contrastive juxtaposition to the enactment of prohibited desire in rape. It establishes a textual norm of self-control over behavior coded as illicit. None of this Oedipal or Electral material is found in Ovid. All is Chrétien's 'invention', *Crestien's* reflection on Ovid's text as his material.

37 Badiou, *Saint Paul*.
38 Editor's note: Excursus III will return to the issue of cultural relativism versus universalism.

Waiting for Pandion to decide on Procne's request, Tereus is at a loss. Putting his arms around Philomena, Tereus, full of desire, sighs and weeps. He cannot wait until he has her in the power of his will ('a sa volenté', ll. 457–61). His only pleasure is staring at the girl's noble body and face, seated next to him at dinner: *that's* his drink, *that's* his food. He flatters her, he serves her, and does his best to make himself attractive to her. No one knows why except himself: he *does* know what he's doing, his behavior is conscious and intentional. He will not renounce the great crime he intends to commit whenever he can, but how hard the wait (ll. 596–607).[39] The internal monologue of obsessive, frustrated desire, as well as the later dialogue of sadistic masculine desire on the point of forcibly inflicting itself on a woman moments before the rape, are remarkable manipulations of indirect and direct discourse. Again, they are Chrétien's invention: they have no equivalent in Ovid, whose ample, curling hexameters delight in the forbidden, in displaying the prohibited.

Pandion's hand-over of Philomena to Tereus is a complex narrative act, simultaneously personal and political. The key phrase is: 'sa fille lui a baillie' (l. 673). In the Middle Ages, the *bailli* is a representative of a lord who manages the latter's estate.[40] *Baillier* is to turn over something or someone to another's power, governance, and responsibility. *Baillier* assumes assurances of safe return. Even today, in contemporary twenty-first-century French, a *bail* is a contract of lease. Tereus gives Pandion assurances that, once the visit to her sister finished, he will bring back Philomena safe and sound. He stresses the value of his word, his trustworthiness. He specifies he will do exactly the contrary of what the reader knows he is planning to do. The narration leaves the reader/auditor in no doubt regarding Tereus's falseness. But he gives all the formal assurances that could be demanded, short of actually turning over hostages, a feudal military norm. He speaks not only as Pandion's son-in-law, his elder daughter's husband, but as a king, a head of state, negotiating the contract of a diplomatic agreement:

> 'Biaux sire, quar la me bailliez
> Par tel couvent c'ançois quinsaine
> La vous ramerrai toute saine;
> Et de ce que je vous promet,
> Ma foi en ostage vous met
> Et tous les diex en cui je croi.
> Par sairement et par ma foi,
> Le me bailliez seürement.' (ll. 534–41)

> ['Fair Lord, please turn her over to me
> On condition that before two weeks
> I will bring her back to you all safe;
> And this I promise you,
> Placing my faith as your hostage

---

39 Cf. Chrétien's later treatments of frustrated desire *within observance of social codes* in *Cligès*.
40 One such *bailli* will be Philippe de Beaumanoir, who will collect and publish the customary laws of the principality he had governed in the most famous *coutumier*, but far from the only one: it is a superb work of thirteenth century legal anthropology.

> And all the gods I hold dear.
> By oath and by my faith,
> Give her to me with all surety.']⁴¹

Tereus is possessed by *amour* as madness, as *folie*. During the ensuing formal banquet, the text amplifies the themes of desire and obsession. Tereus spent the night sleepless, so greatly did his madness work him. When Pandion escorts his guest, much as he regrets it, he has to be true to his word: 'Convient qu'il tiengne verité' (l. 671). Again, the contrast with Tereus is marked. Pandion acquits his promise and turns over his daughter: 'Si a son couvent aquité, | Que sa fille li a baillie' (ll. 672–73). Philomena herself was sure of going and returning in safety. How could she have thought of the gruesome thing being prepared for her (ll. 678–83)? Pandion takes leave of his daughter. He commends her to the traitor: 'Si la commande au traïtor' (l. 703).

The ideology of the feudal system identifies property rights, political power, and familial structure. In the process of state-formation, the identification of power structures shifts to monarchy, initially conceived as a form of feudal *dominion*. Philomena, in her doting father's word, is a *bien*: the word still used in modern French for property as real estate. Pandion hands over both rights of lordship and responsibility for the safety of his 'goods', his *bien*, his beloved daughter. The discussion with Tereus has been a negotiation, the result of which is to pass lordship over Philomena to Tereus. Pandion, against his desire, places his younger daughter in the power, the *dominion*, of another king who has furnished all customary assurances for the safekeeping of the person entrusted to him.⁴² The process concludes.

Tereus now has the force and governance of Philomena: 'or a la force et la baillie' (l. 715). The displacement to Thrace (theoretically crossing the Aegean Sea northward to the landmass between the Aegean and the Black Sea) is cursorily narrated (ll. 716–21). It is uneventful: the text notes it and goes on to the next segment.

The Narration of Evil: Failed Seduction and Rape

The text does not even mention touching land. Tereus immediately leads Philomena to a deserted house in the forest, far from towns, fields, and clearings, far from paths or roads of any kind. The presence or absence of civilization is a constant in the author's narrative sitings: it will be crucial in the *Lancelot*, the *Yvain*, and the *Perceval*. The absence of civilization can be an occasion for hospitality and reciprocal succour; it can be the highly ambiguous *gaste forest* [wilderness]; or, as in *Philomena*, it can be a location of monstrosity, the occasion for barbarity.

Narrative barbarity is not synonymous with inchoate textuality. On the contrary, the rape episode in *Philomena*, in its presentation of modern, calculating evil, while it does present complex issues of *literary* interpretation, is well plotted. Its complexities

---

41 Editor's translation.
42 Woman as chattel has a different resonance in feudalism than in capitalism. The notion of responsibility for the chattel's welfare is perhaps stronger in the Middle Ages.

are neither those of theology, however, nor of contemporary theory. Tereus, alone with Philomena, entirely unsuspecting, leads her into the solitary house he has chosen for his project. A passing comment may reflect a historical reflection on the perpetrators of the genocide of 1096: 'En mal fere a trop douce chose | Au malfaitour qui faire l'ose' [there's a sweetness in evildoing | for the evildoer who dares the doing] (ll. 753–54). Evil here is not referred to theology, to original sin, to a curse on mankind. Evil is a human act, perpetrated against another human. Evil is referred to human nature. One thing is requisite for evil: a basic degree of daring, of courage, to break ordinary social, moral rules. Beyond that, however — the lesson is grievous — there is gratifying pleasure for the perpetrator in doing the evil act.

The principle is shocking to a liberal conscientiousness, brought up in a comfortable belief in a supposedly Rousseau-istic goodness of the human being, backed by belief in liberal democratic socialization. It is equally shocking to a consciousness, either Jewish or Christian, viewing the human as created in the image of God. Quite possibly a thoughtful Jewish historical consciousness, growing up in the wake of 1096, further immersed in a wash of semi-manichean Catholic theology, common in the eleventh and early twelfth century, might have found the notion of a self-rewarding taste for evil less perplexing than a modern liberal consciousness does.

The text does not pronounce on the universality of such a principle. Other subjects in *Philomena* — the weavers, for instance — will not exemplify it. Tereus does, however. For Tereus, who has been characterized as evil since the beginning of the text, 'there is a certain sweetness in evildoing', in itself, and perhaps for its own sake? The quality of Tereus's act, the quality of Tereus himself, will be a topic further explored by Chrétien's text, as it extends into its historical co-text.

Tereus is evil, so says the text. But, says the narrator, at least Tereus has this much of 'courtesy' ['de tant fait viaux que cortois'] (l. 763), that, before raping her, he propositions his victim. *Courtoisie*, in other words, is merely a matter of superficial manners, with no inherent moral value. Tereus is evil, but Tereus has the courtesy to proposition the woman he desires. If she yields, he obtains what he wants: a good lay without bother. If she does not yield, fine, he rapes the victim: simple. 'Courtesy', in other words, is a notion possessed of somewhat restricted pretension in this text. Evil and *courtoisie* cohabit. Might some irony hover about *courtoisie*?

The narrator observes moral distinctions both in the narrative articulations of his text and in its verbalization.[43] Tereus tells Philomena he 'loves' her, and asks her to accept his suit, to accept him as her 'ami' — *ami* having, of course, the same ambiguity in Old French as in modern French: 'friend' and 'lover' both. Presumably, it shares the restricted artificiality, perhaps the utter hypocrisy, of 'cortois' above. Additionally, Tereus asks the matter be kept secret. Philomena responds by citing Cordelia ('I love your majesty | According to my bond, no more, no less', *King Lear*, I.i):

> 'Je vous aim bien si com je doi
> Ne je ne m'en quier ja celer,

---

43 The word 'moral' is used here in its French sense, fusing morality and psychology.

> Mes se me volez apeler
> D'amour qui soit contre droiture,
> Taisiez vous ent, je n'en ai cure.' (ll. 772–76)

> ['I love you indeed as bound by duty,
> Nor shall I hide from it
> But if you call me for a love
> that runs counter to right rule,
> keep still, be quiet, I do not care for it.']

Is this the secrecy of an ethics of 'courtly love'? Or is it, as in Andreas Capellanus, a strategy calculated to continue an activity which, if publicly known, is forced to end?[44] The discourse is the object of a moral distance marked by parody and revulsion.

Philomena refuses Tereus and foreshadows the narrative. She refuses to betray Procne, unless overwhelmed by force: 'se n'en suis parforciee' (l. 787). The text draws closer to its verbal climax. Self-defense is useless. Tereus: 'Tout ferai quan que mes cuers pense' [I will do all that my heart thinks] (l. 794). The heart, in Old French, is not just a physiological organ, it marks the site of psychic life, of need and desire, of intentionality and willful decision-making.[45] The heart is the site of personal integrity, the wholeness of the subject who acts, whatever his moral divisions. I will follow my desire, asserts Tereus, echoing Lacan: Tereus is nothing if not faithful to his desire. Tereus's assertion implicates his entire self, moral, psychological, and ethical.

Already, *Crestiens li gois* announces the complexity of the novelist Chrétien de Troyes. Rape will be the climax of the first episode. Together with its sequela, however, the rape begins to constitute the subject of the second episode, which will fold back over the first and produce its horrifying vengeance in the third — at least as horrifying as the rape itself. Criticism that sees *Philomena* as only a story of female victimization by rape castrates the text: it stops at one third of the narrative, and excises, among other things, a female communal organization both in labor and in semiotization that transcends class distinctions, as well as a violent sororal vengeance over male domination. In fact, the narrative is more complex even within the rape episode itself. Tereus first attempts to seduce Philomena, and fails miserably. The rhetoric of the rape inscribes the physical fact of forcing Philomena, of 'exploiting' her. The text has previously labeled the perpetrator and the act itself evil. It will do so emphatically again after the fact, in terms both legal and political.

The orificial act itself offers the pornographer a rich descriptive field, as the marquis de Sade will demonstrate.[46] In *Philomena*, it is represented minimally with the least verbiage possible. Most of the description is pathemic, going quickly to Philomena's horrified reaction:

> Lors li fet force et cele crie
> Si se debat et se detuert

---

44 Monson, *Andreas Capellanus, Scholasticism, and the Courtly Tradition*, p. 277.
45 Haidu, *The Subject Medieval/Modern*, p. 253.
46 'Orificial' is a key term in Burns, *Bodytalk*.

> Par poi que de paour ne muert;
> D'ire, d'angoisse et de dolour
> Change plus de cent fois de coulour,
> Tramble, palist, et si tressue
> Et dist qu'a male hore est issue
> De la terre ou elle fu nee
> Quant a telle honte est demenee. (ll. 798–806)
>
> [He forces her, she screams,
> she fights and twists
> and almost dies of fear,
> of anger, of anguish, of pain,
> she changes color a hundred times,
> trembles, pales, drenches in sweats:
> Damns the day she left
> the land of her birth,
> to be led to such shame!]

The discovery that rape is not primarily about sexual pleasure is not a modern one. Philomena's rape is not a form of lovemaking, nor is it a form of sexuality, it is an exercise of power over an object of desire constituted as such by her beauty, signaling an assemblage of cultural values. The text implicitly treats that beauty as a demonstration of power by its submission, when the tyrant attacks beauty, using sexuality as an instrument. When love exists between freely-consenting lovers, the beloved's bestowal upon the lover of the freedom of her body is a bestowal of power freely consented, an incomparable gift: it is a gift of beauty, and pleasure, and power, as parts of love. The seizure of the body substitutes an exercise of power for the commonality of desire and pleasure which, Andreas Capellanus reminded us, is part of the essential definition of love. The substitution is criminal, but it is a substitution of something supplementary into the position of primacy, a supplemental substitution which makes the act the most profoundly repugnant to the victim. The exercise of power in lovemaking is itself a universal shared by male and female, writer and reader, narrator and auditor. The 'small variation' in the relationship of power and pleasure which normally operates by mutual consent (the switch of primacy and secondarity) produces the catastrophe of rape in the absence of consent. This is 'catastrophe': the topological singularity in which a small displacement, a substitutive displacement from hierarchical subordination to the position of primacy, produces a radical discontinuity, the catastrophic event that destroys a world.[47]

---

[47] Rape is thus a variant of torture, on which see Elaine Scarry's classic *The Body in Pain: The Making and Unmaking of the World* (Oxford: Oxford University Press, 1985).

Philomena's Indictment

From the very beginning, *Philomena*'s narrator insists on the note struck within the first dozen lines of his text: the personage called 'Tereus' figures evil, and that evil is political.[48] Tereus is a 'tirant felon' (l. 11). The narrator repeatedly returns to the notions of criminality, of tyranny, of betrayal, as Tereus's constitutive qualities. Variants of the phrase 'the felonious tyrant' ('fel tirans') occur three times (ll. 548, 631, and 966). The repeated conjunction of the two terms makes of them what Kenneth Burke identified as an associational 'cluster': each of its elements alone implies the other by equivalential association.[49] When *tirans* occurs alone twice (ll. 12, 682), when *fel* or *felon* occurs alone more than a dozen times, each implies the other: each term alone implies the presence of the other and of the full phrase, *li fel tirans*.[50] Other terms also occur occasionally to qualify Tereus or his acts: *traitor* and *trahir* fifteen times; *vilain*, *vilaine*, or *vilainement* five times.[51]

Philomena addresses the existence of evil. So does Philomena, in a savage indictment of Tereus that is simultaneously moral, legal, political, and intensely passionate rhetoric:

> 'Ha! fet elle, *fel* deputaire,
> *Fel* ennuyeux, que veulz tu faire?
> *Fel* mauves, *fel* desmesuré,
> *Fel* traïtre, *fel* parjuré,
> *fel* cuivers, *fel* de pute loi,
> *Fel*, dont ne plevis tu au roi
> Que tu honor me porteroies
> Et qu'a lui me ramenerois
> Saine et haitie en mon païs?
> Tu li juras, et sel *traïs*!
> *Traïtres*, mes peres te crut,
> Qui ta *traïson* n'aperçut,
> Pour ce que devant lui ploroies
> Et pour ce que devant li juroies
> Sor tous les dieux en cui tu crois.'
> (ll. 807–21, my emphasis)

> ['Ah! she said, you whoring *felon*,
> perfidious *felon*, what have you done?
> Evil *felon*, overweening *felon*,
> treacherous *felon*, perjurious *felon*,

---

48 A recent work of criticism, with an important insight as to the violence of medieval passions, re-invents a doubly fictional Tereus: at some imaginary time prior to the beginning of the actually existing fictional tale, he is said to have been 'a decent man' and 'a good husband' before 'being attacked by love' (Adams, *Violent Passions*, p. 67).
49 See, for example, Kenneth Burke, *The Philosophy of Literary Form: Studies in Symbolic Action* (Baton Rouge: Louisiana State University, 1941), pp. 29–30.
50 *Fel/felon*: ll. 548, 606, 631, 904, 966, 1273, 1289, 1291, 1302, 1303, 1327, 1457, 1460.
51 Variations on *trahir*: ll. 543, 631, 703, 712, 713, 739, 810, 816, 817, 827, 862, 1065, 1300, 1321, 1460; variations on *vilain*: ll. 214, 215, 216, 220, 472. *Vilain(e)* also occurs non-pejoratively as the social category of the widow and her daughter, charged with watching over Philomena (ll. 869, 1084, 1103, 1250, 1254, 1258). This second use also bears political value: see the Conclusion.

duplicitous *felon*, whoreson *felon*,
felon, didn't you swear to the king
you would treat me with honor
and bring me back to him
safe and sound to my own land?
Then you swore, now you betray him!
Traitor, my father believed you,
Not recognizing your *falseness*,
because you wept before him,
because you swore before him
on all the gods you credit.']

Within six lines, Tereus is called a *felon* nine times; in eleven lines, he is called *felon* and *traitor* eleven times. Philomena's *acte d'accusation* takes us outside the expected moral space of modern gender discourses, into a legal and political space of medieval power relations which the narrator's vocabulary had indicated from the very beginning. The qualifying statements of the villainous subject's victim reiterate the narrator's judgments from the beginning of the text. From beginning to end of the first episode, its villainous subject Tereus is declared to be evil: the story he performs demonstrates his evil. On this point, narrative and discourse more than reinforce each other. As Roberta Krueger and Colette Storms have understood, *Philomena* is an intently moral text, whose significance exceeds and transcends that of the personal evil inherent in the individualized personation of narrative.[52]

What is the signifying status of the terms *fel*, *tirant*, and *traitre*? Narrative imposes a vocabulary and syntax of individual characters.[53] A focus on the narrative's individualizing nature, manifested as characters, narrative subjects, or agents, can readily suggest taking these valorial terms — *fel*, *tirant*, *traitre* — as merely intensifying, hyperbolic variants of 'bad', referring to Tereus's reprehensible acts. The moral, personal, individual dimension of signification is unquestionable. But all three terms also incorporate another dimension, a legal and political dimension of signification. Even in poetry, 'felony' is 'an active, disruptive force, damaging relations based on fealty, chivalry and love'. The figure so characterized receives a strong negative marking: '*Felon* remained a strong term of reproach and condemnation, indicating behaviour or character disloyal to God, king, feudal lord and vassal, lady and poet-lover'.[54] The three terms together insist on the radical disruption of the polity's fundamental bond which had been signaled at the text's beginning, perhaps threatening its destruction.

That political dimension is emphatically signified without being allegorized, thanks to the repeated use of those qualifying statements. The juridical-political

---

52   Krueger, '*Philomena*'; Storms, 'Le Mal dans *Philomena*'. The term 'personation' is taken from Thomas Hobbes, *Leviathan*, ed. by Richard Tuck (Cambridge: Cambridge University Press, 2002), ch. xvi.

53   A different problem from that of 'the birth of the individual in the twelfth century', though not unrelated!

54   Glynnis M. Cropp, 'Felony and Courtly Love', in *The Court Reconvenes: Courtly Literature Across the Disciplines*, ed. by Barbara K. Altmann and Carleton Carroll (Cambridge: Brewer, 2003), pp. 73–80 (p. 79).

dimension is also insisted on by the victim's enraged accusation. In fact, Philomena does not bemoan the affront either to her person, to her womanhood, or to the universal principle of self-determination in sexual congress, instanced by both Hugh of Saint Victor and Andreas Capellanus, and to which she would be amply entitled. The core of Philomena's accusatory charge against Tereus is that he did not keep his word, his diplomatic contract with the king her father, the contract which, as we saw, was negotiated with King Pandion at King Tereus's insistent entreaties. The judicial quality of political criminality borne by the repeated term of opprobrium *fel* is defined by that failure at the level of narrative action, and further qualified — again, repeatedly — as the traitorous betrayal of her father. It is the rape victim who defines her rape as a political crime. The text of the rape victim asks to be taken seriously, that is, literally.

Excursus II: Tyranny, a Detour Through John of Salisbury's *Policraticus*

It is the text itself, the Old French appropriation of Ovid's metamorphosis in *Philomena*, that insistently introduces the political notion of tyranny and the tyrant into the literary domain. Part of modernity's claims to a distinctive scientificity is its assumption that precision is a universal value. Yet vagueness, as we also know, is also a value. There are terms whose value depends precisely on their imprecision. As a term of art, 'tyranny' was vague, imprecise, and subjective. It still is. In the Middle Ages, Jean Gerson complained it could be leveled against any ruler.[55] The term's vagueness more than allows for interpretation: it demands it. The word forces consideration of its accusation in accounting for governance, governance as actually exercised by the regime in power, no matter what regime. The charge of 'tyranny' raises the question of the legitimacy of governance, in the very concreteness of governance.

The issue, in the Middle Ages, was a broad one: political governance was practiced not only by monarchs, kings, or emperors. Feudal nobles filled in the gaps left by the disappearance of powerful, centralized imperial governance by Romans and Carolingians. Ecclesiastical administrators exercised governance as well, within church administration as well as in the secular world as bishops and abbots. In addition, as we will see, 'tyranny' could apply to systems of power that we do not consider 'political' at all. The activity of governance overflowed the current receptacles of political powers, the governments of states. Tyranny could occur in any receptacle, at any level, and in multiple contexts.

The concurrence of multiple forms of political governance was a competition ultimately won by the monarchy: sovereign rule by one. In turn, modernity has substituted 'representative democracy' for 'monarchy' as the only legitimate form of government: rule by the multitude represented by officials selected by

---

55 Jean Dunbabin, 'Government', in *The Cambridge History of Medieval Political Thought c. 350–c. 1450*, ed. by J. H. Burns (Cambridge: Cambridge University Press, 1988), p. 493. For medieval views of tyranny, see John D. Lewis, 'Medieval Theories of Resistance', in *Against the Tyrant: The Tradition and Theory of Tyrannicide*, ed. by Oszcár Jászi and John D. Lewis (Glencoe, IL: Free Press, 1957), pp. 17–34.

vote.[56] This form of legitimacy does not exclude the possibility of tyranny. The importance of 'tyranny' to political theory is not that it designates a particular form of government. It designates today, as in the Middle Ages, a governance whose injustice had become intolerable to the governed. 'Tyranny' signals the appearance in the on-going discussion within any polis whatever of a questioning of the legitimacy of the actual government. This was as true in the Middle Ages as in modern times. It was true for feudal, monarchical, and ecclesiastical government, as for republican or democratic forms of representative elections.

It had not escaped medieval observers that governance was sometimes exercised by bad kings. Some theoreticians cleaved to the legitimation of power: any government was better than none, even if tyrannical. Some rationalized evil governance as punishment for evil subjects: since all humans inherited evil in their genes (not quite a medieval conception), a certain *Schadenfreude* might consider universal tyranny no more than universally deserved punishment. The contrary understanding might be that, absent institutionalized forms of removal to rationalize the process, the violence of tyrannicide was a necessary part of the equation. John of Salisbury wished to consider the question: he mentions a book in preparation, *De exitu tirannorum*.[57]

The problematics of tyranny was inherent in medieval political evolution. The issue became more acute in the initial re-centralization of princely and royal powers as of the eleventh and twelfth centuries. To the magnates of feudal Europe whose power was being displaced, the recentralization of state-formation was a power-grab that naturally seemed tyrannical.[58] On the other hand, independent possessors of powerful castles often behaved as they liked and without restraint, recognizing no superior power to limit their acts or capable of punishing them. Suger, Abbot of Saint Denis and advisor to Kings Louis VI and VII, considered such knights and feudal magnates tyrants.[59] Tyranny could be found throughout all hierarchies of power.

---

56   If Athenian practice is considered the model of democracy, its face-to-face confrontation of citizens is directly contradicted by modern practices of representation. Modern democracy is a complex self-determination-by-representative-interposition that is the opposite of Athenian democracy. 'Democracy', as touted today, is what Althusser identified as 'state ideology', only at the world-level: its world-wide victory has made it the *de facto* political universal ideology, even invoked by the most grotesquely and brutally tyrannous governments.

57   John of Salisbury, *Policraticus*, VIII, 20 & 21, and D. E. Luscomb and G. R. Evans, 'The Twelfth-century Renaissance', in *History of Medieval Political Thought*, ed. by Burns, p. 328. The standard edition is *Policraticus sive de nugis curialium*, ed. by Clemens C. I. Webb, 2 vols (Oxford: Clarendon Press, 1909). The first volume of a new edition by K. S. B. Keats-Rohan was published in the *Corpus christianorum: continuatio mediaevalis*, 118 (Turnhout: Brepols, 1993). All citations from *Policraticus* are taken from *Policraticus: Of the Frivolities of Courtiers and the Footprints of Philosophers*, ed. and trans. by Cary J. Nederman (Cambridge: Cambridge University Press, 2000). No complete translation into English exists. In a large bibliography, I have found particularly useful Cary J. Nederman and Catherine Campbell, 'Priests, Kings, and Tyrants: Spiritual and Temporal Power in John of Salisbury's *Policraticus*', *Speculum*, 66.3 (1991), 572–90, and Nederman's all too brief *John of Salisbury* (Tempe, AZ: Arizona Center for Medieval and Renaissance Studies, 2005).

58   D. E. Luscomb, 'Introduction: The Formation of Political Thought in the West', in *History of Medieval Political Thought*, ed. by Burns, p. 158.

59   R. van Caenegem, 'Government, Law and Society', in *History of Medieval Political Thought*, ed. by Burns, p. 180.

I will return shortly to John of Salisbury's discussion of tyranny: it was key in the history of political theory. But first, the phenomenon raises the question of a remedy, as much as the question of nomenclature (just what is it that defines tyranny?). Once it has been decided that the ruler is a tyrant, what is the remedy? Does a remedy exist? Can a remedy be imagined? Given the characteristics of a tyrant, submission by flattery and tyrannicide were both the extremes and the likeliest reactions. Isidore of Seville was convinced that even if he was an evil ruler, the tyrant had to be endured, since he possessed God-given power.[60] Giles of Rome argued against the imposition of limits on kingship, and thought a degree of princely tyranny preferable to the evils that arise from disobedience.[61] On the other hand, the welfare of the community was the determining criterion for Thomas Aquinas in his *Summa theologica*: tyrannical government could be overthrown without incurring mortal sin, if the results were more favorable to the community than the continuance of the pre-existing tyranny. Despite its backing by Cicero, John of Salisbury, and Aquinas, however, tyrannicide met with general disapproval.[62] The concept of tyranny was useful above all in exhorting kings to do their duty.

Tyrannicide became a crucial issue in the wake of a royal assassination in 1407: the heir apparent, Louis of Orléans, associated with popular discontent, was killed on a Paris street at the orders of Jean sans Peur, duc de Bourgogne. Jean was defended by Master Jean Petit, who argued, citing John of Salisbury, that this particular tyrannicide was justified. The theoretical opinion of the twelfth century retained judicial pertinence two and a half centuries later. Earlier, Jean Gerson, Chancellor of the University of Paris, had seriously entertained arguments about tyrannicide. At the Council of Constance in 1414, however, he took a different position. He condemned Jean Petit's defense, and argued for a condemnation of tyrannicide. A good academic, Gerson now thought that before committing tyrannicide, the matter should be discussed by 'a council of prudent and learned experts'.[63] In other words, political assassination was referred to committee.

The crucial discussion had occurred in the twelfth century, in the *Policraticus* of John of Salisbury. John, secretary to Theobald of Canterbury and friend of Thomas Becket, combined wide classical readings, biblical scholarship, and patristics with practical experience in politics, diplomacy, and ecclesiastical administration, both local and international. The resulting *Policraticus* is long and prolix: some 250,000 words touching on many topics. Sometimes it is a mirror of princes, sometimes a wide-ranging, unsystematic, moral and philosophical disquisition (not entirely dissimilar to Montaigne's essays). Only occasionally does it touch on its announced topic, that of 'courtiers'. Within its huge edifice, the space directly devoted to the problem of tyranny is relatively small: it is not unimportant for all that.[64]

---

60 Isidore of Seville, *Sententiae*, III, 48.10–11; P. D. King, 'The Barbarian Kingdoms', in *History of Medieval Political Thought*, ed. by Burns, p. 143.
61 Kate Langdon Forhan, *The Political Theory of Christine de Pizan* (Aldershot: Ashgate, 2002), p. 41.
62 Dunbabin, 'Government, Law and Society', pp. 494–95.
63 Forhan, *Political Theory of Christine de Pizan*, p. 85. Unless I am mistaken, the conservative Christine de Pizan, in spite of her use of the *Policraticus*, avoids the topics of tyranny and tyrannicide.
64 It looms large in his letters as well. Editor's note: see for instance, *The Letters of John of Salisbury*,

John of Salisbury's notion of tyranny is unusually broad: it extends well beyond the political domain of public, governmental power. In part, this is due to the fact that his political and moral philosophies are 'inextricably interwoven'.[65] The personal and the political, severed by a traditional modern episteme, are different aspects of the same. A personal act has political implications; a political act is defined in moral and ethical terms. The exercise of power in the *Policraticus* concerns deontology in general: politics, ethics, and morality. It presents the same end result as *Philomena*, but in reverse order: the identification of the personal and the political in the issue of 'tyranny'. The political is personal.

The tyrant can be found in any walk of life: not only in the public sphere of political governance, but also in the private sphere of personal relations as well as ecclesiastical governance. John of Salisbury spends almost as much time discussing ecclesiastical tyranny as political tyranny. Bishops, abbots, popes were often eminences of power, administrators engaged in the political governance of secular communities. According to one of their own, they were as subject to the temptations of immoderate exercise of power as their secular counterparts. John of Salisbury, a churchman who ended life as Bishop of Chartres, assesses the tyranny of his colleagues:

> Even among the priesthood many may be found who are driven by all their ambition and all their talents so that they can be tyrants under the pretext of exercising their duties [...]. Priests should not be indignant with me [...] if I acknowledge that even among them one can find tyrants.[66]

The exercise of power over others is governance: its transformation into tyranny is an ever-present potential, wherever and by whomever that power is exercised. The churchman, the husband, the father, the would-be lover, is as much a potential tyrant as the monarch.

John's discussion of the tyrant and tyranny addresses all forms of power; his discussion of tyrannicide, however, addresses only the political. It has occasioned widely divergent scholarly interpretations. For one scholar, John asserts the citizen's 'duty to kill [the tyrant]'. For another scholar, the proper reading of John's text enjoins 'thou shalt NOT slay a tyrant'.[67] Whatever John of Salisbury's most profound beliefs in the matter, the *Policraticus* certainly contains declarative assertions as to the justifiability of tyrannicide. It defines the tyrant from the people's perspective, as

---

ed. by W. J. Millor and C. N. L. Brooke, 2 vols (Oxford: Clarendon Press, 1979), II, 429–30 (Letter 234), 455–58 (Letter 239), & 615–19 (Letter 281).

65 'Introduction', in *Policraticus*, ed. by Nederman, p. xxiv.

66 John of Salisbury, *Policraticus*, VIII, 17 (*Policraticus*, ed. & trans. by Nederman, pp. 193–94). Further references to Nederman's English translation will be given in the main text.

67 A classic article is Richard H. Rouse and Mary A. Rouse, 'John of Salisbury and the Doctrine of Tyrannicide', *Speculum*, 42.4 (1967), 693–709. More recent contributions are: Cary J. Nederman, 'A Duty to Kill: John of Salisbury's Theory of Tyrannicide', *The Review of Politics*, 50.3 (1988), 365–89; Jan Van Laarhoven, 'Thou shalt NOT slay a tyrant! The So-called Theory of Johannes of Salisbury', in *The World of John of Salisbury*, ed. by Michael Wilks (Oxford: Boydell & Brewer, 1984), pp. 319–41. Laarhoven's point, that John does not present a *developed theory* of tyrannicide, strikes me as correct, but of limited import: it does not invalidate the view that John presents the *opinion* that tyrannicide may be justified. Editor's note: Irene O'Daly treats the issue of tyrannicide in *John of Salisbury and the Medieval Roman Renaissance* (Manchester: Manchester University Press, 2018), chapter six.

'one who oppresses the people by violent domination' (VII, 17, p. 190), a definition broad enough to be widely applicable. The binary contrast with the good prince is striking:

> As the image of the deity, the prince is to be loved, venerated and respected; the tyrant, as the image of depravity, is for the most part even to be killed. The origin of tyranny is iniquity and it sprouts forth from the poisonous and pernicious root of evil and its tree is to be cut down by an axe anywhere it grows. (VIII, 17, p. 191)

Stressing that he is not addressing 'private tyrants' but 'those [tyrants] who oppress the republic,' John states that 'it has [always] been honourable to kill them if they could not otherwise be restrained' (VIII, 18; p. 205). The following chapter cites history to the effect 'that it is just for public tyrants to be killed and the people to be liberated for obedience to God' (VIII, 20, p. 207).

Finally, the authority of the Bible is cited to justify tyrannicide in the title of this same chapter: 'That by the authority of the divine book it is lawful and glorious to kill public tyrants, so long as the murderer is not obligated to the tyrant by fealty nor otherwise lets justice or honour slip' (VIII, 20; p. 206). The reservation is not without weight. As in Suger, the notion of 'tyrant' was often applied to feudal magnates who forcibly extended their authority, over ecclesiastical territory and against the Church's power.[68] John's reservation states that the vassalic subordinate of such a magnate is not licensed to kill his own lord, his feudal superior. That category removed, the license of tyrannical assassination would appear to apply to knights or nobles whose vassalic duty is to another lord, as well as to commoners, secular persons who are neither knights nor aristocrats: peasants and burghers. Whether the license to kill applies as well to ecclesiastics is perhaps moot.

Farther on, John asserts the need to avoid conflicts with the obligations of feudal or religious oaths. Nevertheless, 'tyrants are to be removed from the community [...] they are to be removed without loss to religion and honour' (VIII, 20; p. 209). And without repeating the prescription of tyrannicide, the following chapter observes that, one way or another, 'the end of tyrants is confusion [...] all tyrants reach a miserable end' (VIII, 21; p. 210).

The historical fact is that tyrannicide was more than a matter of discussion in the Middle Ages. Tyrannicide was practiced, 'on the ground', and with remarkable frequency. Murders of feudal lords were sufficiently common to occasion the development of a ritual; the judicial punishment for such ritualized murders of tyrants appears to have been surprisingly light.[69] And, as we have seen, tyrannicide was also practiced at the highest level, as when the duke of Burgundy had the heir to the French throne assassinated. If distasteful, killing the tyrant was not only imaginable: it was a necessary conceptualization within a system of monarchical power lacking alternative courses of remedial action against oppressive exercises of absolute power.

---

68 John Dickinson, 'The Mediaeval Conception of Kingship and Some of its Limitations, as Developed in the *Policraticus* of John of Salisbury', *Speculum*, 1.3 (1926), 308–37 (p. 325, n. 1).
69 Robert Jacob, 'Le Meurtre du seigneur dans la société féodale: la mémoire, le rite, la fonction', *Annales ESC*, 45.2 (1990), 247–63.

That the proliferation of classical language, religious references, the rhetorical arsenal of techniques of indirection, and the complex structure of dialectical argumentation characteristic of John of Salisbury, lead to uncertainties of meaning and ambiguity, strikes me as a valid point. It seems unquestionable, however, that at a minimum, the author wants to posit the question of tyrannicide, and to have it considered seriously by his readers. Its very recurrences, whether taken at face value or subordinated to the structures of complex arguments, testify to the presence of the idea of tyrannicide as a problem for judgment. The author's endorsement of tyrannicide has been argued, but not the presence of the idea as a topic posited for serious consideration.

It is possible to downplay 'John's exhortations to tyrannicide' as 'more a matter of principles than of practical politics', but only if one disregards the pointed conclusion of the *Policraticus* as a whole in its historical context.[70] In spite of the universal relevance of the concept of tyranny, the ultimate relevance of the book's theorization comes to rest squarely on the figure of the king. Not the abstract figure of 'the prince' (as in 'mirrors of princes') but the reigning monarch, Henry II, King of England and Duke of Aquitaine (including all of western France from Normandy to Gascony, Brittany to Bourges), a king of great power, ever working to increase that power by the expansion of old institutions, the invention of new ones (sometimes at the expense of existing feudal and ecclesiastical institutions), and conquering new territories by brute military means. At the end, the *Policraticus* addresses Henry II, with whom John of Salisbury entertained turbulent relations.[71] The king's recent deeds, John says, fail to live up to the promise of his beginning.

The huge *Policraticus* comes to a point and that point is Henry II. If he was praised earlier (VI, 18), he is now limned as having fallen off from that high, earlier standard. Invading the south of France, he is:

> Thundering near the Garonne River [...] besieging Toulouse with a successful blockade [...] he terrorizes not only Provence all the way to the Rhone and the Alps but he has aroused fear in the princes of the Spanish and the French (as though he were presently threatening the whole world) by destroying fortifications and subjecting peoples. (VIII, 25; p. 230)

Though the last pages of the *Policraticus* seem to come to a polemical point, nearly turning the book into the world's longest political pamphlet, the *Policraticus* cannot be reduced to the status of a political broadside. It is too important for that, and far too long. But its meandering and inventive theoretical discourse of political philosophy — including the consideration of tyranny, the tyrant, and tyrannicide — finally designates a potential and particular target. The punch line, of course, is in the parenthesis: as the reigning King of England and Duke of Aquitaine, Henry II, once a great king, has now become a threat, not just to his own people but to the entire world.

---

70 Luscomb and Evans, 'The Twelfth-century Renaissance', pp. 328–29. See also the initial round in the modern exchange, Rouse, 'John of Salisbury and the Doctrine of Tyrannicide'.
71 See Nederman, *John of Salisbury*, pp. 17–36.

The treatise's ambiguity may be willed, a calculated, self-imposed imprecision the author adopted in the hope of remaining within relatively secure boundaries: in other words, in the hope of remaining alive. Naming a contemporary, real-life king a tyrant, after all, is a hazardous exercise. The somewhat elusive but suggestive treatment of tyrannicide may have been a humanist shot across the bow to a king whose fiscal, bureaucratic, and military expansions threatened the established order, and especially ecclesiastical interests: its imprecision may have been a willed, strategic ambiguity. In fact, John of Salisbury dedicated the *Policraticus* to Thomas Becket. His hopes of influencing the king may have backfired in the murder of his friend Becket in 1170, eleven years after the publication of the *Policraticus*.

★ ★ ★ ★ ★

Did *Crestiens li gois* know the *Policraticus*? Directly, or by hearsay? Does *Philomena* specifically allude to John of Salisbury's complex treatment of tyranny in repeatedly, insistently calling Tereus a 'fel tirans', a 'tirant felon'? These questions, perfectly valid, are unanswerable. *Philomena* and the *Policraticus* exist in close chronological proximity to each other. The *Policraticus* was 'published' — made public — in 1159; the composition of *Philomena* occurs on a continuum from 1160 to 1170 according to existing scholarship. I will suggest 1171, for historical reasons. Thus, the *Policraticus* precedes the poem by one to eleven years. The documentary evidence to make the case of influence or intentional allusion simply does not exist. What can be asserted more surely is that the *Policraticus*, along with contextual historical information, signals that the question of the limits of legitimacy in governance was a question raised, not only in the historical, institutional structures of governance themselves, but in the political practices of the populace and in the reflection of its intellectuals. The code of tyranny was anchored, not only in the problematics of institutional structures, but also in praxis, ideology, and cultural representation. If not all agreed on what remedial action was appropriate, the existence of the problem seems largely recognized. A broad and imposing intertext of tyranny is unquestionable. How much more powerfully raised would the question of radically unjust governance — tyranny — be for Jews or post-pogrom converts and their children?

Furthermore, given the broad notion of tyranny John of Salisbury propounds, including both the political and the personal, its applicability to Tereus's rape of Philomena in the solitude of a house lost in the Thracian woods, where the King of Thrace enjoys the absolute power of violence over a victim handed over to his sovereignty, seems self-evident. Tereus is a tyrant. He is a tyrant as husband and brother-in-law, violently imposing his will on a family dependent in his charge. He is a tyrant as king who formally gave his word to another king to protect the young woman he took in charge, giving his word to bring her back safe and sound. His culpability thoroughly established by the narrative, Tereus is passible of judgment for his act on both personal and public counts. In narrative logic well before Dostoyevsky, crime leads to punishment. 'Crime and punishment' defines the narrative logic of *Philomena*, even if, in the absence of an available system of justice under established governance, the only available justice is that, universally available, of barbaric vengeance. The principle of tyrannicide, as discussed in the *Policraticus*, could readily justify killing the tyrant Tereus.

Delingualization

Philomena's indictment of Tereus, aside its rhetoric, is also a speech act. It is a narrative integer. As such, it warns Tereus of the danger Philomena represents. Tereus measures the danger Philomena represents as the living witness to the crime he has just perpetrated on her. That it is a crime is unquestioned. No justification of the act is proffered, nor can one be. It is totally unjustified. Tereus's logic is obvious. To prevent Philomena from bearing witness against him, he cuts out her tongue, to leave her imprisoned in a lost Thracian farmhouse in the care of two weavers, a mother and daughter, nameless servants.

Her tongue cut out, Philomena weeps, screams, brays like an animal. Ovid has the tongue, cut off from its root, fall to the ground, and still shivering, murmur on ground blackened with blood: like a mutilated snake's tail, it palpitates and dying tries to rejoin the person it belonged to. Ovid's has been termed a 'baroque cruelty'.[72] It could figure as fetishized phallicism, or a symbolic castration similar to Yvain's lion, the tip of its tail cut off, reminiscent of a circumcision. *Crestiens li gois* suppresses the detail. His substitute is less palpitating, perhaps more cruel, and far more puzzling as to meaning: 'La langue li traist de la goule | S'en trenche prez de la meitié' [He pulls her tongue out of her maw | And cuts off nearly half of it] (ll. 854–55). Having raped her, Tereus cuts out Philomena's tongue, to prevent her bearing witness against him: a 'delingualization'. But why half? Why not simply excise the tongue entirely? Why the detail of the half?

The first narrative subject of the author's first narrative, Tereus is a radical inversion of the literary 'heroes' that Chrétien de Troyes will author in the future: Erec, Alexander, Cligès, Lancelot, Yvain, Perceval, and Gauvain. None is quite perfect, all are admirable. Oddly enough, the text of *Philomena* does not rely on the implications of shared social codes or religious values to identify the subject Tereus as evil and repugnant: it repeatedly states the fact of his moral negativity quite directly and baldly. If the adaptation erases one trace of Ovid's 'baroque cruelty', it amplifies the discursive sadism of the rapist so as to stress his moral repugnance. The first narrative sequence of the text establishes the episodic subject as emphatically an anti-hero: a personage of evil, whose acts are recognizably evil and are labeled as such by the text.

The text also performs a rather different narrative manoeuver with the subject of the narrative as a whole. Philomena, the unique feminine beauty radiant with culture and knowledge at the beginning, stolen from her land by dissemblance, raped and mutilated, undergoes a radical desubjectification. At this moment, hers is an absolute destitution, a total dispossession not only of goods and wealth, but of personal dignity and any sign of personal worth. The remainder of the narrative

---

72 G. K. Galinsky, *Ovid's Metamorphoses: An Introduction to the Basic Aspects* (Berkeley: University of California Press, 1975), pp. 129–32.

will see not just a turn-around, but a radical resubjectification of the person. Only it is a resubjectification into a subject whose narrative program is highly problematic. It will entail alliance with the two wordless weavers left as jailers, an alliance that transcends class difference. It entails the invention by Philomena of a new mode of semiosis for the speechless that is a model for the oppressed by radical dispossession. It also entails alliance with her sister Procne in a narrative program of incestuous familial revenge that is, if anything, more horrifying than the criminal rape she has suffered. Philomena's resubjectification prefigures the invention of a poetry of persecution as well as a politics of cruel, vengeful revolution.

(iii) Episode 2: Resubjectification, Semiotics, and Class Transcendence

The final segment of the poem narrates the revenge wreaked on Tereus for his crimes in episode 1: that revenge occurs in episode 3. That defines the dynamic of the narrative. Between the episodes of the crime and the revenge, however, episode 2 occurs. Its narrative function is instrumental: to reunite Philomena and Procne for their revenge against Tereus. It is, however, amplified into a major narrative sequence. A minor instrumental segment in the Ovidian source is turned into a major episode in its medieval appropriation.

The narrative function of episode 2 is the communication of Philomena's message to Procne, so that the two sisters may be reunited to enact their collective revenge. Its amplification introduces a theme at first foreign to the 'crime-and-vengeance' scenario: the invention of a particular form of semiosis. A narrative instrumentality gives rise to developments that come very close to the poetic subject. Without obvious connection to either rape or bloodthirsty vengeance, the amplified moment of communication interposes semiosis invented between the two moments of horror. Furthermore, that semiotic invention is associated with an apparently foreign political theme, the association of the subject with the two weavers assigned to guard Philomena, in a project of liberation transcendent of class distinctions.

The creation of representation stands between crime and punishment. A representation of representation within an aesthetic of conventional repetition defers the repetition of horror in a revenge of horror. The principle of repetition determines a second coming, as horrendous as the first. Structurally, the second half of the poem (what ensues after the crime itself) thus breaks into two episodes, followed by an epilogue:

i. instrumental program of communication = the invention of semiosis;

ii. enactment of vengeance;

iii. epilogue

While the narrative dynamics are clear, the point of the detour is not.

Silence and Semiotic Invention

The celebrated invention of a new culture and a new literature by the twelfth century's vernacular writers proceeded in part by the appropriation of their classical heritage in a combination of translation, adaptation, and revision. It also proceeded by archiving the representation of oral textuality in writing, and incorporating traditions from colonized territories.[73] These complex processes incited the inscription in their narratives of a heightened consciousness of semiotic processes: social marginality is a particular site of cultural exploration where semiotic models are tried, tested, and fleshed out. The twelfth was *the* century of literary and cultural experimentation par excellence, a fact not always perceived by moderns confused by the period's conventional alterity. Social marginality had its role to play in the cultural renascence of the twelfth century.

The heightened consciousness of semiotics is intensified when the text's implicit critique or resistance takes a distancing perspective on its own historical society and installs a critical reflexivity in general. But the condition of writing disaster — an implacable imposition on the subject of both impulse and topic — means manoeuvering inside the fragile construction of the bubble of semiosis. The artificiality of the forms of human semiosis, their status as mere convention, their resultant fragility stand naked to the subject who faces the looming ferocity of historical repetition: the friable constructions of semiosis are always erected against the principle of repetitive disaster, the principle that past disaster inherently announces its repetition as futurity.

That subject lives a double bind. The natural impulse of expression is doubled by an imposed duty to speak — to address the disaster, to mourn the dead and cry the lost — but simultaneously, the subject is doomed to silence, lest advertising presence itself bring repetition, not to mention persecution. The dual stricture of speech and silence produces an imperative of silent speech, imposing itself on the curly-headed writer who contemplates the past with the staring eyes and open mouth of amazed horror as catastrophic wreckage piles up at his feet, the violent whirlwind of history threatening to catch him up and propel him into the future backwards.[74] This is the birth of covert indirection in language: the necessity of saying things that cannot be said, for ultimate reasons, for reasons historical and political, and the desire for personal survival always honored in Judaism. Resistance and critique are indirect. They are not discursively formulated in directly theoretical or philosophical terms. They operate in a shadowed silence that marks their presence-in-absence.

The problematics of interpreting silence as meaning is thematized by the text. During an early moment of dalliance between Tereus and Philomena — a verbal jousting that, in another story, could figure as discursive foreplay and suggest a less than total innocence in Philomena — the question arose of interpreting the silence with which Pandion greeted Tereus's request (ll. 296–319). Tereus, desiring

---

73 Haidu, *The Subject Medieval/Modern*, p. 97.
74 The reader will recognize the paraphrase of Walter Benjamin's inexact description of Paul Klee's 'Angelus Novus' in *Illuminations*, ed. by Hannah Arendt and trans. by Harry Zohn (New York: Schocken, 1969), pp. 257–58.

a favorable reply, cites the proverb: 'who keeps silent grants the wish'. Philomena casts doubt that Pandion's is an affirmative silence. She responds: I don't think so, that interpretation doesn't sound right. The problematic of the unsaid, and perhaps the unsayable, is textualized. The silence of the unsaid is not meaninglessness. What needs to be communicated cannot be said. But something is there, unsaid — so far. The verbal text is a construct around the unsayable. The major part of Chrétien de Troyes's first novel, *Erec et Enide*, will be constructed around the imposition of silence on the female subject by her husband's order. Perceval's silence will also be in obedience to a male figure's rule of silence. In the following century, the *Roman de silence* is constructed around a rule of silence imposed by the female subject's father.

The interpretation of silence can be thought a problem of hermeneutics, of course: what does silence mean, from the perspective of the *Vorhaben* of a preestablished religious faith? Outside the subject position of being the destinatee of a text, or its willed narratee, the application of hermeneutics to a text of alterity is dubiously appropriate.[75] The question posed by the characters, however, refers to the king's silence before a concrete request in a secular world. It is closer, paradoxically, to the documentary silence around the 'Final Solution': the absence, in spite of extensive, centralized bureaucratic structuration of the extermination process, of a written order to proceed to the extermination of the Jews. *Philomena*'s silence is the physically imposed silence of a tyrant on his subject-prisoner. Tearing out a prisoner's tongue is a crude, savage form of sovereignty: tyranny as mutilation. Did it look back to something in the writer's constitution as subject, back to a formative historical trauma, and forward to an equivalent, possibly inverted, horror? Mutilation may be constitutive of subjectivity, a formative desubjectification.

Silence also marks social and political ineffabilities in the historical world which link writer, text, and audience. As we have seen, a self-preserving hesychasm may be at work in John of Salisbury's huge amplification of ambiguity in the *Policraticus*. The creation of a secular culture during the twelfth century relocated the theological problematics of silence, of the unsaid, of the ineffable, of the unsayable, into the domain of vernacular secular writing as it developed within the polities of the nascent state-form. But the impossibility of certain utterances may also have been political and historical. The shape or structure of the problem remains the same — text woven around unspecified meaning — but the import of the issue changes. The present text addresses, not the silence of a deity, but silence as enmeshed in sublunar, social, and political life. From within the context of historicality, the new culture addresses an ultimate issue formerly in the exclusive domain of theology and doctrine.

If the twelfth century moves ineffability from theology into politics, in that twelfth-century context, the problematics of silence replayed in secular, vernacular texts retains the potential of religious resonances.[76] That is the potential of

---

75 Peter Haidu, 'The Semiotics of Alterity: A Comparison with Hermeneutics', *New Literary History*, 21 (1989–1990), 671–91.
76 Such 'resonances' or 'reverberations' are very different from what is called 'allegory' in a

secondarity, semiosis at a second level. Beyond denotation, beyond association, semiosis produces simulacra that refract human life and are to be contrasted to social 'reality', including its religious ideologies. Does *Philomena* reverberate theologically? A religion whose god had entered the life of his people, made a pact with them and addressed their leader directly, had given birth to a religion that claimed to supersede its origin as a religion of *deus absconditus*, an absent and silent god whose will is by definition unascertainable. Theology is entirely nourished by the issues of God's silence. The enormous and unique development of Christian theology and doctrine results from that originary silence, and attempts to compensate for it. Jews had benefited from discourse with God, and were capable of questioning and arguing with Him. His silence was not originary; His presence was. Allowing horrors to visit his chosen people was incomprehensible and personal both. The secular, vernacular encoding of the silence of torn flesh unquestionably reverberates with theological associations, even when it avoids turning into allegory. It only requires the conjunctive power of the reader or auditor.

Resubjectification, Imprisonment, and the Feminine Nodule

In his later work, Chrétien de Troyes will develop a structural technique of separating a long narrative into a sequence of discrete episodes. *Philomena* is much shorter than the later novels (less than a quarter of their typical length). The difference is that between a novel and a novella. The technical necessity of separating a long narrative into sectioned episodes is not as apparent. The episodic principle is already at work in *Philomena*, but the separation of narrative modules is less precise. In fact, the narrative implies its second half at the end of its first half.

As we have seen, Philomena responds to the carnal violence she suffers in a discourse of anguished intensity within the rape scene of episode 1. Something radically different occurs simultaneously. Philomena responds to her victimization with a verbal, accusatory counter-violence that shifts the text's narrative ground. Her discourse of accusation seals the transformation of her rape from a personal, sexual crime to incur a specifically political and diplomatic dimension. The political and legal isotopy has been present since the beginning. At this point, that political and legal isotopy becomes dominant.

Rape, as a political crime, as a personal variant of tyranny, legitimates counter-violence. Whether it legitimates the particular counter-violence actually deployed raises the question of proportionality, or does it? A principle of exchange lies at the basis, not only of civilized economic life, but of justice as well. The effect of Tereus's barbaric horror, the compound of rape and mutilation, has created a new barbarism out of the civilization signaled by Athens, Pandion, and the discourse of *amour*. Does proportionality end at civilization's edge?[77]

---

medieval context, but close to what Angus Fletcher once called 'allegory', see *Allegory: The Theory of a Symbolic Mode* (Ithaca, NY: Cornell University Press, 1982).

77 Editor's note: for further discussion and undermining of the opposition between civilization and barbarism, see Excursus III.

By the very fact of her victimization at the end of episode 1, Philomena is transformed into the vengeful narrative subject of episodes 2 and 3. The violated, victimized object of the antagonist's action in spite of her protests, becomes the extraordinarily resourceful subject of semiosis and vengeance of those episodes. The previously-noted syncretism of Tereus as villainous subject is doubled, paralleled, and narratively balanced by Philomena's syncretism as object-turned-subject. The vengeful subject of episode 3 comes to the textual surface at the end of episode 1, in Philomena's indictment. The limited political optimism of *Philomena* is that the perpetrator's sadism incites the victim's rebellion. The personal story of 'crime and vengeance' is also the political story of rebellion against tyranny. But the horror of the crime is such that it transcends all civilized limits, in the retaliatory vengeance as well as in the crime itself.

After rape and the mutilation that leaves her speechless, Philomena is imprisoned in the solitary house lost in the woods that was the scene of her rape. Silence becomes a pragmatic problem. Ovid briefly sketches Philomela's situation in nine hexameters (ll. 572–80): guards preclude flight, thick stone walls surround her, the muted mouth cannot speak, but great is the ingenuity of suffering, and unhappiness is the mother of invention. Philomela hangs a cloth on a primitive loom, and across its white threads she weaves purple letters that recount the crime. She entrusts the completed work to an uncharacterized woman who carries it to Procne. The Old French poet amplifies this kernel of nine hexameters to a narrative segment of 368 octosyllables (ll. 867–1235). The expanded component gives the story a completely new dimension. The Latin poet assumes the existence of both language and loom-work. The medieval poet narrates their invention. The Latin poet leaves the status of woman where he found it. The French poet textualizes the formation of a feminine community that transcends class distinction. Language and the communal labor of women across class distinctions are narrative inventions of the young twelfth-century Jew.

The medieval poet concretizes Ovid's abstract 'custodia' (*Metamorphoses*, l. 572) by inventing not one, but a duo of guardians: an old woman and her daughter. Neither is named, but both play the kind of role that Chrétien de Troyes later will relish. The older woman is quickly characterized as a 'vilaine', an ambiguous word that can be either a social class determination or a negative judgment: a peasant or commoner, or an ugly, morally reprehensible person. The feudal ideology of the extractive class tends to fuse these meanings. Chrétien de Troyes's irony famously inverts the relation of feudal superiority and the *vilain*'s inferiority when the knight Calogrenant narrates his encounter with a rustic giant of a man in *Yvain*. That anti-feudal inversion is anticipated in *Philomena*, where the anonymous mother and daughter, formally servants of the tyrant, are paradoxically good and deontologically inventive. They manage to keep faith with their lord and master's injunction not to let their charge wander away from the house and yet serve Philomena by facilitating both the creation of her message and its communication beyond her prison. The old *vilaine* and her daughter actantialize the ambiguity Chrétien exploits in language. Chrétien loves to demonstrate feminine wit and the spunky resolution of agents caught in narrative double binds, as with Enide, Fenice, Lunete, and Blancheflor.

Is that part of his Jewish heritage, fused with a political openness to working-class culture?

In fact, the concretization of the function of 'guarding' the prisoner allows the creation of a small female nodule, in the house lost in the forest, a female nodule of weavers. This small community of women weavers in *Philomena* grounds a more complex narrativity. The nameless *vilaine* and her daughter own the materials and tools their noble prisoner needs to borrow in order to create her message. The traditional task assigned women by their subordination within patriarchy, weaving cloth, is turned to the constitution of a small sorority that transcends class. That trio (the imprisoned princess, muted by savage delingualization, seemingly desubjectified, together with the two nameless working women, weavers by trade, caught in subjugated servitude) allows for the forced invention of semiosis, as the message composed transcends the walls of the prison and opposes a female subject of vengeance to a male tyrant.

The literary lineage of this feminine nodule will be the three hundred noble *serves* and the sororities clustered around Laudine and Lunete in the *Yvain*, and perhaps that of Marie de France's *Fresne*. Finally, the *vilaine* is the earliest of Chrétien de Troyes's characters who, faced with the double bind of contrary injunctions, manages both to satisfy unjust superiors and yet to retain moral standing. Her most fully-developed literary progeniture will be Lunete, and beyond Chrétien de Troyes, Molière's multiple *soubrettes*. The Middle Ages was far from exclusively misogynous.

Semiotic Inventions and Fascism in Medieval Praxis

Tereus returns to his wife Procne and asserts that Philomena has died.[78] Back in the solitude of the woods, Philomena wants to inform Procne of her real situation. Lacking speech, messenger, and means of writing, she needs a stratagem ('engin', l. 1073). The text elaborates a sequence of stratagems that, in the face of muteness imposed by violence, signal an acute semiotic consciousness.

Philomena's successive semiotic stratagems to overcome her muteness are *Crestiens li gois*'s inventions: none occurs in Ovid. Ovid's Philomela writes a message in purple letters to communicate with Procne: she 'writes' letters in threads. *Crestiens* performs a more radical substitution, familiar from honorable classical antecedents: the substitution of visual representation for language. Following Penelope's example in the *Odyssey*, Philomena weaves a tapestry with a supply of colored threads provided by the old *vilaine*, a narrative fabric in which her entire misfortune is manifested:

---

78 Jacques Derrida stated that the 'lie', defined as individual intentionality, was strictly speaking never possible to prove (*Histoire du mensonge: prolégomènes* (Paris: L'Herne, 2005), p. 22) and then went on to explore the difficulties of that impossibility. That impossibility may or may not hold in 'real life'. In narrative, however, the lie is eminently provable. It is an essential resource of fiction, as it is of quotidian life and politics. No one doubts the existence of the lie as a social fact. Only a reduction of the issue to individual consciousness allows its denial, and the undifferentiation of text and social reality.

> [...] une cortine ouvree
> [...]
> Que toute sa mesaventure
> Iert sa serour magnifestee. (ll. 1095, 1098–99)

Had the author seen the embroidery of the Bayeux 'tapestry'? Does he refer to it in noting its multiple colors: indigo, red, yellow, and green? Perhaps, but there is a difference. Philomena's weave does not record the past to glorify or legitimate the present. She tells her story to provide a road map marking her exact location in the present. Finally, Philomena signs off on the work: the tapestry-text signals its authorship, just like Christian the Goy within *Philomena*.[79] When Procne receives the work, she will understand it immediately: it is a communication device that is pragmatically successful. Neither tapestry nor text glorifies or 'aestheticizes rape'. The description of the event is in the verbal narrative itself, where it needs to be, not in its visual *mise en abyme*. The text does not tarry on the description of the woven text: the medieval writer gives a skeletal summary of narrative events that are the content represented by the tapestry (ll. 1122–33). Functionally, Philomena's tapestry is a call for help that communicates essential information: what happened and the enunciator's location.

The work cites an identifiable, traditional equation of the visual and the verbal, as in rhetorical ekphrasis, and reverses it: the written narrative includes the visual representation of its own evenementiality. The verbal text rediscovers and recreates a visual form of semiosis in translating from one language to another, from Latin to French. But the text goes much farther in its concrete imagination of the process of inventing semiosis. The tapestry completed, the message woven, Philomena still needs to have it carried and delivered to Procne. How does a mute communicate to the old woman weaver her desire or her intent that she desires her daughter to carry the semiotic object just fabricated to Procne in a nearby city? Since she is unable to speak, she needs new signs. Indeed, she needs new systems of signs, a new and different means of communication.

First, Philomena touches the old woman, perhaps on the shoulder: physical touch is itself a means of communication, an index. If it does not communicate discursive content, it minimally calls on the other's attention. Secondly, Philomena comes to semiotic invention proper: 'de tout son estouvoir | Fist *nouviax signes*' [out of the depths of her necessity | she invented new signs] (ll. 1146–47, my emphasis)

If speech defines the human, rendering one unable to speak robs the person of the specification of the species. The infliction of muteness by delingualization is a dehumanizing mutilation; it is a species desubjectification. The re-invention of semiosis replaces desubjectifying violence. But the human is more than language. If language is the privileged mode of human semiosis, it is not the only one. Language subtracted, something remains that seeks language. Something in the human

---

[79] As if to nudge the reader with the joking detail, the difference is that Philomena's work is signed at one end (ll. 1120–21), not in the very center, where *Crestiens li gois* signed his. The Bayeux work (embroidery in fact), unfinished in its present state, may have been complete originally: Wolfgang Grape, *The Bayeux Tapestry: Monument to a Norman Triumph* (Munich: Prestel, 1994), p. 23. Was it signed?

privileging of language precedes language. As the text inscribes the invention of semiosis, so does it present the pre-existence of something outside the text. The text constructs multiple semiotic means of referring to the *hors-texte*. Philomena's invention of semiosis responds to a need that is pre-semiotic, but which must inscribe itself in semiosis. Philomena invents new signs, and hence a new sign system, in order to inscribe what precedes signs, sign systems, and signification: human need.

Tereus's savage mutilation of Philomena attempts to mute her humanity, to render her unable to speak in claiming justice. She is now unable to represent herself to claim justice. The self-evident injustice comes remarkably close to Jean-François Lyotard's definition of discursive fascism as stripping away a complainant's ability to represent himself or herself, including by the power of speech.[80] 'Fascism' is not quite part of the medieval experience, its conceptual vocabulary, or its self-consciousness. It requires willful anachronism to speak of fascism in a medieval context. Nevertheless, parts of the complex phenomenal bundle we call 'fascism' exist in medieval textuality and in medieval history.

Similarly, Michel Foucault taught us that the ability to speak is not only a matter of learning language and rhetoric: it is also a question of social entitlement.[81] Whether we can speak and make ourselves heard is a matter of our subject position in a world of discursive institutions and the rights and privileges they grant. If the equation between narrative subject and writing subject is recognized, the muteness physically inflicted on Philomena stands in for an incapacity to speak imposed on the writer. Chrétien's predilection for covert or indirect speech — as in irony — is more than a matter of ornamental style: it is a matter of survival, a survival beyond the physical assured by converted parents, but a survival to which the words 'spiritual' or 'religious' do not do justice. In our vocabularies, perhaps 'culture' or, better, 'mode of being' come closest. Philomena, muted by delingualization, stands in for the convert's inability to speak directly.

It is not pure victimization, however. Philomena must present her case in ways other than speech. Other forms of signifying are required and are to be invented. It is their multiplicity that generates an understanding of semiosis, and a general semiotics.[82] Here, however, a peculiar problematic occurs. It inheres in a supposed connection between discursive forms and political forms, the political significance of literary forms. The author's texts are characterized by 'openness': they are open to various interpretations. But the term 'open' is suspicious. It is suspicious insofar as together with its binary opposite, 'closed', it has political reverberations I do not wish to invoke. 'Open' and 'closed' textuality is a covert allegory for 'open' and 'closed' societies. Textual 'openness' is not correlative with political democracy; textual closure is not coordinate with totalitarianism. A closed political culture,

---

80 Jean-François Lyotard, *Le Différend* (Paris: Minuit, 1984), pp. 22–27.
81 The *locus classicus* is the lecture originally given in English: Michel Foucault, 'What is an Author?', in *Textual Strategies*, ed. by Josué Harari (Ithaca, NY: Cornell University Press, 1979), pp. 141–60.
82 This is close to the realm explored by Henry Louis Gates, Jr., in *The Signifying Monkey* (New York: Oxford University Press, 1988).

with generally shared codes of value and interpretation, can readily foster open texts. Democracies, reputed to be 'open' polities, experience no difficulty in generating closed texts. Indeed, democracies require closed texts like constitutions and contracts. Democracies like totalitarian systems require the communication of messages with specifiable content, which in turn requires 'closed' systems of semiotics. Both 'open' and 'closed' texts are produced and circulated in all kinds of polities. There is no perfect equivalence between forms of language or literary forms and political forms or systems of values. The texts of the author Chrétien de Troyes, like novels in general, frequently represent the function of communication. Successful communication requires closed semiosis. Within a text of open semiosis, such as *Philomena*, 'closed' communicative messages also are created and exchanged.

Necessity enforces semiotic creativity: the invention of new forms of semiosis is inherently linked to the narrative reality of representation of need and (in)ability under conditions of dehumanization and desubjectification. Philomena, the possibility of speech ripped out of her mouth, needs new sign systems to communicate. Philomena invents new sign systems. One is touching another person to communicate a call for attention, a primary, corporeal interpellation. Another such new sign system, not described, is an indexical sign system such as was developed in the Middle Ages for monks.[83] Such a sign system works as a modern sign-language for deaf-and-mute subjects.

Chrétien's semiotics is not merely expressive: it allows for a pragmatic communication system. It requires an interpreter who grasps specific content in the functioning of a closed sign system. Chrétien's text understands this meta-semiotic principle. Philomena's new sign system works pragmatically, the narrator tells us. The old *vilaine* grasped everything Philomena signed, says the text, *she understood all her signs*: 'tous ses signes entendoit' (l. 1188). *Crestiens*, writing a disaster of incommensurability which cannot be specifically delineated, insists on the pragmatic closure of the semiotic systems used to communicate specific needs. Philomena and her *vilaine* can communicate, the latter understands whatever Philomena asks, and Philomena metalinguistically understands that her interlocutor understands her. Visual images and digital, iconic, and indexical sign systems together substitute for the abstract symbols of verbal signs.

The continued substitutive invention of new modes of semiosis — new 'languages' — occurs within a 'translation' of Latin into medieval French, the substitution of one verbal system for another. Within the verbal system of French, the narrative fields three familiar forms of semiosis: visual representation, manual or digital signs, both successfully negotiated as substitutes for the abstract, verbal signs of language. It is rather as if the author had decided to slip into his text examples of each category in the inventory of signs defined by C. S. Peirce as 'iconic' signs, 'indexical' signs, and 'verbal' symbols, all three substituting for each other, within the substitution of one set of verbal symbols (medieval French) for another (classical Latin). Furthermore, the text incorporates Peirce's triad of signs within a narrative which responds to the categories of Greimas's narrative semiotics: the two forms

---

83 Constable, *The Reformation of the Twelfth Century*, pp. 198 & 290.

of semiotics are not exclusive of each other when the task is the representation of human experience.[84] The aptness of both theoretical forms of modern semiotics, Peirce and Greimas, to the twelfth-century writer's narrative invention leads to speculation about the question of transcendence and universalism in the human sciences. The minimal claim to be made is that advanced modern forms of semiotics are textually present *in* narrative *nuce* in the twelfth century, even if not theorized. Not only sign systems, but a meta-semiotic consciousness, are born out of the experience of evil. And what better site than the self-reflexive consciousness of a passionate young Jewish convert, appropriating Ovidian metamorphosis to render the horrifying dehumanization of the 1096 holocaust through the narrative of rape, invented covert semiosis, and equally horrific vengeance?

If the text considers the semiotics of philosophical pragmaticism and narrative semiotics as not exclusive of each other, but rather as interpenetrating systems of signification, neither is semiotics exclusive of moral or historical or political evaluation. In a passage of minor moral significance but fairly complex syntax, the narrator explains that the old *vilaine* understands and has no hesitation in doing what her prisoner asks, which is to have her daughter bring the 'tapestry' to Queen Procne, because nothing but good is intended. As in Peter Abelard's *Ethics*, the act is judged, not objectively, but according to subjective intention. The old peasant woman transfers to Philomena as logical assumptions the givens of her own life. You sew and weave to earn your keep, for money. The principle is transferred from the *vilaine* to Philomena. Weaving and embroidery are labors that deserve reward. It is for the hope of the reward which such a work deserves that Philomena wants her tapestry presented to the queen, thinks the *vilaine* who earns her living by such labor.

> Cele entent sa volenté toute
> Mes nulle chose ne redoute
> A fere ce qu'ele commande,
> Ne ne set pour quoi plus atande,
> Quar ele n'i entent se bien non,
> Ains cuide que pour guerredon
> Et pour esperance d'avoir
> C'on doit de tele oeuvre avoir
> Vueille qu'el li soit presentee. (ll. 1197–1205)

> [The *vilaine* completely understands Philomena's intention,
> But has no fear
> in carrying out her command,
> nor does she know why she should delay any longer,
> for she has only good intentions.
> Rather the *vilaine* thinks that for compensation
> and in the expectation of payment
> that one should receive for such work,
> Philomena wants the tapestry to be presented to Procne.][85]

---

84   There is a question of priority: which mode of semiotic analysis gives form to the discussion. Since the text under discussion is defined as narrative, narrative semiotics has priority here. A philosophical discussion might invert the hierarchy.

85   Editor's translation: in Chrétien's verses, the fluid play of feminine pronouns and verbs

Monetary reward for weaving or writing (the symbolic equivalence of the two is well-known to the Middle Ages) also anticipates the theme of the writer's anticipated reward from his patron, a theme found again in the *Perceval* prologue: the laborer is worthy of his or her hire. The visual representation of Philomena's story, with its narrative map and signature, then becomes the script for Procne's narrative rescue of her sister: the visual representation of past narrative events becomes the occasion for a moral response in future narrative. The communication of that representation is made possible by the agency of a lowly peasant woman. Is *Crestiens*'s acknowledgment of the multitude continuous with Chrétien's?

Attentive reading of *Philomena* reveals the text's awareness that rape is always a political issue. *Philomena* recognizes as well the necessity of actualizing female communicative resourcefulness in a situation of dire need through semiotic invention and a sisterhood that transcends class distinctions. Nevertheless, the unfortunate phrase does point to an issue of towering importance: the representation of evil — a transcendental problem of aesthetics that has returned to the forefront precisely with fictionalized representations of the Holocaust.

Excursus III: Alterity, Cultural Relativism, and Universalism

The fundamental dynamic of *Philomena* is 'crime and vengeance'. That vengeance is a punishment obtained, not through judicial process, but as personal revenge. The possibility of institutional justice was jettisoned by the original crime. Along with institutional justice, one might think civilization itself had been jettisoned. A new barbarism was created. The text, however, is more specific, narratively speaking. In its specificity, peculiarly enough, it is also more resonant, historically and theologically. The third episode of *Philomena* is the vengeance wrought upon Tereus. Its complexities elude the simple binarism of barbarism vs civilization as external to each other. Indeed, ingurgitation is its theme, literally and symbolically. A short excursus into alterity and cultural relativism will set the stage for understanding how the third episode problematizes the justice of revenge and forces reflection on revenge as 'justice' in theological discourse and history. No difference is made here between revenge and vengeance.

The relativism of legal systems and the notions of justice they try to specify is a truism in the Middle Ages as in modernity. Against all expectations of entrenched ideological uniformity defined by the dogma of a single, established Church, an awareness of cultural relativism and the alterity of other legal systems exists in the Middle Ages. The European 'Middle Ages' cover a multiplicity of cultures, marked by different degrees of mixture and assimilation. Some flourished, some were wiped out, all survivors changed.

Alterity is an essential epistemological condition of medievalism. It is used here to designate complex relationships of cross-cultural epistemology. Alterity designates the objective reality of cultural difference, including the difference

---

with implicit subjects (standard practice in Old French) seems to highlight the sorority Haidu is describing; the proper names added to the translation aim to guide the reader through the series.

in semiotic modes of signification, and the resultant epistemological problematic for modern readers addressing the texts of medieval culture.[86] Those texts are antecedent to our own textuality, but continue to nourish modern textuality. Yet they operate in ways that are profoundly different from modern textuality. Identifying and measuring the problematic mix of continuity and difference is the challenge to the conscientious medievalist. Cultural and legal differences were known and recognized, as operating within the same society, within the same polity. Perspectivalism was a cultural, intellectual, and literary fact in a historically evolving society.

Medieval texts, in fact, also mark this more tempered view of alterity as a feature of human variability. They may even internalize it, not as an insignificant detail, but as a substantive split within the subject, whether individual or collective. Systems of law recognize the de facto differences of people living under those laws. In the early medieval period, individuals of different origins living in the same locality were judged according to their law of origin. In the central Middle Ages, an effort at ordering the enormous variability of local, oral, customary legal systems was integral to the process of state-formation beginning in the twelfth century, both in the work of Gratian and his school and in the *coutumiers*, among which Philippe de Beaumanoir's collection of customary laws (1283) is the best known. New sub-polities were created by regional rulers, endowed with a relative autonomy which allowed them to levy taxes, police themselves, and impose justice on their populations, in exchange for payment of a collective tax to the ruler, a one-time or periodic payment. The Jewish communities in northern France, often initiated by the invitation of a local, regional lord as of the ninth or tenth century, may have provided the model for communes in the twelfth century.[87] Their relative autonomy was itself an economic good, bought and paid for in direct collective taxation.

Philomena identifies its own narrative content as one of criminality, incorporating law and justice as criteria of judgment signaled by the narrator's lexemes: felon,

---

86   To my knowledge, the term 'alterity' was introduced to the discussions of modern medievalism in 'Making It (New) in the Middle Ages: Towards a Problematics of Alterity', *Diacritics*, 4.2 (Summer 1974), 2–11, my review of Paul Zumthor's *Essai de poétique médiévale*. The term identified the cultural difference between the medieval text and the modern reader. Zumthor himself had not used the term in the *Essai*. Hans-Robert Jauss picked up on the term in *Alterität und Modernität der mittelalterlichen Literatur: gesammelte Aufsätze 1956–1976* (Munich: Wilhelm Fink, 1977). The first chapter was translated as 'The Alterity and Modernity of Medieval Literature', *New Literary History*, 10.2 (1979), 181–229. I returned to the epistemological question in 'The Semiotics of Alterity'. The article by Paul Freedman and Gabrielle Spiegel, 'Medievalisms Old and New: The Rediscovery of Alterity in North American Medieval Studies', *The American Historical Review*, 103.3 (June 1998), 677–704, deals with the prehistory of the question, stopping short of contemporary developments. A recent overview is Vincent Ferré, 'Altérité ou proximité de la littérature médiévale? De l'importation d'une notion "européenne" en Amérique du Nord', *Perspectives médiévales*, 37 (2016) < http://journals.openedition.org/peme/9609 > [accessed 17 March 2019].

87   This hypothesis would have to be grounded in: Agus, *Urban Civilization in Pre-Crusade Europe*; Amnon Linder, 'Introduction', in *The Jews in the Legal Sources of the Early Middle Ages*, ed. by Amnon Linder (Detroit, MI: Wayne State University Press, 1997); as well as Salo W. Baron, *A Social and Religious History of the Jews*, 2nd edn, 18 vols (New York: Columbia University Press, 1952–1983).

tyrant, traitor, etc. Medieval *loi* has a broader meaning than in modern French or English. *Loi* does mean 'law', of course, but it also includes custom, habit, mores, practices, social and cultural norms. In fact, *loi* sometimes best translates as 'culture' or 'civilization' — a particular but generalized way of doing things, a way of living, with a certain coherence, possibly the coherence of contradiction.

The text insists on the distinction between its own moral codes and the codes of the diegetic universe depicted. To recapitulate the moral dialectic up to this point:

1. The text, as of the first moment, establishes that Tereus's desire is to do something evil and criminal, something morally repugnant and socially reprehensible. That judgment is maintained in the narrative perspective from beginning to end.

2. The second moment temporarily relocates Tereus's desire from the here and now of the medieval enunciating culture to a hypothetical culture of alterity, that of the enunciated diegetic world which the narrative constructs for a brief hypothetical moment. That other culture, the 'pagan' culture of the fiction, valorizes what may appear as a garbled Epicureanism which licenses all desire. The auditor or reader is thus faced with a contradiction, in the text and perhaps in his own putative reaction, an ideological contradiction.

3. The third moment of the textual dialectic is to render moot the distinction at the basis of the contradiction, the multiple semiotic worlds of culture it limns, and the plural moralities engendered by its multiculturalism. Let us leave their law and their culture, says the poet-author-narrator. After all, citing a developing cultural discourse, who could resist *amour*? Who could prevent love from wreaking its will? Too bad that Tereus left Thrace — reminding us that Tereus is a cultural Other — to seek out Philomena, for love has now declared war on him. Tereus is trapped. Tereus is in a bad way, for the flame sprung in the heart quickly catches fire and burns (ll. 233–41).

Finally, cultural differences and their alterities are moot and irrelevant. 'Love', desire, is the driving force in play. Against desire as *amour*, no system of law or ideological values, no cultural comparatism can obtain.

Nor will cultural relativism be valid at the end of *Philomena*. But the apparent detour through cultural relativism is not pointless. It establishes the bi-valorization of the narrative, according to two scales of cultural values: the code of enunciation *versus* that of 'paganism'. This text insists on the implication of different codes of value and yet posits an element that both subtends and transcends their opposition. *Amour* is a violence that overcomes both rationalities of enunciation and paganism. No matter the scale of values meant to harness it, it is a power whose violence overcomes all ideological constraint. And it is a universal. At least, it is presented as a universal.

The beginning of *Philomena* is narrated in a manner which delegitimizes the evil it represents and condemns it insistently. The text stands out as a profoundly serious moral exploration. It shows the rape of Philomena as proceeding from what is claimed to be a universal human experience: a passionate desire inspired by beauty and accomplishment. To assert they issue from passion does not legitimate crimes of passion.[88] The assertion does recognize the troubling truth that they issue from a sufficiently common experience to render the threat of their evil effects potentially universal. The text's complicated dialectics proceeds by exemplarity, and has the effect not of morally justifying evil, but of 'naturalizing' it, that is, showing its 'flame' catching fire in the ground of a potentially universal experience. That the experience is potentially universal does not mean 'we are all rapists'. It does imply that rape is one possible reaction to something all may experience: being 'struck' by beauty as if by lightning.

Philomena is demanding. The moral and philosophical implications of the text are grounded in the paradoxical universality of the condition under which evil comes into existence and flourishes. Foregoing theological distinctions, the condition of desire or 'love', canonized by the Church as *caritas*, praised in secular love poetry, practiced in friendships at court, is also entangled as discourse, emotion, passion, and practice with decried vulgar, carnal fuck-desire. That vulgar, carnal fuck-desire can be a value of its own; it can be enveloped in the tenderness of love; it can be sublimated in the complexities of *fin'amors*, or love of the other as *caritas*, or the face-to-face ethics of an Emmanuel Levinas. At the beginning, however, is the surge of that endlessly ambiguous word 'love' — as ambiguous as the 'thing' itself. 'Love' is hard to counter as a motive force, whether turned to good or evil, both because of its force and its multiplicities. Particularly if, for *'amour'*, or 'love', we substitute 'sex'. Isn't the ambiguous slippage of love, desire, sex, and the Levinassian ethics of the face, isn't that slippage a universal? Isn't setting a text of any period face-to-face with the pertinent universal the very point of writing, at all periods, as Aristotle suggested? Does the juxtaposition of a multicultural perspectivalism, even at the beginning of the poem, with a potential universalism, suggest the breadth of a certain literature of ineffability?

Procne's long apostrophe to death, when she believes her sister to have died (ll. 954–1004), invokes *loi* in passing and cites *'notre loi'* in the sense of 'our custom':

> '[...] il est escript *an nostre loi*
> Que noire vesteüre port
> Qui ire et angoisse a de mort.'
>   (ll. 1002–04, my emphasis)[89]
>
> ['it is inscribed in our *law*
> That [one who grieves] wears black clothes
> Of anger and fear at death.']

The practice is specific to those living under 'nostre loi'; it does not necessarily apply to other populations. People practicing under different *lois*, people in different

---

88   Though certain laws and legal traditions have in fact done so, e.g., killing a wife and/or her lover caught in flagrant adultery.

89   'Writing' here ('escript') is to be taken broadly, as 'encoded' or 'represented': see also l. 1131, cited below. Editor's note: Baumgartner's edition gives l. 1004 as 'D'ire et d'angoisse et de mort', the whole phrase modifying 'noire vesteüre'. Haidu follows De Boer's emendation ('Qui ire et angoisse a de mort'), which Baumgartner's note acknowledges as workable. Haidu's translation seems to mix original text and emendation, the choice of 'anger and fear' offering a particular slant to the suffering and anguish evoked by the binomial 'ire et angoisse'.

cultures, have different practices and customs. Oddly enough, wearing black clothes as a sign of mourning is common in historical France as well as in the text's diegesis of fictional Thrace.

After the black clothing is brought, Chrétien textualizes alterity in an extended description of a pagan ritual. This description does not come from Ovid. It is an invention of the medieval writer, *Crestiens li gois*, emphasizing cultural differences in religious ritual praxis.[90] The law, or rule, or custom that is cited is one maintained by the pagans for their ancestors, the sacrifice of a living bull to Pluto, lord of the 'dÿables'. The ritual ends with an ugly representation of the one who disposes of souls in burning hell and of the devils who guard them: 'une ymage laide a veoir' (l. 1044). The 'ymage' can be hypothesized as a statue of Pluto, to whom Procne addresses an intense prayer.

The text presents this as a pagan ritual, but the description of souls burning in hell, the devils escorting them, the Devil who oversees the whole process, might remind the twelfth-century reader or auditor who had traveled of sights on the pilgrimage road to Compostela, such as the tympanum at Conques, or, closer to home, the west wall of Saint Lazare at Autun, a little to the south of Troyes. Saint Lazare had been completed a generation earlier; its west porch hosts one of the most imposing medieval representations of the Final Judgment. The identity of the presiding deity is different; the scene, the action, and the effect, the entire representation, are quite similar.[91] Again, a cultural entity assigned to the culture of alterity returns home to the culture of enunciation.

Procne pitifully implores mercy for Philomena:

> 'Dieux qui d'enfer ez rois et sires,
> Pluto, de l'ame aies merci
> De cele pour qui je fais ci
> Ce sacrefice et ce servise,
> En quel que leu que li cors gise.' (ll. 1052–56)
>
> ['God, lord and king of hell,
> Pluto, have mercy on her soul,
> For whom I here make
> this sacrifice and service,
> wherever she may lie.']

And so does Procne make sacrifice for her sister's soul, notes *Crestiens li gois* with harsh irony. Procne's grieving and apostrophe to Death are pointless, since in fact, as the reader knows in a triangulation that will become familiar to readers of Chrétien de Troyes, her sister is not dead at all. Chrétien de Troyes's irony will be empathetic; *Crestiens li gois* has not yet achieved the same aesthetic distance.

---

90   See Baumgartner's note to ll. 1010–56 for distant analogies in other twelfth-century texts (*Pyrame et Thisbé, Narcisse, Philomena*, ed. by Baumgartner, p. 225).

91   Saint Lazare bears the same mixture of the macabre and the erotic as *Philomena*: see the famous relief of a pubescent naked Eve, originally posted at the lintel of the entry to the church, now exhibited at the nearby Musée Rollin.

Procne honors her 'dead' sister Philomena according to her own, pagan *loi*, by performances rendered logically absurd by the fact that Philomena, though raped, mutilated, and imprisoned, is far from dead, but alive in a house in Thrace. Procne's apostrophe to Death and her ritual sacrifice to Pluto are rendered doubly absurd by their exercise on the occasion of a death which is fictitious, and by the repeated suggestion that the alterity itself is factitious. The passage has no narrative functionality; it does not advance the story. There is a structural point, however. It inscribes an example of cultural relativism. The narrative has gone out of its way to posit a cultural alterity, in addressing a death which is not one. To that first irony is added the second level of irony: the 'return' of the supposed alterity of the 'target' culture, marked with 'difference', to the enunciating culture, whose ritual burial representations reduplicate their supposedly pagan counterparts. As with the mourning color of black, the 'alterity' of Hades shuttles back home to Hell.

The external culture of alterity, other by reason of time, language, and the practices of religious ritual, is perhaps not a culture of alterity at all. Or perhaps the correct phrasing is that its alterity, if accepted as such, is to be found closer to home: perhaps 'alterity' is inscribed in the enunciating subject and in the enunciating culture as well. Either way, the simple, exclusive binarism of 'us' vs 'them', which instantiates the radical form of alterity, is undermined. It is invoked to be dismissed. It is posited to be negated. Under the problematics of multiculturalism, of cultural alterity, an older issue re-appears, that of the universality of certain principles. The negation of the negation is not irrelevant to the history of Jewish-Christian dialectics.

If Procne's phrase 'nostre loi', asserting a perspective of alterity, hesitantly differentiates it from *loi* as the culture of the audience, it does not provide an identity for the culture cited. Tereus's identity as a Thracian is repeatedly mentioned by Chrétien, but unelaborated. This absence of definition is the deliberate result of a subtraction from Ovid's text. Ovid repeatedly identifies Tereus as a 'barbarian'. The Roman poet calls Tereus 'barbarus' when he exults on embarking Philomela on his ship leaving Athens (*Metamorphoses*, l. 515). After the rape, Philomela exclaims 'What barbaric acts!' (ll. 533–34). The loom on which Ovid has her 'write' her message to Procne is a crude 'barbarian' loom (l. 576). Ovid, writing at the end of the Roman colonization of Thrace, insists on the barbarian isotopy, on the Thracian Tereus's barbarian identity and moral status: the shift from 'foreign' to repugnant, which has become properly suspicious to a post-anthropological modernity, is traditional and obvious.

Having suppressed all verbal reference to 'barbarity', *Crestiens li gois* makes the gesture of a limited cultural relativism that appears to allow for alterity, but erases the verbal tags that allow for an externalizing rejection of that alterity as 'barbarous', only to have the alterity revealed as a practice of the subject of the instance of enunciation. The Ovidian horror subsists, but in moral form rather than as a feature of genetically determined cultural alterity. The reflexive return of the shuttle of 'alterity' to the self means that the problematics attributed to the 'Other' turn out to be those of the subject of enunciation: 'ours'.

Instead of the word 'barbarian', the medieval text repeatedly names the geographical site of 'barbarism': Thrace. The first reference to Tereus's Thracian origin occurs at the end of the narrator's substantial commentary on the 'vilonie' of that love. The narrator comments that Tereus made a mistake in leaving Thrace:

> Mar issi Thereüs de Trace
> Pour aler Philomena querre,
> Qu'Amours a vers lui prise guerre. (ll. 236–38)

> [Alas that Tereus left Thrace
> To go seek Philomena,
> For Love has declared war on him.]

Tereus's face to face with the conventionalized description of Philomena's beauty is the 'barbarian' encounter with the most refined cultural moment of the new civilization aborning that Chrétien de Troyes will celebrate in the prologue to *Cligès*. One feature of this new civilization, part and parcel of state-formation, is its discipline of carnal desire, and its ideology of subordinating the violence of warrior passion to the weakest of the weak: women. That ideology was identified by the Middle Ages as *fin'amors*. Largely promulgated and propagated in the fictional bodies of lyric and narrative representations, above all those of the Chrétien de Troyes who wrote *Philomena* as *Crestiens li gois*, it was the most exquisite imaginative fantasy of the transfer of the conjunction of power and knowledge, *imperium studii*, to the West.[92] As the ideology of idealizing fantasy — rather than a representation of reality — it provided performative models of behavior that over centuries actually helped to modify behavior.[93] But the dialectic of the text suggests its focus is not on an encounter of barbarian East and civilized West. Rather, it is the encounter of the self with its own 'alterity', its buried but persistent 'barbarity'.

This internalization of a supposed 'cultural' difference throws a shadow on the proffered, hypothetical cultural relativism. While cultural relativism is more than conceivable in the medieval intellectual context (it *is* textualized, frequently), what it is meant to explain — the barbarity of certain human behaviors — is not left in the safe receptacle of exteriority. The fact that morally repugnant behaviors, hypothetically ascribed to externalized Others, are internalized *within* the culture of enunciation throws a shadow on the notion of the relativistic interpretation of cultural difference.

The suppression of Ovid's identification of the Thracian as a barbarian, along with the repeated feints toward a notion of cultural alterity which repeatedly lead back to specifics in the culture of enunciation, undermine the concept of alterity, not by denying it, but by repeatedly demonstrating that the traits or practices assigned to alterity are, in fact, those of the collective social subject. As literary

---

92 Sharon Kinoshita, 'The Politics of *Translatio*: French-Byzantine Relations in Chrétien de Troyes's *Cligès*', *Exemplaria*, 8.2 (Fall 1996), 315–54.
93 The phrase 'representation of reality' refers to the subtitle of Auerbach's *Mimesis*. Medieval texts do not proffer a representation that mimics pre-existent social reality in details of everyday life: they construct a representation refracting that reality, whose juxtaposition with a 'lived reality' leads to discussion, evaluation, and a potential signification of critique.

technique, this is of a piece with Chrétien de Troyes's repeated constructions of Arthurian and Byzantine diegeses, which, though far more complex, always point back to the cultural position of enunciation, as past, present, or future, either as critique or as prospective postulation. The literary strategy has implications which are simultaneously ideological, philosophical, and theological. They are also 'political', in a broad sense of the word: they envisage a complex polity of multiple subjectivities.

By contrast, the communicative semiosis of Philomena's 'cortine ouvrée' is limited and pragmatically successful: it enables Procne to rescue and free her sister and bring her to Thrace to 'do justice'. The thinking of 'after-death' is evacuated, and replaced by the task of 'doing justice' in the here-and-now of this world. 'Justice' is variable in different cultures or civilizations. In medieval French, one might have said that 'justice' was different under different *lois*. 'Justice' is a major preoccupation of medieval rulers and of vernacular writers as well: Chrétien de Troyes's most accomplished novel, the *Yvain*, will end on an issue of justice. Imposing justice, justice as a relative universal by virtue of being universal under a given rule and within a given territory, helps legitimate political rule insofar as it brings a relative peace. 'Justice' as an essential component of a state is an ideologically charged universal.

(iv) Episode 3: Vengeance, Justice, Universalism

As noted, Philomena's suffering — her rape, delingualization, and abandonment — beggars language: 'a world is shattered' by torture.[94] But *Crestiens* chooses not to dwell on Philomena's victimhood. Rather than expatiate on the passive phase of the character that makes of her Tereus's victim, the author focuses on the narrative action of the story he inherits: Philomena, together with her sister Procne, turns into a most aggressive and emphatically active narrative subject of revenge. The moral or ethical quality of this action, if not of her agency, is what is doubtful.

Philomena is marked by different strata of juridical culture. The text pinpoints the primary human sentiment at the basis of revenge, vengeance, and justice: severe personal loss occasions a meld of anger, anguish, and pain or grief, which requires the salve of recognition, acknowledgment, and compensation. In Procne's apostrophe to Death, the griever wears black clothes as a sign of 'ire', 'angoisse', and 'dolour' (distress, anguish, and sorrow, l. 999). The anthropomorphic logic of a narrative of 'justice' demands that for a harm incurred, another harm be performed on the person who initiated the harm. Procne and Philomena's revenge carries out a narrative program of a 'justice' prior to any institutionalized system of justice. Early in the anthropological history of mankind, the sense of personal loss takes form as an exchange pattern. The narrative pattern of loss followed by compensatory recognition, acknowledgment for damage suffered, is fused with an economic exchange pattern.[95] For a harm endured, another harm is exchanged.

---

94   Scarry, *The Body in Pain*, pp. 3–11.
95   The Code of Hammurabi specifies both legal punishments and ordinary labor wages.

The perpetrator of the initial harm suffers, in a second moment, the retaliation of a retributive harm, conceived as an exchange.

The problem with revenge lies in the indeterminacy of retribution. Non-governmental retaliation incurs several possible negatives: the avenger running amok, the disproportion between initial harm and avenging harm, and the possibility of its unending extension. In the Middle Ages, the injured party is not only an individual; it is also a collective unit of uncertain contours: 'family' is widely extended, from 'blood' relations to a broad population of affines. The 'exchange pattern' of vengeance can extend across populations, territories, and time. Hence what seems to modern readers an obsessive concern with revenge stories, as in certain *chansons de geste* like *Raoul de Cambrai*.[96] That vengeance was a problem was widely recognized in medieval texts of all kinds.[97]

Rather than recognizing revenge as a form of justice necessitated by specific historical circumstances, modernity contemns revenge narrative as external to and contrary to justice. For modernity, justice can be served only in the form it recognizes as its own, as an activity of the state, conceived as a form of impartiality that guarantees the process of justice. In recorded history, governance and justice are closely imbricated. At least since Hammurabi, governance regularly gloms on to doing justice as a defining function. But of course, particular forms of governance disintegrate, disappear, and 'die'. That evacuation may be externally caused, as by 'barbarians'. It may be internally caused, as by poisoned lead pipes bringing water to Rome in its famed viaducts. Or it may be internally caused as a more profound moral and social implosion of the existing system. When governance is identified with an individual ruler (chieftain, prince, king, monarch, sovereign, or feudal magnate claiming the ban), a ruler demonstrably corrupt like Tereus, justice hovers unmoored in the black hole of tyranny.

In that juridical gap, Procne's first thought, after having rescued Philomena and brought her to the palace, is for the necessity of revenge in return for Tereus's

---

96 Sarah Kay, *The Chansons de geste in the Age of Romance: Political Fictions* (Oxford: Oxford University Press, 1995). These 'political fictions' explore major issues of the polity, e.g. justice. Procne's vengeance incorporates an ideology amply represented in the ambiguous politico-fictional texts that are the *chansons de geste*. The third episode of *Philomena* is thus in part the normalized encoding that follows on Philomena's rape and mutilation. That normalized encoding is what permits the text of *Philomena* to raise fundamental issues of the polity.

97 In addition to a wide range of vernacular texts, vengeance also drove theology, both Jewish and Christian, see Philippe Buc, *Holy War, Martyrdom, and Terror: Christianity, Violence, and the West* (Philadelphia: University of Pennsylvania Press, 2015). On medieval Jewish themes of vengeful violence, see Elliott Horowitz, *Reckless Rites: Purim and the Legacy of Jewish Violence* (Princeton, NJ: Princeton University Press, 2006), and Israel Jacob Yuval, *Two Nations in Your Womb: Receptions of Jews and Christians in Late Antiquity and the Middle Ages*, trans. by Barbara Harshav and Jonathan Chipman (Berkeley: University of California Press, 2006). See general and varied studies of medieval vengeance in *La Vengeance, 400–1200*, ed. by Dominique Barthélemy, François Bougard, and Régine Le Jan (Rome: Ecole Française de Rome, 2006), as well as *Vengeance in the Middle Ages: Emotion, Religion and Feud*, ed. by Susanna A. Throop and Paul R. Hyams (Farnham: Ashgate, 2010). Professor Throop is also author of *Crusading as an Act of Vengeance* (Farnham: Ashgate, 2011), a title to be juxtaposed to that of Jonathan Riley-Smith (Throop's dissertation director): 'Crusading as an Act of Love', *History*, 65.214 (1980), 177–92.

felony (ll. 1286–91).[98] The revenge pattern embodies the redistribution of harms as a personal right which, whether in literature or in society, constitutes the basis of justice in the absence of governance. In this particular case, the aggrieved are the ruler's wife and his sister-in-law: the case accuses the tyranny of the sovereign himself.

It is not revenge as justice that is the focus of the third episode of *Philomena*, however, grim and horrifying as it is. What the text of *Philomena* displays is not the pleasure of rape, nor victimization, nor the pleasure of revenge: it is the sequential narrative pattern that includes all three, a narrative that concludes in a particular act. That particular narrative act leads the author to a condemnation. The author, *Crestiens li gois*, who has narrated the story from Philomena's point of view up to now, condemns the final act of his narrative subject, in a judgment that has every appearance of an absolute universal. While much of Chrétien de Troyes's textuality is associated with nuance, complexity, and ambiguity even unto paradoxicality, here we come on to a declarative deontological statement that is clear and univocal.

Law, Revenge, and Justice

The institutionalization of justice, like the institutionalization of the church, implies the possibility of corruption in the eyes of those who are administered in the name of 'justice', sometimes by officials, secular or ecclesiastical, who operated (as John of Salisbury pointed out) as 'tyrants'. Though governance is not the overt topic of *Philomena*, its textualization encodes governance, unjust governance that is, with several terms: 'fel tirans', 'tirant felon' most notably, but also *traitre, trahison*, etc. Those codes, frequently repeated, endow the narrative of rape, mutilation, and cannibalistic infanticide with a political dimension. As noted earlier, another such term is *baillir*, or *baillier*, not a term that inherently bears a negative marker, but it does mark the presence of an activity of governance, governance by representation. The *bailli* was the prince's administrative representative, performing 'justice', accounting, and profitability.[99]

In *Philomena*, *baillir* designates the fiduciary relationship in which Pandion entrusts his younger daughter to Tereus (ll. 541, 562, 673, 715). That he does so occasions the ironic use of a proverb, the technique termed *paroemia* by medieval treatises of grammar and rhetoric, frequently used in Chrétien's *Cligès*. In turning his daughter over to the traitor Tereus, Pandion misplaces his trust: 'Si la commande au traïtour. | Ensi *a fet dou leu pastour*' [he entrusts her to the traitor | and *makes of the wolf a shepherd*] (ll. 703–04, my emphasis). The shepherd-wolf, who has been handed a trust: his betrayal of that specific trust defines him as 'traitor'. The tyrant is termed a traitor who will betray his function of trust and safe-keeping by rape and mutilation.

---

98 The theme of felony returns in the internal monologue regarding her son (ll. 1302–03), and again in that of revenge and felony (ll. 1326–27).
99 The nascent bureaucracy of state in France of the twelfth century, was organized with two superior levels, reporting to feudal or royal superiors: the provost (< *praepositus*), and the superior functionary to whom were entrusted basic tasks of governance. The *bailli*, well known to earlier feudal princes, grew substantially under Philip II.

The exercise of justice, a specific aspect of governance, becomes identified with governance itself.[100] More than a function of governance, it is identified with sovereignty. *Joustisier*, doing justice, means governing, with the potential of exercising violent force over those held in 'subjecti̇on' (l. 430), those thrown under the heels of the sovereign. Rape becomes a form of 'justice' in the degraded sense that the 'force' of the sovereign is indistinguishable from sovereign 'violence' and substitutes for the consent of the governed, in this case the woman who is the object of the tyrant's desire. Tereus rapes Philomena, after the attempt to obtain her willing surrender, and in spite of her pleading. Three verbs of overlapping meanings occur in close order in the narration:

> [...] cil toute voies l'*assault*,
> Si l'*esforce* tant et *joustise*
> Que *tout a force* l'a conquise
> Et trestout son bon en a fet. (ll. 836–39, my emphasis)

> [he *assaults* her,
> he *violates* her and '*justices*' her
> so that he conquered her *with violence*
> And took his pleasure on her.]

'Justice' undergoes deconstruction by narrative, a reduction similar to *amour*. As 'love' was reduced to carnal desire, so *joustise* is nothing more than the violent law of the pleasure of the stronger. Christian the Jew deconstructed language before Jacques Derrida, by narrative means rather than analytic discourse.

Justice is more insistently political than 'love', but it is subject to modulation. Friendly relations between states or princes, i.e. relations of peace, are marked in medieval French by the use of *aimer*.[101] *Justice* is less directly related to violence when used of the old woman's supervision of the mute, distraught woman she guards.

> [...] rest en tel *joustise*
> Qu'el n'a congié ne loisir
> De fors de la maison issir. (ll. 1080–82, my emphasis)

> [she remains under the *rule of justice*:
> she has neither permission nor occasion
> to go out of the house itself.]

Justice is ambiguous. It incarnates a human ideal, a hoped-for universal, a universal desire for equity and fair play. It is connected to governance, and sometimes identical with it. It is sometimes criminal. Like love and sovereignty.

---

100 The topic of medieval governance is now magisterially treated by Bisson, *The Crisis of the Twelfth Century*.
101 Old French *aimer* is an etymological compound of Latin *amo*, *amare*, and *aestimare*.

Vengeance and the Universal: Mother Murders Child

The *vilaine*'s daughter brings the tapestry to Procne, who then follows her on the return to the house in the forest. Procne frees her sister and brings Philomena back to Tereus's palace. Procne will stand next to her son, reflect, and 'do justice' by avenging her sister: she decapitates Ithys, which leads to the clearest formulation of *Crestiens li gois*'s universalism, its most tellingly paradoxical example.

It is possible to read *Philomena* in purely linear fashion, as a succession of horrendous acts, one more dreadful than the other. But the text specifies that its final act is conceived as vengeance for the earlier rape and mutilation. The final episode folds back over the first and responds to the initial crime. The horrendous nature of the vengeance problematizes the principle of revenge itself — the available form of justice.

As it occurs in the text, the notion of revenge first presents itself to Procne as something desired but unattainable. In an apostrophe, she addresses her sister:

> 'Suer, fet elle, moult sui dolente
> Quant si afolee vous truis
> Ne *vengier* ne vous sai ne puis
> Dou *felon* qui ce vous a fait.
> Diex doinst que tel *loier* en ait
> Comme a sa *felonie* avient!' (ll. 1286–91, my emphasis)

> ['Sister, said she, it grieves me,
> that I find you so deeply harmed,
> but can find no *vengeance*, and know of none,
> against the *felon* who did this to you.
> God grant he is *paid back*,
> as his *crime* deserves!'][102]

Procne herself, in the last line quoted, defines the principle of proportionality: may the vengeance fit the crime! The languages of criminality, betrayal, revenge, and commerce are intertwined.

At first, the notion of vengeance presents itself as negated: Procne does not know how to achieve it, nor is she capable of it. At that point, by unfortunate happenstance, the means of vengeance presents itself. Her son Ithys comes to her. She will kill him in his father's stead. The son will be sacrificed to avenge the father's crime. The absurdity is also a horror: mother-love transformed into barbaric vengeance. Yet, it is not without recalling an analogous transformation of mother-love in the historic experience forced upon the Jewish people in 1096, as told in the Hebrew chronicles. The narrative logic is different, but Procne will wreak harsh, pagan 'justice' with the same act by which Jewish mothers, sanctifying God's name, avoided the murder of their Jewish children by the unsanctified, uncircumcised Christian Crusaders, or even worse, their capture and indoctrination as Christians. In *Kiddush Hashem*, the Jewish mothers killed their own children; Procne will kill her son and — in a bitterly, cruelly ironic savagery unknown to the Hebrew

---

102 Editor's note: literally, 'as befits his *felony*'. Procne, like her sister, insists on the motif of *fel/felon/felonie* strongly associated with Teseus as a tyrant so evil, so powerful he seems impregnable.

chronicles but part of the legend retold by Ovid — she will serve up the son as dinner to his father.

As Procne resolves to avenge her sister, her son approaches. He was beautiful beyond measure, 'beaux estoit a desmesure' (l. 1293), just as the sacrificed children in the Hebrew chronicles were 'comely'. Bad luck ('mesaventure') brought him on the scene at that moment (ll. 1292–95). His mother sees her son approach and mutters under her breath an astonishing displacement, something unheard of: a 'merveille' (l. 1297), a word translatable as 'marvel' or 'miracle', a *merveille* that only the devil could inspire.

> 'Ha! fet elle, chose samblable
> Au traïtour, au vil dÿable,
> Morir t'estuet de mort amere
> Pour la *felonie* ton pere.
> Sa *felonie* comperras,
> Pour son *forfait* a tort morras,
> Qui ne l'as mie deservi,
> Fors seulement c'onques ne vi
> Ne Diex ne fist, mon escïant,
> Chose a autre miex resamblant,
> Et pour ce te vueil decoler.'
> (ll. 1299–1309, my emphasis)

> ['Ha! said she, you thing that resembles
> the traitor, the foul devil,
> You'll die bitter death
> for your father's *felony*,
> His *felony* you'll pay for,
> For his *crime* you'll wrongly die,
> You don't deserve it,
> But I have never seen
> Nor did God ever make
> Two things of closer resemblance,
> And that's why I'll cut your neck.']

The technique of inner monologue will be emphatically developed in *Cligès*. The personage is split into speaker and listener: a linguistically split subject, in accordance with the inner division of self-reflexivity.

The speech, to put it mildly, is paradoxical: a revenge that abandons all claim to justice. The murderess intends to murder her son on the ground of resemblance (fairly common between fathers and sons). The Old French is closer to 'thing *that is like*' than the English 'thing *that resembles*': it has more to do with being than appearance. Ithys does not just *look* like Tereus, he *is* like Tereus. But the speech immediately corrects that impression. If Ithys actually *were* like Tereus as a male, or as his genealogical descendant, if Ithys were a potential tyrant and rapist, might that not justify killing him? But in fact, Procne specifies the killing will be a murder, an intentional, unannounced killing, unjustified, that Ithys her son does not in the least deserve: 'For his crime you'll wrongly die, | You don't deserve it'. Again, she insists that the resemblance between father and son is striking. Physical resemblance is the only basis for the murderous revenge.

The murderess's own words declare her vengeance unjust. That injustice is not excused by being located in the laws or customs of a particular culture of alterity, a culture that is 'other' to the codes of the text. Alterity and 'cultural relativism' have been recognized in the text, even if rendered with some dubiety and ambiguity. But now, the narrator is charged with telling the end of the story, and the relativism of cultural alterity is not at all in question. On the contrary, as against a cultural or moral relativism, universality is textualized.

Mother slaughters son in one line: 'A a l'enfant coupé la teste' [she cut off the child's head] (l. 1332). The murder of Ithys by his mother Procne is the inescapable climax of the story, given in his source, the text of Ovid. However distasteful, however repugnant, it is unavoidable. Or is that turning things upside down? Was that murder, the murder of a beautiful child by its mother, was that murder in fact the reason for choosing this among Ovid's *Metamorphoses*? Retelling the mother's dreadful revenge on her son may not be an unfortunate appendix to the rape-story of Philomena. The end of the story narrates the revenge for the acts narrated in the beginning. The connection between end and beginning is 'organic'. Logically, the end responds to the beginning. Anthropomorphically, the end avenges the beginning. Crime and punishment respond to each other, separated in the text only by the invention of semiotics, the principle of representation. Is it possible that this particular representation of metamorphosis was chosen for 'translation' specifically *because* it narrates a child's murder by its mother? Responding to the murder of her children by Rachel of Mainz?

Crestiens li gois's telling of the end is more laconic than the beginning. Whereas the writer allowed himself luxuriant rhetorical verbalizations growing out of the construction of narrative strategies — like the conventional developments on beauty, love, and death early in the text — now a pall falls on narration. The narrative stands alone, bare bones and minimalist, nearly skeletal. At the end, a cold, neutral narration asserts itself, with the effect of a Houellebecquian 'objectivity' in mid-twelfth century, communicating distaste without comment, except for the final judgment, even as it indulges in sadistic manipulation.

Crestiens li gois subtracts and adds to his Latin source-text in ways that radicalize the narrative. Ovid first constructs a conflict between Procne's anger and maternal love, shows her alternating between 'ira' and 'matrem pietate' (ll. 627 and 629), wrath and maternal tenderness. The Latin poet then offers a quasi-legitimation of her anger by assimilating it to a natural process, by introducing a simile which compares Procne to a tigress on the Ganges, dragging a newborn fawn, still nourished by its mother's breast-milk, which the tigress has taken from the mother-deer, through thickening forests. The poetic presence of the tigress interrupts the mother-son bond, as if to suggest disculpabilization for the child's death. *Crestiens li gois* omits the simile and erases almost all trace of Procne's inner conflict. Finally, the Old French author simplifies the murder itself. Ovid's mother kills her son with two sword strokes: one on the torso, where chest joins the flank, and a second stroke to the throat. The French boy dies of a single stroke: his mother cuts his throat. Chrétien de Troyes will specialize in psychic conflict; here, *Crestiens li gois* reduces psychic conflictuality, stressing the evil of the narrative act.

Christian the Jew suppresses Procne's passion, torn between maternal love and the imperative of vengeance, as well as a naturalization that almost excuses the murder. In their place, he inserts a consideration of which there is no trace in Ovid: the humanization of the boy Ithys. The beauty and the sweetness of Ithys, the victim, are the inventions of *Crestiens li gois* — Jewish topoi of child descriptions. The boy Ithys runs to his mother. He kisses her and hugs her lovingly. Procne nearly extracted herself from the thought she had entered, or perhaps she should have done so. Either way, the boy's sweetness towards his mother is affecting. In Ovid, that sweetness feeds Procne's alternating anger and maternal love. In the Old French text, that sweetness has a very different effect. It is ideational: it allows entry of the dialectical opposite of the cultural relativism sketched out earlier, *Crestiens li gois*'s universalism:

> Tant la baisa et conjoÿ
> Que Progné se dut estre ostee
> Dou penser ou elle iert entrée,
> Si com requiert *Drois et Nature*
> *De toute humaine creature,*
> Et si com Pitiez le desfent,
> Que *mere ne doit son enfent*
> *Ne ocire ne desmembrer.* (ll. 1312–19, my emphasis)

> [He kissed and hugged her.
> It should have extracted Procne
> from the thought she had entered,
> as demanded by *Right and Nature*
> *of all human creatures,*
> and as *Pitiez* forbids it,
> for *a mother must not her child*
> *kill or dismember.*]

Justice and Nature concur with the universal emotion of 'Pitiez', a term left untranslated. Its polysemy names in simultaneity three concepts that semantic evolution has separated: the pity one human feels for another who is in a bad way, the empathy of identification which bears the concept of a universal community, and the fact that this *pitiez* or empathy is — in Judaism as much as in Christianity — the love of the proximate person God demands of man and woman: piety as religious charity. The three senses of *pitiez* feed into the universal rule: mothers must not kill or dismember their children.

The universals of Law and Nature rejoin the knotting of the pathemic, the political, and the religious named by *Pitiez*. The notation that the resulting injunction would address 'toute humaine creature' is almost superfluous. One possible reflection here is that the young writer has not yet attained the delicate touch of sophistication the master of the medieval verse novel will exemplify. Or is it that his moral consciousness, lost to a modernity abandoned to wealth, power, and careerism, is more insistent than his art? Or finally, does the emphasis on the human underline that the text designates the human institution of Law, a rule of Nature shared alike by Judaism, Christianity, and pagan practices, and the human potential of psychological identification with the other, without specifying the divinity that fails? In any case, by rights, by nature, by pity or piety, Procne ought to have renounced her project: 'a mother must not her own son | either kill or dismember'. Whether the origin of the morality is law, nature, the psychology of identification, or piety, the text — incidentally, as if in passing — invokes a univocal universal: a mother shall not kill or dismember her son. Anywhere. At any time. As a universal. Stated by *Crestiens li gois*.

The narrator, who has accustomed the reader or auditor to distantiating commentary that criminalizes Tereus as anti-hero and tyrant, now engages a different strategy, both rhetorical and dialectical. Rather than a political judgment within a particular set of customs and *lois*, the text asserts a universal rule that condemns what Procne is about to do. The discourse of the text now asserts, not a relative universal within a given community, but the force of a universal. The text asserts an absolute injunction by the conjoined forces of Law as a form of universal Justice, Nature, and the emotion that justice, nature, and religion inspire: Pity or Piety.

The mother's resolve to murder her son, to commit infanticide on her own progeniture, incites its rejection in the name of the universal, formulated as literal rule. The narrator's discourse, the narration of the text, banishes cultural relativism from any account of her crime. Cultural relativism cannot provide a rationalization of that crime, or a possible legitimation. What is quite remarkable is that, within the minimalist narrative technique of the third episode, the discourses both of the narrative agent (Procne, who acts in the stead of her sister Philomena) and the narrator (who stands in for the author) remove all legitimation for the actual vengeance against Tereus. The revenge enacted lacks all purchase on the realm of justice. It lacks any justification in the character of the child being killed or in the moral consciousness of the murderous mother. Procne knows the vengeance is undeserved: she says so. Procne's infanticidal bloodthirst for vengeance stands out from the narrative discourse: it is evil. The criminal act is the same as that of the mothers in the Hebrew chronicles; its motivation is radically different. The religious justification offered for Rachel's act of sanctification in the Mainz Chronicle is entirely absent here.

Procne in the French text makes evil palpable as the product of revenge. The text insists on the horrendous evil of revenge. As beauty in the first episode produced a desire that led to rape, so family identification, as in feudal honor, leads to the horror of a mother killing her son in the final episode, where beauty characterizes the victim — as beauty characterized the victims of *Kiddush Hashem* in 1096. That evil is confirmed by the gruesome second act of vengeance, where the French author follows his Latin source fairly closely, except in intensifying Procne's cruelty. Procne and Philomena together prepare dinner for Tereus, boiling part of the boy's corpse, roasting the rest, serving it to his father without identifying the dish (as if doubling the mutilation that followed Philomena's rape). *Crestiens li gois* socializes Ovid's text: he adds details to Procne's stratagem that intensify its cruel irony. The wife seduces Tereus, promising to dine alone with him. At his insistence, she then includes Ithys. Urging Tereus to come to table, the narrator tells us 'he cannot know for what a dish she invites him, don't think she's telling him it's his son she feeds him!' (ll. 1366–69).

Procne makes herself as pleasing as possible, sets the table with a white cloth, and brings her husband his son's leg. The text specifies that the father cuts, and eats, and drinks. Then he 'asks for what he's looking at': 'Et demande ce que il voit' (l. 1380). He repeats to Procne, he wants his son. Where's Ithys? You promised he would be here with us (ll. 1381–83). At this point, the discourse turns to the most gruesome irony anywhere in Chrétien de Troyes. To Tereus's request for Ithys, his wife responds:

> 'Sire, tous en seroies saoulz,
> Fait Progne, n'aiez tel besoing.
> Ithis n'est mie de ci loing.
> S'il n'i est ore, il i sera,
> Que gaires ne demorera.' (ll. 1384–88)

> ['My lord, you'll soon have enough,
> says Procne, don't worry.
> Ithys is not far;
> He's not here right now, soon he will be,
> he'll hardly delay.']

She brings him a roasting skewer of meat, and while he cuts and eats the meat, he continues to urge her to go bring him his son. It is unpleasant for me not to see him, says Tereus. At that point, says the narrator, Procne can no longer hide what food she serves him:

> 'Dedens toi as ce que tu quiers,
> Mes n'i est mie tous entiers:
> Partie en as dedens ton cors,
> Et partie en as par defors.' (ll. 1403–06)

> ['You have in you what you seek,
> Just not quite entirely:
> A part you have inside yourself,
> A part you have outside yourself.']

Procne's allegory is immediately understandable to the reader, but Tereus needs further information. At that point, Philomena returns, marking the sisters as a dual subject. She runs out towards Tereus from the adjoining room where she was hiding and throws Ithys's bloody head at his face.

There is no gainsaying the horror of the story or the cruelty of its narration. In spite of long-standing caution about assigning intent to long-dead medieval authors who left no trace of documentary evidence of their intent in writing, an exception may be valid here: assigning the intent of causing horror to the present author does not seem hazardous. The writer goes out of his way to strip what rationalizations might be found for Procne's behavior in his source. He strips away any possible humanization, any possible disculpabilization found in his source, from her decision to sacrifice her son to her vengeance. If Chrétien de Troyes pitched his later texts as idealizations of human behavior (possibly hoping for a performative effect on feudal society), *Crestiens li gois*, using the same verse form, the same narrative type and conventions, renders human behavior as cruel, barbaric, savage, and quite outside any justifiability, even for a sisterhood as sympathetic as he had rendered Philomena and Procne. As sympathetic, as justifiable ... ?

(v) Epilogue: *auctor ex machina*

The end of the play, in Greek tragedy, was where the playwright might choose (if the myth allowed it) a dramatic ending: the god came down from the sky in a specially-constructed apparatus, to resolve the issue of the play — the *deus ex machina*. The Middle Ages did not have the texts of the Greek tragedies, but medieval novels developed an analogous structure in the epilogue.

The *deus ex machina* in *Philomena* occurs in the epilogue as a triple metamorphosis. The metamorphoses are the hook by which the story figures in Ovid's anthology of metamorphoses, eventually included in the fourteenth-century *Ovide moralisé*. That 'hook' is turned, by both the Latin author and the Old French author of the twelfth century, into a minuscule, terminal self-reflective surface which mirrors the preceding narrative even in ending it, transposing the human changes of narrative action into species metamorphosis. It is a *mise en abyme*, but in a concluding position rather than within the narrative.

The *mise en abyme* performs a function that is not inherent to its defining reflexivity. It is more than a summary reflection in terms transposed from narrative to symbol. It is the moment when the hitherto shadowy figure, hidden in the folds of narrator/ reciter/ commentator/ questioner/ author, comes out of hiding, comes out *tout court*, to perform a final turn, a pirouette that changes things. The end, which narrates the metamorphoses into birds of the three principal characters of the story, itself operates a metamorphosis on the preceding story. The structural metamorphosis *Crestiens li gois* performs in his epilogue announces a technique that recurs in Chrétien's *Cligès* and *Yvain*.

In both these later works, the author inaugurates a particular technique: the concluding narrative twist that ends the narrative without resolving its issues, letting both author and public off the hook. That sudden twist provides relief from the dark, troubling seriousness of the text, a relief whose irony takes the form of a humorous release of tension. It is a surprise, a sudden appearance from the narrative wings of the voice that has been controlling and commenting on the narrative. It is the sudden appearance, marking the narrative's limit, hovering both in the text and outside it, of a character that is to have a long progeny: the *auctor ex machina*.

In *Philomena*, the epilogue is bipartite. The medieval author switches Ovid's order. Where the Latin transforms first the sisters and then Tereus, the medieval text places Tereus's transformation first. The Latin poet names Tereus's bird an 'epops'. *OED* records the following description for 'hoopoe':

> I saw to-day a pair of hoopoes on the road [...] I could see the beautiful orange crest of the male, with its black tip going up and down as he walked, and after he flew into the tree he continued his cry of 'uup, uup'.

Ovid manages an ornithological description that also ridicules the character, with its crest, its disproportionately long beak, and a head that looks as if wearing armor, suggesting the pompous, arrogant aggressor Tereus has been.

Chrétien changes not only the order, but the descriptive register of the former Tereus. Tereus turns into a bird puzzlingly called an 'hupe coupee' (l. 1448). Instead of Ovid's ridiculing description, he offers a moral devaluation. In medieval bestiaries, the hoopoe is presented as a very dirty bird that feeds off excrement, which fits the immediate context.[103] The narrator, siding with the bestiaries' moral perspective, says Tereus is transformed into an 'hupe coupee', a dirty, disgusting, small, and ragged bird ('Ors et despis, petis et viaus', l. 1446), 'on account of the sin and the shame | of what he had done to the young woman' ('Pour le pechié et por la honte | Qu'il avoit fet de la pucele', ll. 1450–51).[104] That *Crestiens li gois* sides more with contemporary bestiaries than either classical or modern descriptions is hardly surprising. What makes one wonder, however, is the transitional line which moves from the assertion he became a 'cut hoopoe' — whatever that means — to the moral description (ll. 1448, 1450–51). That transitional line is either ironic or a lie: 'Si com la fable le raconte' (l. 1449) [Just as the fable tells it]. Either the 'fable' is Ovid's version, the expected meaning in view of the usual association of classical pagan texts with fabulation, and in that case the medieval text traduces its source, or, more surprising, 'fable' might refer to the bestiary used by the author, presumably for its moral truth value. Either way, the transition — between the 'fact' of metamorphosis and its significance, between the narrative signifier and its signified — troubles the relationship between language and meaning.

Indeed, 'hupe coupee' is already a puzzlement. While *hupe* readily translates as 'hoopoe', just what the significance of 'the cut' might be is open to question. While there is no confirmation of such an association in *Philomena* itself, one might link the 'hupe coupee' to the notion of the lion with the tip of its tail cut off, in Chrétien de Troyes's *Yvain*. If the conjecture of the author as a converted Jew is retained, one might wonder if the notion of 'the cut' was not an absurd but risible response to an aleatory phonetic association of *hupe* with the *hoopah*, the canopy under which takes place a Jewish marriage: 'the cut' being that of the groom's circumcised penis — not irrelevant either to his identity or to the notion of a wedding. Whether the dual reference to Judaism of the 'hupe coupee' is then taken as redundant assertion of the Jewish isotopy or as an oxymoron would be a purely subjective judgment, of course. Either way, the invocation of a Jewish wedding could refer to the ill-omened wedding at the beginning of *Philomena*, or to the total narrative. Again, whether such reference would be one of analogy or of contrast is an open question.

After Tereus's transformation, the second part of the epilogue tells of the two sisters' metamorphoses. Again, the changes wrought on the Latin source are telling. Ovid's metamorphosis of Pandion's two daughters has them suddenly take off on

---

103 See Baumgartner's note to l. 1448 (*Pyrame et Thisbé, Narcisse, Philomena*, ed. by Baumgartner, p. 253).
104 Editor's note: in some contexts, polysemous *pechié* in Old French simply means 'misfortune', but Haidu's translation as 'sin', its other common meaning, brings out the moral perspective he emphasizes here.

wings and hover momentarily in the air, before flying off, one (Philomela?) towards the forest, the other (Procne?) — her breast still bearing the traces of Ithys's murder, her plumage spotted with blood — flies under the eaves. The two disappear into the whirring flight of two avians, unnamed, without species identity, but bearing markers of the preceding narrative as they are joined by the more specifically named and described bird named 'epops', the 'hupe' of *Crestiens*'s text.

In addition to *Philomena* and the five longer verse novels that survive, Chrétien de Troyes is also the author of lyric love poems, the first in Old French to follow the model of *fin'amor* proposed by the troubadour lyric, where the theme of spring's renewal is associated with that of love. The epilogue to *Philomena* now cites that double tradition, but turns it to moral interpretation. In the medieval text, Procne is turned into a swallow, the sign of spring; Philomena is turned into a nightingale, whose song is that of *fin'amor*. It is the nightingale that sings here, but her song is not of love.

Her song is not at all the traditional love-song: it is radically reinterpreted, or inverted, reiterating the narrator's insistent political vocabulary at the text's very conclusion:

> Encore, qui creroit son los,
> Seroient a honte trestuit
> Li desloial mort et destruit,
> Et li felon et li parjure,
> Et cil qui de joie n'ont cure,
> Et tuit cil qui font mesprison
> Et felonnie et traïçon
> Vers pucele sage et cortoise,
> Quart tant lor grieve et tant lor poise
> Que quant il vient au prin d'esté,
> Que tout l'iver avons passé,
> Pour les mauvés qu'ele tant het,
> Chante au plus doucement qu'el set
> Par le boschaige: oci! oci!
> De Philomena lairai ci. (ll. 1454–68)

> [Even today, if you trust her recommendation,
> they would be shamefully
> condemned to death and destruction,
> the felons, the forsworn,
> those who care not for joy,
> and all those who commit outrage,
> felony and treason
> towards a proper and courteous young maiden,
> for it weighs and grieves them
> when spring comes to summer,
> after we've passed winter,
> on account of the evil ones she so hates,
> she sings as sweetly as she can

throughout the underbrush: Kill! Kill!¹⁰⁵
Of Philomena I cease here.]

That long, lithe, sinuous sentence of perverse syntax, mingles literary themes of springtime and love with the political and judicial moralism of the preceding narrative, and the paradoxical concluding mixture of sweet gentleness with the hatefulness of the lovebird's final hortatory command: 'Kill! Kill!' Whether this is to be seen as citation of the preceding narrative, or affirmation of its murderous universality, is an open question. Perhaps its answer is: both!

The paradoxical quality of the epilogue fuses with its lyric breath, and envelops the reminder of the tale's moral content in the shimmering gauze of an inclusive linguistic skein — an inclusivity which, rather than mark a concluding, charitable forgiveness, insists by contrast on the horror narrated by marking its repetition. Philomena-the-nightingale's final song returns us to the thematics of the preceding novella: beauty inspires a passionate desire that overwhelms all decency, obligation, and respect for the other, for that other face which signals the ethical question in the face-to-face of human relations; a passionate desire that turns to utter ugliness, as strategically calculated mutilation for the sake of self-preservation follows upon rape, and is incited to sadistic reiteration of the violation by the victim's grief. Nothing in the sinuous sweetness of the final enunciation masks the evil recounted: the epilogue asserts the mingling of evil and beauty in the bitter moral hybridity of the human.

The *auctor ex machina*, rather than removing or transcending the content of his narrative, gently reinserts its poison.

---

105 Editor's note: The antecedent for the plural object pronoun in 'Quart tant lor grieve et tant lor poise' might be understood as the disloyal lovers rather than the birds, as Haidu's translation suggests. In that case, 'grieve' and 'poise' become active verbs and the nightingale, like Philomena in the final act, becomes an agent who torments those guilty of *felonie*. The nightingale's 'oci' might be heard in Old French as 'kill' or 'killed', both relevant to the horror of Philomena's tale and Rachel of Mainz's story.

CONCLUSION

Chrétien de Troyes: Singular Universal

It is the conjecture of this book that the writer Chrétien de Troyes was the second or third generation offspring of the social catastrophe visited upon the Jews in the First Crusade holocaust. His survival allowed identification with other victims of dispossession in his world: women, subjects of rape, peasants or *vilains*, poverty or labor expropriation. This polyvalent potential of social identifications came at the cost of personal desubjectification, repeatedly marked in his texts by episodes of torture, madness, and finally the non-socialization of Perceval.

The process marked as 'conversion' from Judaism to Christianity, rather than a social positivity, can be reconsidered as a form of social subtraction tantamount to enforced universalization. Forced Christianization subtracted full adhesion to Judaism, without producing full adhesion to Christianity. Such subtraction renegotiates the complex field of identity, historical personhood, and the much-decried notion of the universal. It is perhaps in this work of subtractive negation that the generic appears, forced into bare existence by a historic process of stripping away. The resultant hybrid identity (or perhaps the lack thereof) in the historical circumstances which were Chrétien's, forced the construction of a fictional universe whose representations comported universalist values from which analytic critique of his own society was possible.

The readings of Chrétien's works in the contextual history suggest the shape of the subjective process of universalization: psychic identification and self-extension of one bearer of the mark of dispossession to other bearers of the mark of dispossession, or to whole groups marked by dispossession. Texts were formed in this process, raising the question of a historical explanation: what were the material conditions that formed the ground on which the mystery of literary genius operated?

Balibar vs Badiou

Forcing their way into the philosophical domain, claims to universality, to universalism, to the universal, arouse suspicion, distrust, unease at the very least. Such universalist claims have often been made from positions of establishment power, subjectivity, and assumed color, ethnic identity, and religious values, imagining the universal as a superior level of transcendence atop prior existents. Another act of imagination is possible. The universal may be reached instead by a process of subtraction, rejoining earlier developments in the present text, grounding it in a continuation of Aristotle's zoologism.

That is the value of Alain Badiou's introduction of the notion of the 'generic', however surrounded by mathematical abstractions it is in his philosophical Platonism. The generic, in ordinary discourse, can be wrenched out of abstraction to reintroduce the necessary dimension of universality to the liberation discourse of identity politics, as valid for human kind as a genus.

Badiou defines 'generic' as the passion for equality; the idea of justice; the will to break off with endless accommodations of servicing property, knocking egotism off its perch; intolerance of oppression; the desire to see an end to the oppressive state; and seeing to the absolute preeminence of the multiple over representation in which the tenacious obstinacy of the activist, engaged by some unpredictable event, is enabled to speak.[1] That is the aspect of Badiou's conception of the generic being invoked here. The generic becomes a form of universalism, or under conditions of history, of acts of universalization.[2]

In the history of philosophical thought, universalism's burials have been shallow and temporary. It is difficult to see how the issue can be avoided in medieval studies. The Catholic Church activated a long history of repression of all other identities, or even unorthodox variants of the central identity, under its universalist claim: 'catholic' derives from *katholikos*, meaning universal. If claims to the universal arouse unease among those who view it with suspicion and distrust, even those who use the notion and the term 'universal' do not agree on it. For the Platonist Alain Badiou, 'the universal is univocal'.[3] For the post-Derridean Etienne Balibar, the universal has an 'insurmountable equivocity' to it.[4] Both Badiou and Balibar conjugate history and philosophy. They do so at fundamental levels but differently. By calling the apostle Paul's Christianity 'the invention of universalism', Badiou repeats Althusser's use of religion as a fundamental example of ideology, in spite of his oft-repeated claims to Platonism and his early attack on Louis Althusser.[5]

---

[1]   Alain Badiou, *D'un désastre obscur* (Paris: Aube, 1991), pp. 13–14. In a passage of complex propositions, highly subject to debate, whose political fundamentalism may shock American sensibilities, Badiou intends to redefine 'communism' as an equivalent of democracy — a sovereign ahistoricism characteristic of Badiou's frequently proclaimed Platonism.

[2]   Editor's note: Haidu's enumeration of the generic's propositions offers a close paraphrase of Badiou's answer to a question: 'What does "communist" signify in an absolute sense? What is philosophy able to think under this name (philosophy under the condition of a politics)?' (Alain Badiou, *Can Politics Be Thought?*, trans. by Bruno Bosteels (Durham, NC: Duke University Press, 2018), p. 115). Badiou ends the passage with a footnote: 'The generic, that is to say the status in thought of the *whatever* infinite multiplicity as materiality of a truth, constitutes the most important concept of the philosophical propositions of my book *Being and Event*, trans. Oliver Feltham (London: Continuum, 2007)'. According to Bosteels, Marx and Badiou share the notion of the generic, but locate it differently: Badiou assigns the generic to 'being qua being as uncovered in a singular truth procedure' (*Can Politics be Thought?*, p. 15).

[3]   Alain Badiou, 'Huit thèses sur l'universel', *Centre International d'étude de la philosophie française contemporaine*, 11 November 2004; the univocality of the universal is thesis 6. Editor's note: in French <http://www.lacan.com/baduniversel.htm> and in English <http://www.lacan.com/badeight.html> [accessed 14 March 2019].

[4]   Etienne Balibar, 'Ambiguous Universality', *Differences*, 7.1 (1995), 48–74 (p. 48); repr. in *Politics and the Other Scene* (London: Verso, 2002), pp. 146–76.

[5]   Alain Badiou on Althusser: *De l'idéologie* (Paris: Maspero, 1976); repr. in *Les Années rouges* (Paris: Les Prairies Ordinaires, 2012). Badiou on Saint Paul: *Saint Paul*. Elsewhere, Badiou's 'description of

Badiou makes the convert Paul's Christianity his model of militant political activism.[6]

In fact, Badiou offers an excellent site to note briefly the fundamental yet necessary equivocity inherent in the concept of the universal itself: the universalist claim to transcend history has a history of its own. Indeed, its historical element is so strong it would be preferable to speak of repeated processes of 'universalization' rather than a static 'universal'. Balibar, commenting Badiou, notes that discourses on universalism and the universal generally take a refutative form: what the Greeks called an *elenchus*, saying not so much what the universal *is*, but what it *is not*, or *not only*.[7] If there is no meta-language of universality, there are possibilities of shift and strategic choices, as when Badiou's essay on Saint Paul opposes a *true* universalism of equality and a *false* universalism, a 'simulacrum' of universalism. The false universalism is that of the liberal world market which relies not on *equality* but *equivalence*, allowing for a permanent reproduction of rival identities within formal homogeneity. Tracking subalternity back to the European philosophical tradition's categories of the One and the Multiple (so that we could speak of a universalism of the One and a universalism of the Multiple), Balibar notes that multiplicity exceeds every possibility of subsumption and therefore of denomination. This long story traces back to conflicts between monotheistic and polytheistic religions in the ancient world. It also dominates the oppositions of the Enlightenment's 'war of universals' between followers of Kant's univocal, monotheistic universality of the categorical imperative, and Herder's historicist, polytheistic concept of world history, where unity exists only as the absent cause of the harmonic multiplicity of cultures. When Derrida and Habermas, cosmopolitan post-Kantians of different orders, joined together after 9/11, it was not only *against* a certain form of sovereign unilateralism and the generalization of the warlike model of politics, but *for* a certain construction of a global, transnational, and transcultural public sphere.

Theoretical antitheses can shift a dialectical politics of universality, leading Balibar to name 'the *institution* of the universal'. With great delicacy and caution, he suggests that there emerges an inherent right to the assertion of the principle of 'equaliberty' through collective, emancipatory insurrectionary actions in reaction to unjust impositions. Masses confer this right upon themselves: they grant themselves rights as a kind of limit-institution, a naturalistic form of the discourse on human

the Truth-Event bears an uncanny resemblance to Althusser's "ideological interpellation"': Slavoj Žižek, *The Ticklish Subject: An Essay in Political Ontology* (London: Verso, 1999), p. 128.
6 On Saint Paul, see also Daniel Boyarin, *A Radical Jew: Paul and the Politics of Identity* (Berkeley: University of California Press, 1994); Boyarin's admirably reserved review, 'Neither Greek nor Jew: Review of Alain Badiou's "Saint Paul: The Foundation of Universalism"', *Bookforum* (April/May 2006), 12–13; and Jacob Taubes, *The Political Theology of Paul*, trans. by Dana Hollander (Stanford, CA: Stanford University Press, 1993).
7 Etienne Balibar, 'Opening Statement: A Dialogue Between Alain Badiou and Etienne Balibar on "Universalism"', University of California Irvine, 2 February 2007 <issuu.com/ivanradenkovic/docs/balibar-debating-with-alain-badiou-on-universalism> [accessed 2 February 2020]. Balibar refers to his previous essays: 'Racism as Universalism', in *Masses, Classes, Ideas: Studies on Politics and Philosophy Before and After Marx*, trans. by J. Swenson (New York: Routledge, 1994), pp. 191–204; 'Ambiguous Universality'; and 'Sub Specie Universitatis', in *Topoi*, 25.1–2 (2006), 3–16.

rights. Equaliberty asserts that humans are free and equal *by nature,* a right that takes historical form when universality grounds itself not in a theoretical essence, but in the *contingent* struggle of insurrection itself.[8]

Balibar concludes not that civic universality is an absurd myth, but precisely that it exists as a tendency, an effort and, following Spinoza, a *conatus*. The driving force within this tendency remains the force of the negative, expressed in Jacques Rancière's formula of 'la part des sans-part' [the share of the shareless] and what is perhaps his model: 'le pouvoir des sans-pouvoir' [the power of the powerless] in Merleau-Ponty.[9] Balibar's cautious delicacy leads him to conclude on a note of political responsibility that recognizes the risks of past history:

> Universalistic ideologies are not the only ideologies that can become absolutes, but they certainly are those whose realization involves a possibility of radical intolerance or internal violence. This is not the risk that one should avoid running, because in fact it is inevitable, but this is the risk that has to be known, and that imposes unlimited responsibility upon the bearers, speakers and agents of universalism.[10]

What strikes me in Balibar's exposition is the dual movement towards naturalization and historicization of the universal. The refutative nature of universalist discourse indicates that it arises in a natural reaction to growing, unjust impositions become intolerable to those who are forced to endure them by violence: that is, the dispossessed. The universal, grounded in human nature, thus becomes the name of a historical process — it would be preferable to speak of universalization, rather than a static universal — driven by the necessity of refuting and repulsing established powers experienced as tyrannous.

The Singular Universal

An intriguing formula occurs in the text of a former colleague at Yale, the late, regretted Naomi Schor, in a discussion of Jean-Paul Sartre's Jewish problematics, a formula oddly pertinent to present issues: that of a 'singular universal'.[11] According to Sartre, identity was thrust on French Jews by others, a view later subjected to extensive criticism. But French universalism was already in crisis, partly as a result of Sartre's critique. A double problematic was at work: universalism as against

---

8 'La Proposition d'égaliberté' is the title of Balibar's essay, originally published in *Les Conférences du Perroquet*, 22 (Paris: Le Perroquet, November 1989), and a book, *La Proposition d'égaliberté*, which includes that essay among others, now published in the collection *Actuel Marx confrontation*. It is translated as '"Rights of Man" and "Rights of the Citizen": The Modern Dialectic of Equality and Freedom', in *Masses, Classes, Ideas: Studies on Politics and Philosophy Before and After Marx*, trans. by J. Swenson (New York: Routledge, 1994), pp. 39–59.
9 Jacques Rancière, *Disagreement: Politics and Philosophy*, trans. by Julie Rose (Minneapolis: Minnesota University Press, 1998); Maurice Merleau-Ponty, 'Note sur Machiavel', in *Eloge de la philosophie et autres essais* (Paris: Gallimard, 1989), pp. 287–308 (p. 306).
10 Balibar, 'Opening Statement', p. 8.
11 Naomi Schor, 'Anti-Semitism, Jews, and the Universal', *October*, 87 (Winter 1999), 107–16. See Jean-Paul Sartre, *Réflexions sur la question juive* (Paris: Gallimard, 1946); *Anti-Semite and Jew*, trans. by George J. Becker (New York: Schocken Books, 1995).

particularism, universalism as against differences, paradoxically setting Right and Left against each other as representatives of different strains of a national heritage since the Revolution. France had insisted on public assimilation, relegating the separatism of identity to the private sphere. This placed Jews in the double bind of being free to practice their faith in the privacy of their home, while performing as abstract rights-bearing individuals in public.

Sartre denounced Christianity's expropriation of the universal, its claim to occupying the position of the universal, relegating all others to positions of alterity (developments well-known to medievalists). The Jew was thus forced to assimilate into *francitude* in order to become universal, Judaism per se being implicitly defined as a tribalism. This supposedly binary opposition of universalism and particularism left the position of neither Christianity nor Judaism very clear. Catholicism's derivation from the Greek *katholikos* gave it an etymological claim to universalism, casting Judaism into a position of particularism. In *Difficult Freedom* (1963) Emmanuel Levinas repeatedly asserted the universality of Judaism as revealed in that very particularity, the view echoed forcefully in Daniel Boyarin's assertion that '"true Jewishness" [...] paradoxically consists of participating in a universalism'.[12]

'Universalism' and 'particularism' were themselves unstable terms. Following Pierre Birnbaum,[13] Naomi Schor insisted that French Jews do not require assimilation into national identity to access the universal: they assimilate because they are always already universalists.[14] If universalism was an outdated concept for Sartre, inadequate to the heterogeneity of modern societies, his was not a simple-minded rejection of the concept. Sartre invoked a distinction between two forms of universality, concrete universality and abstract universality.

In a little-known text (a talk delivered at Levinas's invitation after the publication of *Anti-Semite and Jew*), Sartre returns to the opposition between the concrete, 'aligned with ethnic particularity and pride', and the abstract, 'aligned with assimilation, denial, and inauthenticity'.[15] As Schor points out, Sartre insists that the rights the Jews possess, they have as Jews, not as abstract persons:

> 'This is a question of *concrete democratism*'. In opposition to [any] 'abstract liberalism' [...], what Sartre propounds is a concrete liberalism, with the emphasis on concrete. What Sartre condemns in universalism is its tendency to lead to abstraction; universalism is, however, acceptable if it is concretized, i.e. encompasses historical specificity and all manner of material differences.[16]

In spite of his fulminations, Sartre returns repeatedly to the question of the universal. His most explicitly universalist text was written for a conference on Kierkegaard sponsored by UNESCO in 1964. On the occasion of that lecture,

---

12   Boyarin, *A Radical Jew*, pp. 94–95. Boyarin discards prior essences and meanings in a dissolution of Jewish identity that seems to spiritualize and allegorize it in a move of European culture familiar even today.
13   Pierre Birnbaum, 'Grégoire, Dreyfus, Drancy et Copernic: les juifs au cœur de l'histoire de France', in *Les Lieux de mémoire*, ed. by Pierre Nora, 3 vols (Paris: Gallimard, 1992), III, 561–613.
14   Schor, 'Anti-Semitism, Jews, and the Universal', p. 111.
15   Ibid, p. 112.
16   Ibid., p. 113 (my emphasis).

in its very title, Jean-Paul Sartre used the phrase that appears in the title of this conclusion: 'The Singular Universal', signifying 'what transforms the contingent, aleatory, insignificant singularity of the individual into a meaningful and concrete universal'.[17] That transformation is not always easy and pellucid. The universal depends on singularity to manifest itself: 'there is no incarnation of the universal but in *the irreducible opacity of the singular*'.[18] Indeed, one might add, it is only singularities that construct the universal.

Schor concluded her essay in 1999 by acknowledging that Sartre could not have foreseen 'the spectacular rise of particularism that has marked our era'. Noting 'identity politics' in passing, Schor ends with the assertion that:

> Today's Jew is no longer as he was for hundreds of years, the paradigmatic stranger, the unassimilable Other. That role has been reassigned today to the immigrant, notably to the members of Islam. But that is another story. If Sartre were alive today we could imagine him writing a *Réflexions sur la question musulmane*.[19]

Sartre's *Réflexions sur la question juive* was written and published in 1946, at the end of the Second World War, following revelations of the full horrors of the Holocaust. The role of the Other in defining the victim is to be understood in that historical context.

If it is only singularities that construct the universal, it must be singularities in concert, singularities activated by collective values and enthusiasm, that (dis)allow engagement with other similar singularities in collectivity. Indeed, the concept of the singularity as an individual radically castrated from the collective and cast into a multitudinous desert entirely on its own may have passed. Yet, paradoxically, the singular universal has a historical role that is undeniable. Male or female, the singular universal arises, writes texts that survive the racisms of time to bond, puzzle, amaze, and incite, across centuries of alterity. To cite an earlier passage and add to it: the refutative nature of universalist discourse indicates that it arises in a natural reaction to growing, unjust impositions become intolerable to those who are forced to endure them — the dispossessed. Universalization thus becomes the name of a historical process driven by the necessity of refuting established powers experienced as tyrannous. The universal is the implication of equaliberty that arises as the dialectical counterclaim to dispossession.

Race, Racism, and Chrétien the Convert

As noted in the Introduction, the historical processes in which Chrétien de Troyes took part were epochal and trans-individual. Though his texts, upon attentive reading, reveal a remarkable, critical historical awareness, the historical processes in which he participated necessarily transcended what the individual could consciously

---

17 Jean-Paul Sartre, 'The Singular Universal', in *Between Existentialism and Marxism*, trans. by John Mathews (New York: Pantheon Books, 1974); cited by Schor, 'Anti-Semitism, Jews, and the Universal', p. 113.
18 Schor, 'Anti-Semitism, Jews, and the Universal', p. 114 (my emphasis).
19 Ibid., p. 116.

perceive. To attempt to circumscribe our present understanding of his texts in the twenty-first century to a hypothetical projection of what might have been thinkable at the time by institutionalized clerics under the name of 'historicism' is rank ideological manoeuvering. To the extent possible, the historical critic negotiates the multiple differences between his own consciousness, that of his subject, and the multiple potentials of the historical period with sensitivity and respect. That is his ethics, as well as his *raison d'être*.

Our own understanding is itself historical. No historian or critic can claim to abstract himself or herself from being historically situated. Calling it a 'Copernican Revolution', Balibar has made the crucial distinction in anthropology's study of the human, displacing its earlier focus from the pseudo-scientific topic of 'races' to the study of racism in three historical forms:

— European anti-Semitism leading to the Nazi genocide;

— Colonial rule over so-called 'subject races' by supposed 'superior races';

— American racial laws and practices of segregation on the basis of the black-white color divide.[20]

Thus, Jews, colonized Africans and Asians, and American slaves were three different historical forms of oppressive racism. The study of these historical forms of racism provided the foundations for a politics of human rights by an institutional decision that followed upon the disaster of World War II: that of UNESCO in 1950 and 1951, following a commission of the United Nations based on the Universal Declarations of Human Rights.[21] Racism was redefined by UNESCO as including anti-Semitism, the racial prejudices of world-wide colonizers of black, brown, and yellow races, as well as the American re-invention of black slavery after slavery had been abandoned by the rest of the civilized world for centuries. That institutional decision opened a new epistemic and political epoch in human consciousness. As was to be expected, it also opened a period of struggle between those who accepted it and counter-revolutionary forces of the ugliest kind.

Racism uses race as ideology. Philology traces the ideologeme of 'race' back to the late Middle Ages, either in France or in Spain, specifically in relation to anti-Jewish prejudice.[22] The practices of racism are far earlier, of course, as illustrated by the holocaust of Jews in the Rhineland as the first chapter of the First Crusade, well before the invention of pseudo-scientific theories of race and 'proper' anti-

---

20   Etienne Balibar, 'Difference, Otherness, Exclusion', *Parallax*, 11.1 (2005), 19–34; and 'Différence, altérité, exclusion: trois catégories anthropologiques pour théoriser le racisme', in *Néoracisme et dérives génétiques*, ed. by Marie-Hélène Parizeau and Soheil Kash (Quebec: Presses de l'Université Laval, 2006), pp. 27–46.
21   Balibar, 'Difference, Otherness, Exclusion', p. 23.
22   Charles de Miramon, 'Noble Dogs, Noble Blood: The Invention of the Concept of Race in the Late Middle Ages', in *The Origins of Racism in the West*, ed. by Ben Isaac, Yossi Ziegler, and Miriam Eliav-Feldon (Cambridge: Cambridge University Press, 2009), pp. 200–16; David Nirenberg, 'Was There Race Before Modernity? The Example of "Jewish" Blood in Late Medieval Spain', in *The Origins of Racism in the West*, ed. by Isaac, Ziegler, and Eliav-Feldon, pp. 232–64. See also Peter Biller, 'Proto-racial Thought in Medieval Science', in *The Origins of Racism in the* West, ed. by Isaac, Ziegler, and Eliav-Feldon, pp. 157–80.

Semitism: the Middle Ages knew only anti-Judaism, after all.²³ Equipped with merely medieval *scientia*, a millenium of theologically-derived ideology, and readily manipulated hate, anti-Judaism provided ample ideological basis for Count Emicho and other 'Christian' magnates to murder all Jews within their reach in the spring of 1096.²⁴ The practice of genocide may require ideology to cover its foundation in hate, aggression, and economic and political self-interest. Arguably, at certain moments in history, the relationship between ideology and the fundamentals of political economy is inverted. Is it the case that Christian ideology of anti-Judaism, developed over the preceding millenium, is considered the primary cause of the genocide of 1096, rather than the combination of ordinary human hate, aggression, and self-interest, whipped up by feudal magnates inspired by crusading ideology and rebelling against the initial constrictions of state-formation?

Chrétien de Troyes, a Jew in History

The literary production of the convert evolved dialectically in relation to the evolution of the polity. The genocide remembered is inscribed in Philomena's rape as tyranny, an internal exclusion from the rule of law within Christian polities, analogous to the Jews' internal exclusion — an internal exclusion whose millennial ambiguity led to the monstrosity of 1096 as holocaust. If this youthful metamorphosis of an Ovidian metamorphosis registered horror at recent history, perpetrated on Jewish bodies by Christian universalism forcing unwilling conversion, Chrétien the convert's first full-blown novel in verse, *Erec et Enide*, written slightly later under relatively favorable conditions for the Jews of the kingdom, nevertheless insisted on the theme of poverty even as it celebrated a re-imagined messianic kingship as young, handsome, courageous, and married: Davidic with the twist of utter fidelity by both members of the royal couple-to-be.

For *Erec et Enide*, the author invented a specific narrative structure — a *conjointure* — of which he was particularly proud. He re-employed its formal technicity in the *Yvain*, written under different, more ambiguously difficult political circumstances, which features as an opening act an ironic face-to-face encounter of two major social classes, peasant and knight, in which the ugly, oversized peasant bests the knight in critique by wit, according to the knight's own shame-faced account. This is followed by the main act, in which the knightly protagonist goes mad, seeking no more than married wealth and power in a marginal fiefdom. Yet it is this marginal hero who serves to textualize a critical view of the economic basis of feudalism — the mode of production that sustains him — as well as the messianic liberation

---

23 David Nirenberg, *Anti-Judaism: The Western Tradition* (New York: Norton, 2013). Nirenberg downplays events and documents from outside the Iberian peninsula: see 'The Rhineland Massacre of Jews in the First Crusade'. His study of 'anti-Judaism' is to be inserted in broader traditional studies in the development of Christian anti-Jewish ideology such as those of Anna Sapir Abulafia, *Christians and Jews in Dispute: Disputational Literature and the Rise of Anti-Judaism in the West (c. 1000–1150)* (Aldershot: Ashgate, 1998), and Gilbert Dahan, *La Polémique chrétienne contre le judaïsme au Moyen Âge* (Paris: Albin Michel, 1991).

24 I recall Alain Boureau's comment: 'La haine donc, rien que la haine, toute la haine. Il faut partir d'elle, y retourner, entrer dans son ordre, son univers et son discours' (*L'Événement sans fin: récit et christianisme au Moyen Age* (Paris: Les Belles Lettres, 2004), p. 217).

of a localized labor force, three hundred maidens kidnapped from the nearby countryside and forced to work at starvation wages. Chrétien de Troyes's aesthetic is not socialist realism: the passage is best accounted for in terms of rhetorical ekphrasis. Yet its effect and its significance are undoubted. Within what has been deemed a 'courtly romance' by literary history, is lodged a razor-sharp analysis of the feudal economy and a devastatingly critical representation of its ruling class.

Chrétien's last, unfinished text, the *Perceval* or the *Conte du graal*, remains profoundly ambiguous. It is in the *Perceval* that Chrétien, the Jewish convert, faced universalist issues most urgently. On the one hand, political pressures were mounting against Jews in France, and against converts most particularly. On the other hand, the evolution of his own thoughts, in his texts as thinking-machines in the wake of 1096, had led him to consider issues that were universalist in nature: the problematics of aggressivity in young men, and the effort to both channel and capture that aggressivity in ideological representations that, in turn, seem to take on a life of their own. This dual problematic — male aggressivity itself, and its ideological iconization that takes its own vital course — explains the binary structure of the *Conte du graal*, with its two protagonists, Perceval and Gauvain.

It is in *Perceval*'s Prologue, supplemented by the Hermit's narrativization, that the work of creating universal value can be observed directly. If the operative conjecture of this book is correct, Chrétien is stitching together, in plain sight yet without overt acknowledgment, the Christian and Jewish interpretations of the value of charity as the value that is to be dominant in his fictional universe, incomplete as it remains. The signifier *charité* refers to two signifieds simultaneously: the word invokes both Christian and Jewish religious ideologies to focus and install an ethical, anthropomorphic criterion in its narrative. The value is installed in the Prologue, to be inherently referred to by the narrative until it is most concretely instantiated in the Hermit's relation to Perceval.

The 'singular universal' is that of the writer, replicated by the Hermit and the text both. The text, unquestionably lodged in the codes of its time, reaches beyond those codes to address a question that resounds in current events interweaving issues of race, hate, aggression, justice, and political order, twisted, distant, refracted echoes of 1096. In both twenty-first-century America and eleventh-century Europe, many avoid examining and naming the issues at hand for fear of inciting further unrest, except for historians like Albert of Aachen and Otto of Friesing. Which was *charité*?

★ ★ ★ ★ ★

Clearly, the historical specifics of dispossession vary, whether of Jews, of other racial groups, of women, of those dispossessed by poverty, by enforced labor, by warfare. Care must be taken to account for differences in social systems, economic and political systems of extraction, and semiotic systems of oral and written textualization. Such variability does not create insurmountable barriers of alterity. On the contrary, dispossession per se may give access to others' historical experience that respects their alterity. Such would be the lesson of this book's more hopeful conjuncture.

Chrétien de Troyes was not a revolutionary. Revolution is a socio-political form that comes fully into existence in binary opposition to the modern state — see Lenin, *The State and Revolution* — which was only in early stages of formation at Chrétien's time. Revolution itself would become politically imaginable in the fourteenth century. Two potentialities that are pertinent to revolution do come into appearance in Chrétien de Troyes's fictional texts, understanding narrative fiction as a 'well-fashioned anthropomorphic text': identification across barriers of gender and class, and critique of extractive economic practices at the basis of socio-political structures. Carefully structured narratives wrapped in charm and wit, Chrétien's fictions constitute social acts of cross-class, cross-gender identifications and piercing critique, stripping off elite pretensions at natural superiority. Both identifications and critiques will be at the basis of later revolutionary movements. Revolution may not exist in the twelfth century as a fully achieved social form: social critique and unifying identification do.

APPENDIX

Counting Jews in Medieval History

Rashi, still alive at Troyes in 1096, heard oral stories and received letters from individual correspondents. He referred to the mass slaughter of Jews as 'hereg rav': 'the great killing'.[1] Reliable absolute numbers are lacking: I have seen estimates between 3,000 and 30,000 total Jewish deaths for 1096. Such estimates are unverifiable by nature: general archives of population statistics did not exist in the Middle Ages.[2] However, proportional population estimates do exist for a somewhat later historical moment when better information is available. In 1300, there might have been 100,000 Jews in France and 100,000 Jews in Germany, the combined total population of the two countries being about 26 million at that moment:[3] Jews would have represented about 0.75 per cent of the total population. Another estimate, for one region of France a century earlier, reduces the proportion by one third: 0.25 per cent.[4]

Christianity was not in serious danger of being overwhelmed by waves of Judaizing. The stakes, in truth, were mainly symbolic and ideological. Yet the fear was real. The final, full conversion of the Jews was essential to confirming Christian supersessionist theology, foundational for Christian identity, and integral to Christianity's construction of what the anthropologist Arjun Appadurai calls a 'predatory identity'.[5] In spite of prolonged periods of contact and mutual exchange — which would suggest ample opportunity to get to know the other's humanity as a neighbor — huge majorities can feel threatened and conceive of themselves as menaced by very small minorities.[6] In the symbolic domain, the enormous

---

1   Taitz, *The Jews of Medieval France*, p. 91.
2   Actually, crude beginnings were being made in estate surveys and financial account books for governance: see Haidu, *The Subject Medieval/Modern*.
3   Stow, *Alienated Minority*, p. 7.
4   William Chester Jordan, 'Anciens maîtres/nouveaux maîtres: les juifs de France de l'Ouest et la transition des Angevins aux Capétiens', in *Plantagenêts et Capétiens: confrontations et héritages*, ed. by Martin Aurell and Noël-Yves Tonnerre (Turnhout: Brepols, 2006), pp. 387–94 (p. 388).
5   He develops the notion of a predatory identity in Arjun Appadurai, *Géographie de la colère: la violence à l'âge de la globalisation*, trans. by Françoise Bouillot (Paris: Payot, 2007), pp. 77–90. On 'supersessionism', see Catherine S. Cox, *The Judaic Other in Dante, the Gawain Poet, and Chaucer* (Gainesville: University Press of Florida, 2005), and Steven F. Kruger, *The Spectral Jew: Conversion and Embodiment in Medieval Europe* (Minneapolis: University of Minnesota Press, 2006).
6   Appadurai's analysis in *Géographie de la colère* depends on the existence of the nation-state and the custom of counting majorities and minorities. In fact, it fits medieval Christianity to a T. In 'Conversion, Apostasy, and Apprehensiveness', Stow argues that unwilling or vacillating Jewish converts posed a real threat to Christianity.

asymmetry between the dominant hegemony and the persistence of the tiny minority might actually itself be an additional irritant.[7]

But the stakes were greater than sociology can suspect. The Jew represented something contemporary sociology does not grasp, and which history prefers to avoid as tainted by Marxism: the power of ideology. In a sense, sociology and ideology are contradictory powers. One examines social practices aside from ideational investment. Practically speaking, sociologically speaking, the possibility of a Jewish integration within the framework of Christian society had been amply demonstrated, in Italy, in France, in Germany. Jews and Christians were perfectly capable of residing side by side, individually and in groups, peaceably, albeit with occasional frictions. In fact, that was precisely the problem. What was unacceptable was the Jew's persistence in remaining a Jew. That was unacceptable to the hegemon. It was unacceptable as a matter of 'pure ideology'.

The other is sociology's Other, the ideational investment in behavior that turns behavior into action. The Jew, to the Christian hegemon in the Christian Middle Ages, was, in the very essence of his existence, the negation of Christianity. As his total or ultimate assimilation became inconceivable, his formal acquiescence in the Christian hegemony became absolutely required by Christianity's own ideology. The continued social existence of the Jew demonstrated the contingency of Christianity. Exactly to the degree the Jew could be assimilated in Christian society, assimilation became intolerable, and altericide of the Jew inevitable.

The attempted genocide of 1096 does not compare to the attempted genocide of the Second World War in the total numbers actually slaughtered. The numbers do not compare, but the essential principle at work in the two Events does. In fact, the principle is identical. In both cases, the attempt was made to make Europa *Judenfrei*: to clear the territory of Europe of all Jews and Judaism, at once, and by violent means.[8] In principle, there is no difference.[9]

The attempted genocide of 1096 left Europe's surviving Jews traumatized, even as they returned to their homes as 'Christians', negotiating their liberation from the yoke of enforced Christianity with the help of the Emperor, inscribing their trauma in multiple narrative and lyric texts that have been read with delicacy and literary finesse. The literary *piyyutim* and chronicles structure explorations of trauma, texts bound in the tightest bond to evenemential history. It makes no sense to assign trauma to a textuality unmoored from all connection to history. If trauma is in text, it is because text is historical, and because trauma inhabits text and history. Writing history means writing trauma, Dominick LaCapra reminds us, and the reverse is equally true: touch trauma, you touch history.[10]

---

7   Berel Lang astutely notes that 'for the construction of identity, few relationships that hold together fruitfully can expect to be asymmetrical at their base' ('Hyphenated-Jews and the Anxiety of Identity', *Jewish Social Studies: History, Culture, Society*, n.s., 12.1 (Fall 2005), 1–15 (p. 11)).
8   The medieval genocide was somewhat more respectful of human dignity and free choice than the modern version, by offering its victims the choice between the sword's edge and forced conversion. No such choice was available to Hitler's victims.
9   Cf. Philippe Buc, 'Some Thoughts on the Christian Theology of Violence, Medieval and Modern, From the Middle Ages to the French Revolution', *Rivista di storia del cristianesimo*, 5.1 (2008), 9–28, and more recently his *Holy War, Martyrdom, and Terror*.
10 LaCapra, *Writing History, Writing Trauma*.

In truth, the meanings of the world in which the Jewish trauma evolves after 1096 were not pleasant ones. In the struggle between the 'lachrymose' view of history which makes Jews victims of a devastating teleology, and the sunny, cheerful, optimistic, rosy-tinted historiography favored in recent years that seems to bypass brute historical facts, the choice is not an easy one, in spite of a general movement of historians toward the latter, quite disregarding both the genocide of 1096 and the Holocaust itself. This is not the moment to enter into a substantive consideration of the issues — properly monumental — except to recognize a recent essay that suggests the *Aufhebung* of the binarism, not quite by a dialectical mediation, but at least by a third approach that, while acknowledging recurrent disasters, recognizes the philosophical issue at stake, and restores agency to Jews as individuals and collectives.[11] Aside the question of historical persecutions, difficult to deny, the philosophical issue is that of a teleology which would cast Jews irrevocably into the role of passive victimhood. While Elsa Marmursztejn does not name it, the third way that incorporates both the disasters of history and its moments of triumph is traditionally called 'dialectics', shorn of the cast-iron certainties of both philosophical Idealism (Hegel) and orthodox materialism ('vulgar Marxism'): a non-teleological understanding of contradictories at work in the concrete body of history. Bad things happen, very bad sometimes. That is not a question of destiny, but often of calculated machinations, human passions, and understandable determinations.

If, on the one hand, there is ample evidence of cooperation and collaboration by Jewish and Christian intellectuals, artisans, and craftsmen throughout the twelfth and thirteenth centuries, there is also ample and recurrent evidence of intensifying political persecution and ideological pressure on the Jewish population by Christian monarchs and the Church: both trends are present, both ideologies are in full development. *Either* simple lachrymosity *or* simple rosy-tinted optimism is a half-truth based on denialism.

It is necessary to counter such a simple-minded binarism with the reminder of a few facts, as they concern Jewish history in the twelfth century, dates that continue to deepen the furrow of the trauma of 1096, particularly in the second half of the twelfth century — in parallel with Chrétien de Troyes's career. Within such a sublation, room must be made for the unforeseeable singularities produced by the contradictions of history. The historical fact of forced conversion in 1096 threw confusion at both the forcibly-converted Jews and the Catholic Church throughout the rest of the century. Doctrine and charity, theory and practice, theology and history at odds, subjects were ground in contradiction:

> In practice, even the forcibly converted were bound to their new faith. Yet, in the early twelfth century [...] this was a result that nobody within the church was then strong enough to achieve [...]. As late as 1169, Pope Alexander III implied that however awful to contemplate, converts, even originally willing ones, might return to their faith without reprisal.[12]

---

11 Elsa Marmursztejn, 'La Raison dans l'histoire de la persécution: observations sur l'historiographie des relations entre juifs et chrétiens sous l'angle des baptêmes forcés', *Annales, Histoire, Sciences sociales*, 67.1 (janvier-mars 2012), 7–40.
12 Stow, 'Conversion, Apostasy, and Apprehensiveness', p. 927.

In other words, the results of forced conversion were unenforceable. Whatever the doctrinal turmoil of the Church, some of the forced converts returned to their original Judaism. Others did not, electing to stay where history (not Fate or Heideggerian *Geworfenheit*) had thrown them. Localities, circumstances, chance, and character all had something to do with the choices made by those concerned. Historiographical discussions that have sometimes edged towards the theological have warned against improper use of the 'individual' in medieval studies: surely the choice of whether to remain a Christian or to return to the anterior state of Judaism — a choice between adherence to either of two collectivities — could only present itself as a choice to be made by an individual conscience.

An Incomplete List of Events in the Twelfth Century Concerning Jews and Jewish Converts

1096: the massacres of Jews by Crusaders passing through the Rhineland at Cologne, Speyer, Mainz, Worms, and multiple other places in Europe, including Rouen (Normandy), and also leaving sparse evidentiary traces in Provence and Prague.

1171: thirty or thirty-two Jews are burned at the stake by the Count of Blois for the alleged ritual murder of a Christian, with no substantiation of the accusation ever presented. No body was ever found; the Jews were burned at the stake nonetheless. The Count of Blois was the younger brother of the Count of Champagne. He held Blois as a feudal fiefdom from his elder brother. The latter rescinded his brother's *auto-da-fé*, after the *auto-da-fé*.

1179: Third Lateran Council: forbids Jews and Saracens from having Christian slaves to nurse their children, or for domestic service in general. Placing Jews in the same category as Saracens is itself significant: it ratifies the classification of Jews as enemies of God, targets of crusade.

1180–1182: Philip II kidnaps all the Jews of 'France' while they are at synagogue. While they are in prison, the king blackmails them for ransom, appropriates their real estate and expels them from 'France'. According to his sycophantic biographer Rigord, Philip stripped the Jews of their gold, their silver, and their vestments.[13] The following year, in 1182, Philip expelled the Jews from his kingdom, the Ile-de-France. He canceled the debts of Christian subjects to Jews, reserving a major portion of the entire sum for himself.[14] Philip's haul from the royal extortion, including kidnapping and ransoming his Jewish subjects, amounted to more than the monarchy's budget for a year: it financed his expansionist policies during the

---

13   Rigord, *Histoire de Philippe Auguste*, ed. and trans. by Elisabeth Charpentier, Georges Pon, and Yves Chauvin (Paris: CNRS, 2006), p. 133, n. 32. Rigord places the event in 1180 in order to make Philip's reign begin with the action against the Jews: William Chester Jordan, *The French Monarchy and the Jews: From Philip Augustus to the Last Capetians* (Philadelphia: University of Pennsylvania Press, 1989), pp. 30 & 269, n. 36.
14   The proportion reserved for the king varies: according to different sources, it may be a fifth, a third, or a half.

1180s.[15] It was with the money the King of France stole from the Jews of his kingdom that the king launched the expansions into Flanders and other principalities that formed the nucleus of the later nation-state of France. The expanded medieval monarchy formed the basis of the modern nation-state. Today's France is built on the royal theft of moneys from medieval French Jews.

1190: the York massacre: in Anglo-Norman England, 150 Jews (men, women, children) who had taken refuge at the royal castle named Clifford's Tower are estimated to have been massacred or died by suicide in one night of March 1190, in a re-enactment of *Kiddush ha Shem*. The event is noted by Ephraim ben Jacob of Bonn shortly thereafter.[16]

1192: the *auto-da-fé* of Jews in Bray-sur-Seine, similar to the *auto-da-fé* of the Jews of Blois in 1171. Henry II of Champagne being on crusade, the regency of Champagne is in the hands of Countess Marie, Chrétien's patron. On 18 March, according to Rigord, Philip II, learning that a Christian had been killed by Jews (or at the demand of Jews?) in the town of Bray at the border of Champagne and the Ile-de-France, rode to the town *velocissimo*, without letting his own staff know. The king took possession of the castle of Bray, gathered all the Jews he could lay his hands on in Bray — eighty or more — and burned them forthwith at the stake. Whether this local genocide totally exterminated the Jewish population of Bray is debatable.[17]

There is no documentary evidence placing Chrétien in Bray. The town housed a number of Jews eminent by wealth and knowledge.[18] One may speculate that, a small nest egg in hand, Chrétien may have retired to that commune of distinguished Jews, near the Ile-de-France and Flanders, only to be interrupted in the writing of the *Conte del graal* by Philip's raid. The date coincides with the period in which Chrétien stops writing his last work. Again, there is no evidence, but it is conceivable that the French writer was murdered by the French king, as a Jew.

---

15   John W. Baldwin, *The Government of Philip Augustus: Foundations of French Royal Power in the Middle Ages* (Berkeley: University of California Press, 1986), pp. 152–73.
16   Sethina Watson, 'Introduction: The Moment and Memory of the York Massacre of 1190', in *Christians and Jews in Angevin England*, ed. by Rees Jones and Watson, pp. 1–14 (esp. pp. 1–2 and n. 5).
17   Rigord, *Histoire de Philippe Auguste*, p. 310. The narrative also appears in Ephraim of Bonn: Robert Chazan, 'The Bray Incident of 1192: "Realpolitik" and Folk Slander', *Proceedings of the American Academy for Jewish Research*, 37 (1969), 1–18; and more recently Elliott Horowitz, *Reckless Rites: Purim and the Legacy of Jewish Violence* (Princeton: Princeton University Press, 2006).
18   Rigord, *Histoire de Philippe Auguste*, p. 310, n. 508.

BIBLIOGRAPHY

Primary Works

ALBERT OF AACHEN, *Historia Ierosolimitana: History of the Journey to Jerusalem*, ed. and trans. by Susan B. Edgington, Oxford Medieval Texts (Oxford: Oxford University Press, 2007)

ANDREAS CAPELLANUS, 'De Amore', in *Amours plurielles: doctrines médiévales du rapport amoureux de Bernard de Clairvaux à Boccace*, ed. by Rudolf Imbach and Inigo Atucha (Paris: Seuil, 2006)

CHRÉTIEN DE TROYES, *Œuvres complètes*, ed. and trans. by Daniel Poirion and others, Bibliothèque de la Pléiade (Paris: Gallimard, 1994)

—— *Cligès*, ed. by Charles Méla and Olivier Collet, in *Romans*, Livre de Poche (Paris: Librairie générale française, 1994), pp. 285–494

—— *Philomena*, ed. by Cornélis de Boer (Paris: Librairie Paul Geuthner, 1909)

Eleventh-century Germany: The Swabian Chronicles, ed. and trans. by Ian S. Robinson (Manchester: Manchester University Press, 2008)

HOBBES, THOMAS, *Leviathan*, ed. by Richard Tuck (Cambridge: Cambridge University Press, 2002)

ISIDORE OF SEVILLE, *Isidorus Hispalensis Sententiae*, ed. by Pierre Cazier (Turnhout: Brepols, 1998)

The Jews and the Crusaders: The Hebrew Chronicles of the First and Second Crusades, ed. and trans. by Shlomo Eidelberg (Madison: University of Wisconsin Press, 1977)

JOHN OF SALISBURY, *The Letters of John of Salisbury*, ed. by W. J. Millor and C. N. L. Brooke, 2 vols (Oxford: Clarendon Press, 1979)

—— *Policraticus sive de nugis curialium*, ed. by Clemens C. I. Webb, 2 vols (Oxford: Clarendon Press, 1909)

—— *Policraticus*, ed. by K. S. B. Keats-Rohan, volume 1, Corpus christianorum: continuatio mediaevalis, 118 (Turnhout: Brepols, 1993)

—— *Policraticus: Of the Frivolities of Courtiers and the Footprints of Philosophers*, ed. and trans. by Cary J. Nederman (Cambridge: Cambridge University Press, 1990)

OVID, *Metamorphoses*, trans. by Frank Justus Miller, 2 vols, Loeb Classics (London: William Heinemann, 1916)

Pyrame et Thisbé, Narcisse, Philomena, trans. and ed. by Emmanuèle Baumgartner (Paris: Gallimard, 2000)

RIGORD, *Histoire de Philippe Auguste*, ed. and trans. by Elisabeth Charpentier, Georges Pon, and Yves Chauvin (Paris: CNRS, 2006)

Other Works

ABULAFIA, ANNA SAPIR, *Christians and Jews in Dispute: Disputational Literature and the Rise of Anti-Judaism in the West (c. 1000–1150)* (Aldershot: Ashgate, 1998)

ADAMS, TRACY, *Violent Passions* (New York: Palgrave, 2005)

AGAMBEN, GIORGIO, *Potentialities*, trans. by Daniel Heller-Roazen (Stanford, CA: Stanford University Press, 1999)

AGUS, IRVING A., *Urban Civilization in Pre-Crusade Europe*, 2 vols (New York: Yeshiva University Press, 1965)
APPADURAI, ARJUN, *Géographie de la colère: la violence à l'âge de la globalisation*, trans. by Françoise Bouillot (Paris: Payot, 2007)
AUERBACH, ERICH, *Mimesis*, trans. by Willard R. Trask (Princeton, NJ: Princeton University Press, 1953)
AURELL, MARTIN, *Des chrétiens contre les croisades (XIIe–XIIIe siècles)* (Paris: Fayard, 2013)
BADIOU, ALAIN, *Can Politics Be Thought?*, trans. by Bruno Bosteels (Durham, NC: Duke University Press, 2018)
—— *De l'idéologie* (Paris: Maspero, 1976); repr. in *Les Années rouges* (Paris: Les Prairies Ordinaires, 2012)
—— *D'un désastre obscur* (Paris: Aube, 1991)
—— 'Huit thèses sur l'universel', *Centre International d'étude de la philosophie française contemporaine*, 11 November 2004, in French <http://www.lacan.com/baduniversel.htm> and in English <http://www.lacan.com/badeight.html> [accessed 14 March 2019]
—— *Logiques des mondes* (Paris: Seuil, 1988)
—— *Petit manuel d'inesthétique* (Paris: Seuil, 1998)
—— *Saint Paul: la fondation de l'universalisme*, (Paris: Presses universitaires de France, 1997)
BAHUN, SANJA, *Modernism and Melancholia: Writing as Countermourning* (Oxford: Oxford University Press, 2014)
BALDWIN, JOHN W., *The Government of Philip Augustus: Foundations of French Royal Power in the Middle Ages* (Berkeley: University of California Press, 1986)
BALIBAR, ETIENNE, 'Ambiguous Universality', *Differences*, 7.1 (1995), 48–74; repr. in *Politics and the Other Scene* (London: Verso, 2002), pp. 146–76
—— 'Différence, altérité, exclusion: trois catégories anthropologiques pour théoriser le racisme', in *Néoracisme et dérives génétiques*, ed. by Marie-Hélène Parizeau and Soheil Kash (Quebec: Presses de l'Université Laval, 2006), pp. 27–46
—— 'Difference, Otherness, Exclusion', *Parallax*, 11.1 (2005), 19–34
—— 'Opening Statement: A Dialogue Between Alain Badiou and Etienne Balibar on "Universalism"', University of California Irvine, 2 February 2007 <issuu.com/ivanradenkovic/docs/balibar-debating-with-alain-badiou-on-universalism> [accessed 2 February 2020]
—— 'La Proposition d'égaliberté', in *Les Conférences du Perroquet*, 22 (Paris: Le Perroquet, November 1989); repr. in *La Proposition d'égaliberté: essais politiques 1989–2009* (Paris: Presses universitaires de France, 2015)
—— 'Racism as Universalism', in *Masses, Classes, Ideas: Studies on Politics and Philosophy Before and After Marx*, trans. by J. Swenson (New York: Routledge, 1994), pp. 191–204
—— '"Rights of Man" and "Rights of the Citizen": The Modern Dialectic of Equality and Freedom', in *Masses, Classes, Ideas: Studies on Politics and Philosophy Before and After Marx*, trans. by J. Swenson (New York: Routledge, 1994), pp. 39–59
—— 'Sub Specie Universitatis', *Topoi*, 25.1–2 (2006), 3–16
—— *Saeculum: culture, religion, idéologie* (Paris: Galilée, 2012)
BARON, SALO W., *A Social and Religious History of the Jews*, 2nd edn, 18 vols (New York: Columbia University Press, 1952–1983)
BARTHÉLÉMY, DOMINIQUE, FRANÇOIS BOUGARD, and RÉGINE LE JAN, eds., *La Vengeance, 400–1200* (Rome: Ecole Française de Rome, 2006)
BARTLETT, ROBERT, *The Making of Europe: Conquest, Colonization and Cultural Change, 950–1350* (Princeton, NJ: Princeton University Press, 1993)
BAUMAN, ZYGMUNT, *Modernité et holocauste*, trans. by Paule Guivarch (Paris: La Fabrique, 2002)

BAUTIER, ROBERT HENRI, 'Les Foires de Champagne: recherches sur une évolution historique', in *La Foire*, Receuils de la Société Jean Bodin, 5 (Brussels: Editions de la Librairie Encyclopédique, 1953), 97–145

BECKERMAN, GAL, 'The Agony of Walter Benjamin' (review of *Uncertain Manifesto* by Frédéric Pajak), *New York Times Book Review*, 25 April, 2019, <https://www.nytimes.com/2019/04/26/books/review/frederic-pajak-uncertain-manifesto.html?searchResultPosition=1> [accessed 14 August 2019]

BENJAMIN, WALTER, *Illuminations*, ed. by Hannah Arendt and trans. by Harry Zohn (New York: Schocken, 1969)

—— 'Sur le concept d'histoire', in *Ecrits français*, ed. by Jean-Maurice Monnoyer (Paris: Gallimard, 1991), pp. 425–55

—— 'On the Concept of History', in *Selected Writings*, ed. by Howard Eiland and Michael W. Jennings, 4 vols (Cambridge, MA, & London: Belknap Press, Harvard University Press, 2004–2006), IV, 389–400

BERNARD-DONALS, MICHAEL, 'History and Disaster: Witness, Trauma, and the Problem of Writing the Holocaust', *Clio*, 30.2 (2001), 143–68

BILLER, PETER, 'Proto-racial Thought in Medieval Science', in *The Origins of Racism in the West*, ed. by Ben Isaac, Yossi Ziegler, and Miriam Eliav-Feldon (Cambridge: Cambridge University Press, 2009), pp. 157–80

—— 'Mind the Gap: Modern and Medieval "Religious" Vocabularies', in *The Making of Medieval History*, ed. by G. A. Loud and Martial Staub (Woodbridge: York Medieval Press, 2017), pp. 207–22

BIRNBAUM, PIERRE, 'Grégoire, Dreyfus, Drancy et Copernic: les juifs au cœur de l'histoire de France', in *Les Lieux de mémoire*, ed. by Pierre Nora, 3 vols (Paris: Gallimard, 1992), III, 561–613

BISSON, THOMAS N., *The Crisis of the Twelfth Century: Power, Lordship, and the Origins of European Government* (Princeton, NJ: Princeton University Press, 2009)

BLACKER, JEAN, *The Faces of Time: Portrayal of the Past in Old French and Latin Narrative of the Anglo-Norman Regnum* (Austin: University of Texas Press, 1994)

BLOCH, HOWARD R., *Etymologies and Genealogies* (Chicago: University of Chicago Press, 1983)

BLOCH, MARC, *Apologie pour l'histoire ou métier d'historien*, ed. by Etienne Bloch (Paris: Armand Colin, 1997)

—— *The Historian's Craft*, trans. by P. Putnam (Manchester: Manchester University Press, 1992)

BOUREAU, ALAIN, *L'Événement sans fin: récit et christianisme au Moyen Age* (Paris: Les Belles Lettres, 2004)

BOYARIN, DANIEL, *A Radical Jew: Paul and the Politics of Identity* (Berkeley: University of California Press, 1994)

—— 'Neither Greek nor Jew: Review of Alain Badiou's "Saint Paul: The Foundation of Universalism"', *Bookforum* (April/May 2006), 12–13 <https://www.bookforum.com/archive/apr_06/boyarin.html> [accessed 4 April, 2019]

BRUCKNER, MATILDA TOMARYN, 'An Interpreter's Dilemma: Why are There So Many Interpretations of Chrétien's *Chevalier de la Charrette*?', *Romance Philology*, 40 (1986), 158–80

—— *Chrétien Continued: A Study of the 'Conte du graal' and its Verse Continuations* (Oxford: Oxford University Press, 2009)

—— 'Of Cannibalism and *Cligès*', *Arthuriana*, 18.3 (Fall 2008), 19–32

BUC, PHILIPPE, *Holy War, Martyrdom, and Terror: Christianity, Violence, and the West* (Philadelphia: University of Pennsylvania Press, 2015)

—— 'Some Thoughts on the Christian Theology of Violence, Medieval and Modern, From the Middle Ages to the French Revolution', *Rivista di storia del cristianesimo*, 5.1 (2008), 9–28

BUR, MICHEL, *La Formation du comté de Champagne, v. 950-v. 1150*, Mémoires des Annales de l'Est, 54 (Nancy: Université de Nancy II, 1977)

BURKE, KENNETH, *The Philosophy of Literary Form: Studies in Symbolic Action* (Baton Rouge: Louisiana State University, 1941)

BURNS, E. JANE, *Bodytalk: When Women Speak in Old French Literature* (Philadelphia: University of Pennsylvania Press, 1993)

—— 'Courtly Love: Who Needs It? Recent Feminist Work in the Medieval French Tradition', *Signs*, 27.1 (Autumn 2001), 23–57

BURNS, J. H., ed., *The Cambridge History of Medieval Political Thought, c.350–c.1450* (Cambridge: Cambridge University Press, 1988)

CARRUTH, CATHY, *Unclaimed Experience: Trauma, Narrative and History* (Baltimore, MD: Johns Hopkins University Press, 1996)

CHAZAN, ROBERT, 'The Bray Incident of 1192: "Realpolitik" and Folk Slander', *Proceedings of the American Academy for Jewish Research*, 37 (1969), 1–18

—— 'Ephraim ben Jacob's Compilation of Twelfth-century Persecutions', *The Jewish Quarterly Review*, n.s., 84.4 (April 1994), 397–416

—— *European Jewry and the First Crusade* (Berkeley: University of California Press, 1987)

—— *God, Humanity, and History: The Hebrew First-Crusade Narratives* (Berkeley: University of California Press, 2000)

—— *The Jews of Medieval Western Christendom, 1000–1500* (Cambridge: Cambridge University Press, 2006)

—— 'The Timebound and the Timeless: Medieval Jewish Narration of Events', *History and Memory*, 6 (1994), 5–35

CHAZAN, ROBERT, ed., *Church, State, and Jew in the Middle Ages* (West Orange, NJ: Behrman House, 1980)

COHEN, JEREMY, 'The Mentality of the Medieval Jewish Apostate: Peter Alfonsi, Hermann of Cologne, and Pablo Christiani', in *Jewish Apostasy in the Modern World*, ed. by Todd M. Endelman (London & New York: Holmes & Meyer, 1987), pp. 20–47

—— *Sanctifying the Name of God: Jewish Martyrs and Jewish Memories of the First Crusade* (Philadelphia: University of Pennsylvania Press, 2004)

CONSTABLE, GILES, *Crusaders and Crusading in the Twelfth Century* (Burlington, VT: Ashgate, 2008)

—— *The Reformation of the Twelfth Century* (Cambridge: Cambridge University Press, 1996)

COX, CATHERINE S., *The Judaic Other in Dante, the Gawain Poet, and Chaucer* (Gainesville: University Press of Florida, 2005)

CROPP, GLYNNIS M., 'Felony and Courtly Love', in *The Court Reconvenes: Courtly Literature Across the Disciplines*, ed. by Barbara K. Altmann and Carleton Carroll (Cambridge: Brewer, 2003), pp. 73–80

DAHAN, GILBERT, *La Polémique chrétienne contre le judaïsme au Moyen Âge* (Paris: Albin Michel, 1991)

DAHAN, GILBERT, GÉRARD NAHON, and ELIE NICOLAS, eds, *Rashi et la culture juive en France du Nord au moyen âge* (Paris & Louvain: E. Peeters, 1997)

DERRIDA, JACQUES, *Histoire du mensonge: prolégomènes* (Paris: L'Herne, 2005)

DICKINSON, JOHN, 'The Mediaeval Conception of Kingship and Some of its Limitations, as Developed in the *Policraticus* of John of Salisbury', *Speculum*, 1.3 (1926), 308–37

DRAGONETTI, ROGER, *La Vie de la lettre au moyen âge: le Conte du graal* (Paris: Seuil, 1980)

DUGGAN, JOSEPH J., *The Romances of Chrétien de Troyes* (New Haven, CT: Yale University Press, 2001)

DUNBABIN, JEAN, 'Government', in *The Cambridge History of Medieval Political Thought c.350–c.1450*, ed. by J. H. Burns (Cambridge: Cambridge University Press, 1988), pp. 477–519

EINBINDER, SUSAN L., *After the Black Death: Plague and Commemoration Among Iberian Jews*, The Middle Ages Series (Philadelphia: University of Pennsylvania Press, 2018)

—— *Beautiful Death: Jewish Poetry and Martyrdom in Medieval France* (Princeton, NJ, & Oxford: Princeton University Press, 2002)

ELIAS, NORBERT, *Über den Prozeß der Zivilisation: soziogenetische und psychogenetische Untersuchungen*, 2 vols (Basel: Haus zum Falken, 2 vols (1939)

—— *The Civilizing Process*, trans. by Edmund Jephcott, 2 vols (Oxford: Blackwell, 1969–1982)

FERRANTE, ELENA, *Frantumaglia*, trans. by Ann Goldstein (Rome: Europa, 2016)

FERRÉ, VINCENT, 'Altérité ou proximité de la littérature médiévale? De l'importation d'une notion "européenne" en Amérique du Nord', in *Perspectives médiévales*, 37 (2016) <http://journals.openedition.org/peme/9609> [accessed 17 March 2019]

FICHTENAU, HEINRICH, *Heretics and Scholars in the High Middle Ages, 1000–1200*, trans. by Denise A. Kaiser (University Park: Pennsylvania State University Press, 1998)

FLETCHER, ANGUS, *Allegory: The Theory of a Symbolic Mode* (Ithaca, NY: Cornell University Press, 1982)

FORHAN, KATE LANGDON, *The Political Theory of Christine de Pizan* (Aldershot: Ashgate, 2002)

FOUCAULT, MICHEL, 'What is an Author?', in *Textual Strategies*, ed. by Josué Harari (Ithaca, NY: Cornell University Press, 1979), pp. 141–60

FRAENKEL, BÉATRICE, *La Signature: genèse d'un signe* (Paris: Gallimard, 1992)

FREEDMAN, PAUL, and GABRIELLE SPIEGEL, 'Medievalisms Old and New: The Rediscovery of Alterity in North American Medieval Studies', *The American Historical Review*, 103.3 (June 1998), 677–704

FREUD, SIGMUND, *Group Psychology and the Analysis of the Ego*, trans. by James Strachey, International Psycho-analytical Library, 6 (New York: Liveright, 1967)

GALINSKY, GOTTHARD KARL, *Ovid's Metamorphoses: An Introduction to the Basic Aspects* (Berkeley: University of California Press, 1975)

GALLY, MICHÈLE, *L'Intelligence de l'amour d'Ovide à Dante: arts d'aimer et poésie au Moyen Age* (Paris: CNRS, 2005)

GATES, HENRY LOUIS, JR., *The Signifying Monkey* (New York: Oxford University Press, 1988)

GERVERS, MICHAEL, and JAMES M. POWELL, eds, *Tolerance and Intolerance: Social Conflict in the Age of the Crusades* (Syracuse, NY: Syracuse University Press, 2001)

GOH, IRVING, *The Reject, Community, Politics, and Religion After the Subject* (New York: Fordham University Press, 2014)

GOLB, NORMAN, *The Jews in Medieval Normandy: A Social and Intellectual History* (Cambridge: Cambridge University Press, 1998)

GORDON, PETER E., 'Why Historical Analogy Matters', *NYR Daily* <https://www.nybooks.com/daily/2020/01/07/why-historical-analogy-matters/> [accessed 1 January 2020]

GRAPE, WOLFGANG, *The Bayeux Tapestry: Monument to a Norman Triumph* (Munich: Prestel, 1994)

GRAVDAL, KATHRYN, *Ravishing Maidens: Writing Rape in Medieval French Literature and Law* (Philadelphia: University of Pennsylvania Press, 1991)

GREIMAS, A. J., *Dictionnaire de l'ancien français* (Paris: Larousse, 1968)

GUI, BERNARD, *Manuel de l'inquisiteur*, ed. and trans. by G. Mollat and G. Drioux, 2 vols (Paris: Les Belles Lettres, 2007)

HAIDU, PETER, '1194/1941/1994: Five Bucks and the Suitcases of State', *Suitcase: A Journal of Transcultural Traffic*, 1.1–2 (1995), 28–35
—— *Aesthetic Distance in Chrétien de Troyes: Irony and Comedy in 'Cligès' and 'Perceval'* (Geneva: Droz, 1968)
—— 'Althusser Anonymous in the Middle Ages', *Exemplaria*, 7 (1995), 5–74
—— 'The Columbia Stir Fry', in *A Time to Stir: Columbia '68*, ed. by Paul Cronin (New York: Columbia University Press, 2018), pp. 99–106
—— 'The Dialectics of Unspeakability: Language, Silence, and the Narratives of Desubjectification', in *Probing the Limits of Representation: Nazism and the 'Final Solution'*, ed. by Saul Friedlander (Cambridge, MA: Harvard University Press, 1992), pp. 277–99
—— 'The Episode as Semiotic Module in Twelfth-century Romance', *Poetics Today*, 4.4 (1983), 655–81
—— 'The Hermit's Pottage: Deconstruction and History in *Yvain*', *Romanic Review*, 74 (1983), 1–15; repr. in *The Sower and the Seed: Essays on Chrétien de Troyes*, ed. by Rupert T. Pickens (Lexington, KY: French Forum, 1983), pp. 127–45
—— *Lion-Queue-Coupée: l'écart symbolique chez Chrétien de Troyes* (Geneva: Droz, 1972)
—— 'Making It (New) in the Middle Ages: Towards a Problematics of Alterity', *Diacritics*, 4.2 (Summer 1974), 2–11
—— 'Narrativity and Language in Some Twelfth-century Romances', *Approaches to Medieval Romance*, ed. by Peter Haidu, special issue of *Yale French Studies*, 51 (1974), 133–46
—— 'A Perfume of Reality? Desublimating the Courtly', in *Shaping Courtliness in Medieval France: Essays in Honor of Matilda Tomaryn Bruckner*, ed. by Daniel E. O'Sullivan and Laurie Shepard (Cambridge: Brewer, 2013), pp. 25–45
—— 'The Semiotics of Alterity: A Comparison with Hermeneutics', *New Literary History*, 21 (1989–90), 671–91
—— *The Subject Medieval/Modern: Text and Governance in the Middle Ages* (Stanford, CA: Stanford University Press, 2004)
—— *The Subject of Violence: The Song of Roland and the Birth of the State* (Bloomington: Indiana University Press, 1993)
HALLWARD, PETER, *Badiou: A Subject to Truth* (Minneapolis: University of Minnesota Press, 2003)
HASKINS, CHARLES HOMER, *The Renaissance of the Twelfth Century* (Cambridge, MA: Harvard University Press, 1927)
HEAD, THOMAS, and RICHARD LANDES, *The Peace and Truce of God: Social Violence and Religious Response in France Around the Year 1000* (Ithaca, NY: Cornell University Press, 1992)
HOEPFFNER, ERNST, 'La *Philomena* de Chrétien de Troyes', *Romania*, 57 (1931), 13–74
HOLMES, URBAN T., JR., 'A New Interpretation of Chrétien's *Conte del Graal*', University of North Carolina Studies in the Romance Languages and Literatures, 7 (Chapel Hill: University of North Carolina Press, 1948)
HOLMES, URBAN T., JR, and SISTER M. AMELIA KLENKE, *Chrétien, Troyes, and the Grail* (Chapel Hill: University of North Carolina Press, 1959)
HOROWITZ, ELLIOT, *Reckless Rites: Purim and the Legacy of Jewish Violence* (Princeton. NJ: Princeton University Press, 2006)
HOUSLEY, NORMAN, *Contesting the Crusades* (Oxford: Blackwell, 2006)
HULT, DAVID, 'Gaston Paris and the Invention of Courtly Love', in *Medievalism and the Modernist Temper*, ed. by R. Howard Bloch and Stephen G. Nichols (Baltimore, MD: Johns Hopkins University Press, 1996), pp. 192–224
IOGNA-PRAT, DOMINIQUE, *Ordonner et exclure: Cluny et la société chrétienne face à l'hérésie, au judaïsme et à l'islam, 1000–1150* (Paris: Aubier, 1998)

JACOB, ROBERT, 'Le Meurtre du seigneur dans la société féodale: la mémoire, le rite, la fonction', *Annales ESC*, 45.2 (1990), 247–63
JAUSS, HANS-ROBERT, *Alterität und Modernität der mittelalterlichen Literatur: gesammelte Aufsätze 1956–1976* (Munich: Wilhelm Fink, 1977)
—— 'The Alterity and Modernity of Medieval Literature', *New Literary History*, 10.2 (1979), 181–229
JOHNSON, HANNAH, 'Massacre and Memory: Ethics and Method in Recent Scholarship on Jewish Martyrdom', in *Christians and Jews in Angevin England: The York Massacre of 1190, Narratives and Contexts,* ed. by Sarah Rees Jones and Sethina Watson (York: York Medieval Press, Boydell & Brewer, 2013), pp. 261–77
JONES, NANCY A., 'The Daughter's Text and the Thread of Lineage in the Old French *Philomena*', in *Representing Rape in Medieval and Early Modern Literature*, ed. by Elizabeth Robertson and Christine M. Rose (New York: Palgrave, 2001), pp. 161–87
JORDAN, WILLIAM CHESTER, 'Adolescence and Conversion in the Middle Ages', in *Jews and Christians in Twelfth-century Europe*, ed. by Michael A. Signer and John van Engen (Notre Dame, IN: University of Notre Dame Press, 2001), pp. 77–93
—— 'Anciens maîtres/nouveaux maîtres: les juifs de France de l'Ouest et la transition des Angevins aux Capétiens', in *Plantagenêts et Capétiens: confrontations et héritages*, ed. by Martin Aurell and Noël-Yves Tonnerre (Turnhout: Brepols, 2006), pp. 387–94
—— *The French Monarchy and the Jews: From Philip Augustus to the Last Capetians* (Philadelphia: University of Pennsylvania Press, 1989)
—— 'Jewish Studies and the Medieval Historian', *Exemplaria*, 12.1 (2000), 7–20
KARRAS, RUTH MAZO, *Sexuality in Medieval Europe* (London: Routledge, 2005)
KAY, SARAH, *The Chansons de geste in the Age of Romance: Political Fictions* (Oxford: Oxford University Press, 1995)
—— 'Who was Chrétien de Troyes?', *Arthurian Literature*, 15 (1997), 1–35
KEDAR, BENJAMIN Z. 'Emicho of Flonheim and the Apocalyptic Motif in the 1096 Massacre: Between Paul Alphandéry and Alphonse Dupront', in *Conflict and Religious Conversation in Latin Christendom: Studies in Honour of Ora Limor*, ed. by Israel Jacob Yuval and Ram Ben-Shalom (Turnhout: Brepols, 2014), pp. 87–97
KING, P. D., 'The Barbarian Kingdoms', in *The Cambridge History of Medieval Political Thought c.350–c.1450*, ed. by J. H. Burns (Cambridge: Cambridge University Press, 1988), pp. 123–54
KINOSHITA, SHARON, 'The Politics of *Translatio*: French-Byzantine Relations in Chrétien de Troyes's *Cligès*', *Exemplaria*, 8.2 (Fall 1996), 315–54
KNUUTTILA, SIMO, *Emotions in Ancient and Medieval Philosophy* (Oxford: Oxford University Press, 2006)
KOSTICK, CONOR, *The Social Structure of the First Crusade* (Leiden: Brill, 2008)
KRUEGER, ROBERTA L., '*Philomena*: Brutal Transitions and Courtly Transformations in Chrétien's Old French Translation', in *A Companion to Chrétien de Troyes*, ed. by Norris J. Lacy and Joan Tasker Grimbert (Cambridge: Brewer, 2005), pp. 87–102
KRUGER, STEVEN F., *The Spectral Jew: Conversion and Embodiment in Medieval Europe* (Minneapolis: University of Minnesota Press, 2006)
LAARHOVEN, JAN VAN, 'Thou shalt NOT slay a tyrant! The So-called Theory of Johannes of Salisbury', in *The World of John of Salisbury*, ed. by Michael Wilks (Oxford: Boydell & Brewer, 1984), pp. 319–41
LACAPRA, DOMINICK, *History in Transit: Experience, Identity, Critical Theory* (Ithaca, NY: Cornell University Press, 2004)
—— *Writing History, Writing Trauma* (Baltimore, MD: Johns Hopkins University Press, 2001)

LACLAU, ERNESTO, *Emancipations* (London: Verso, 1996)
—— *On Populist Reason* (London: Verso, 2005)
LACLAU, ERNESTO, and CHANTAL MOUFFE, *Hegemony and Socialist Strategy: Towards a Radical Democratic Politics*, trans. by Winston Moore and Paul Cammack (London: Verso, 1985)
LANG, BEREL, 'Hyphenated-Jews and the Anxiety of Identity', *Jewish Social Studies: History, Culture, Society*, n.s., 12.1 (Fall 2005), 1–15
LEVY, RAPHAEL, 'Etat présent des études sur l'attribution de *Philomena*', *Lettres Romanes*, 5.1 (1951), 46–52
—— 'Old French Goz and Crestiens Li Gois', *PMLA*, 46.2 (June 1931), 312–20
LEWIS, JOHN D., 'Medieval Theories of Resistance', in *Against the Tyrant: The Tradition and Theory of Tyrannicide*, ed. by Oszcár Jászi and John D. Lewis (Glencoe, IL: Free Press, 1957), pp. 17–34
LINDER, AMNON, ed., *The Jews in the Legal Sources of the Early Middle Ages* (Detroit, MI: Wayne State University Press, 1997)
LUSCOMB, D. E., 'Introduction: The Formation of Political Thought in the West', in *The Cambridge History of Medieval Political Thought c.350–c.1450*, ed. by J. H. Burns (Cambridge: Cambridge University Press, 1988), pp. 155–73
LUSCOMB, D. E., and G. R. EVANS, 'The Twelfth-century Renaissance', in *The Cambridge History of Medieval Political Thought c.350–c.1450*, ed. by J. H. Burns (Cambridge: Cambridge University Press, 1988), pp. 306–38
LÜTTICKEN, SVEN, 'Personafication', *New Left Review*, 96 (November-December 2015), 101–28
LYOTARD, JEAN-FRANÇOIS, *Le Différend* (Paris: Minuit, 1984)
MADDOX, DONALD, *Fictions of Identity in Chrétien de Troyes* (Cambridge: Cambridge University Press, 2006)
—— 'Trois sur deux: théories de bipartition et de tripartition des œuvres de Chrétien', *Œuvres et Critiques*, 5 (1980), 91–102
MALKIEL, DAVID, 'Destruction or Conversion: Intention and Reaction, Crusaders and Jews, in 1096', *Jewish History*, 15 (2001), 257–80
MARCUS, IVAN G., 'From Politics to Martyrdom: Shifting Paradigms in the Hebrew Narratives of the 1096 Crusader Riots', *Prooftexts*, 2.1 (1982), 40–52
—— 'A Jewish-Christian Symbiosis: The Culture of Early Ashkenaz', in *Cultures of the Jews: A New History*, ed. by David Biale (New York: Schocken, 2002), pp. 449–516
—— 'Why Did Medieval Northern French Jewry (Ṣarfat) Disappear?', in *Jews, Christians, and Muslims in Medieval and Early Modern Times: A Festschrift in Honor of Mark R. Cohen*, ed. by Arnold E. Franklin and others (Leiden: Brill, 2014), pp. 99–117
MARMURSZTEJN, ELSA, 'La Raison dans l'histoire de la persécution: observations sur l'historiographie des relations entre juifs et chrétiens sous l'angle des baptêmes forcés', *Annales, Histoire, Sciences sociales*, 67.1 (janvier-mars 2012), 7–40
MERLEAU-PONTY, MAURICE, *Eloge de la philosophie et autres essais* (Paris: Gallimard, 1989)
MICHAUD-QUENTIN, PIERRE, *Universitas: expressions du mouvement communautaire dans le moyen âge latin* (Paris: Vrin, 1970)
MIRAMON, CHARLES DE, 'Noble Dogs, Noble Blood: The Invention of the Concept of Race in the Late Middle Ages', in *The Origins of Racism in the West*, ed. by Ben Isaac, Yossi Ziegler, and Miriam Eliav-Feldon (Cambridge: Cambridge University Press, 2009), pp. 200–16
MONSON, DON A., *Andreas Capellanus, Scholasticism, and the Courtly Tradition* (Washington, DC: Catholic University of America Press, 2005)
MOORE, JOHN C., 'Love in Twelfth-century France: A Failure in Synthesis', *Traditio*, 24 (1968), 429–43

MOORE, R. I., *The Formation of a Persecuting Society: Power and Deviance in Western Europe, 950–1250* (Oxford & New York: Basil Blackwell, 1987)
—— *The Origins of European Dissent* (Toronto: University of Toronto Press in association with the Medieval Academy of America, 1994)
—— 'The Transformation of Europe as a Eurasian Phenomenon', in *Eurasian Transformations, Tenth to Thirteenth Centuries*, ed. by Johann P. Arnason and Björn Wittrock (Leiden: Brill, 2011), pp. 77–98
—— *The War on Heresy: Faith and Power in Medieval Europe* (Cambridge, MA: Harvard University Press, 2012)
MORRISON, KARL, *Conversion and Text* (Charlottesville: University of Virginia Press, 1992)
NEDERMAN, CARY J., 'A Duty to Kill: John of Salisbury's Theory of Tyrannicide', *The Review of Politics*, 50.3 (1988), 365–89
—— *John of Salisbury* (Tempe, AZ: Arizona Center for Medieval and Renaissance Studies, 2005)
—— *Worlds of Difference, European Discourses of Toleration, c. 1100–c. 1550* (University Park: Pennsylvania State University Press, 2000)
NEDERMAN, CARY J., and CATHERINE CAMPBELL, 'Priests, Kings, and Tyrants: Spiritual and Temporal Power in John of Salisbury's *Policraticus*', *Speculum*, 66.3 (1991), 572–90
NIRENBERG, DAVID, *Anti-Judaism: The Western Tradition* (New York: Norton, 2013)
—— 'The Rhineland Massacre of Jews in the First Crusade: Memories. Medieval and Modern', in *Medieval Concepts of the Past: Ritual, Memory, Historiography*, ed. by Gerd Althoff, Johannes Fried, and Patrick J. Geary (Cambridge: Cambridge University Press, Germanic Historical Institute, 2002), pp. 279–309
—— 'Was There Race Before Modernity? The Example of "Jewish" Blood in Late Medieval Spain', in *The Origins of Racism in the West*, ed. by Ben Isaac, Yossi Ziegler, and Miriam Eliav-Feldon (Cambridge: Cambridge University Press, 2009), pp. 232–64
O'DALY, IRENE, *John of Salisbury and the Medieval Roman Renaissance* (Manchester: Manchester University Press, 2018)
O'SULLIVAN, DANIEL E., and LAURIE SHEPARD, eds, *Shaping Courtliness in Medieval France: Essays in Honor of Matilda Tomaryn Bruckner* (Cambridge: Brewer, 2013)
OREN, DAN A., *Joining the Club: A History of Jews and Yale* (New Haven, CT: Yale University Press, 1985)
OTTER, MONIKA, *Inventiones: Fiction and Referentiality in Twelfth-century English Historical Writing* (Chapel Hill: University of North Carolina Press, 1996)
OVER, KRISTEN LEE, *Kingship, Conquest, and Patria: Literary and Cultural Identities in Medieval French and Welsh Arthurian Romance* (New York: Routledge, 2013)
PADEN, WILLIAM D., JR., and OTHERS, 'The Troubadour's Lady: Her Marital Status and Social Rank', *Studies in Philology*, 72.1 (1975), 28–50
QUESSADA, DOMINIQUE, *Court traité d'altéricide* (Paris: Verticales, Gallimard, 2007)
RABINOWITZ, L., *The Social Life of the Jews of Northern France in the XII–XIVth Centuries*, 2nd edn (New York: Hermon Press, 1972)
RANCIÈRE, JACQUES, *Disagreement: Politics and Philosophy*, trans. by Julie Rose (Minneapolis: Minnesota University Press, 1998)
RILEY-SMITH, JONATHAN, 'Crusading as an Act of Love', *History*, 65.214 (1980), 177–92
ROOS, LENA, *'God Wants It!' The Ideology of Martyrdom of the Hebrew Crusade Chronicles and its Jewish and Christian Background* (Uppsala: Uppsala Universitet: 2003; rev. edn. Turnhout: Brepols, 2006)
ROSENWEIN, BARBARA H., *Anger's Past: The Social Uses of an Emotion in the Middle Ages* (Ithaca, NY: Cornell University Press, 1998)
—— *Emotional Communities in the Early Middle Ages* (Ithaca, NY: Cornell University Press, 2006)

Rouse, Richard H., and Mary A. Rouse, 'John of Salisbury and the Doctrine of Tyrannicide', *Speculum*, 42.4 (1967), 693–709

Rubenstein, Jay, *Armies of Heaven: The First Crusade and the Quest for Apocalypse* (New York: Basic Books, 2011)

—— *Guibert de Nogent: Portrait of a Medieval Mind* (London: Routledge, 2002)

Sartre, Jean-Paul, *Réflexions sur la question juive* (Paris: Gallimard, 1946)

—— *Anti-Semite and Jew*, trans. by George J. Becker (New York: Schocken Books, 1995)

—— 'The Singular Universal', in *Between Existentialism and Marxism*, trans. by John Mathews (New York: Pantheon Books, 1974)

Scarry, Elaine, *The Body in Pain: The Making and Unmaking of the World* (Oxford: University Press, 1985)

Scheindlin, Raymond P., *The Song of the Distant Dove* (Oxford: Oxford University Press, 2008)

Schmitt, Jean-Claude, *La Conversion d'Hermann le Juif: autobiographie, histoire et fiction* (Paris: Seuil, 2003)

Schor, Naomi, 'Anti-Semitism, Jews, and the Universal', *October*, 87 (Winter 1999), 107–16

Schwarzfuchs, Simon, *Rachi de Troyes* (Paris: Albin Michel, 2005)

Seaton, Matt, 'Édouard Louis on Fiction and Reality, Reinventing the Self, and Writing Out of anger', *NYR Daily*, 9 February 2019 <https://email.nybooks.com/t/y-26F0F10A68357A5D> [accessed 15 September 2019]

Sehgal, Parul, 'Two Brilliant Siblings and the Curious Consolations of Math', *The New York Times Book Review*, 17 July 2019 <https://www.nytimes.com/2019/07/17/books/review-weil-conjectures-math-karen-olsson.html> [accessed 23 January 2020]

Shepkaru, Shmuel, *Jewish Martyrs in the Pagan and Christian Worlds* (New York: Cambridge University Press, 2006)

Siberry, Elizabeth, *Criticism of Crusading, 1095–1274* (New York: Clarendon Press, 1985)

Smith, Julia M. H., *Europe after Rome: A New Cultural History 500–1000* (Oxford: Oxford University Press, 2005)

Spiegel, Gabrielle, 'Memory and History: Liturgical Time and Historical Time', *History and Theory*, 41 (2002), 149–62

Stahuljak, Zrinka, and others, *Thinking Through Chrétien de Troyes* (Cambridge: Boydell & Brewer, 2011)

Steele, Stephen, 'Qu'est-ce qu'un Chrétien de Troyes?', *Florilegium*, 12 (1993), 99–106

Sternbergh, Adam, 'David Milch Headlines Most Uncomfortable Panel Discussion Ever at "New Yorker" Fest', *Vulture*, 9 October 2007 <https://www.vulture.com/2007/10/three_things_you_would_have.html> [accessed 21 August 2019]

Storms, Colette, 'Le Mal dans *Philomena*', in *Imaginaires du mal*, ed. by Paul-Augustin Deproost and Myriam Watthée-Delmotte (Louvain: Cerf, Presses Universitaires de Louvain, 2000), pp. 103–13

Stow, Kenneth R., *Alienated Minority: The Jews of Medieval Latin Europe* (Cambridge, MA: Harvard University Press, 1992)

—— 'Conversion, Apostasy, and Apprehensiveness: Emicho of Floheim and the Fear of Jews in the Twelfth Century', *Speculum*, 76.4 (2001), 911–33

Strauss, Leo, *Persecution and the Art of Writing* (Glencoe, IL: The Free Press, 1952)

Taitz, Emily, *The Jews of Medieval France: The Community of Champagne* (Westport, CT: Greenwood Press, 1994)

Taubes, Jacob, *The Political Theology of Paul* (Stanford, CA: Stanford University Press, 1993)

Throop, Susanna A., *Crusading as an Act of Vengeance* (Farnham: Ashgate, 2011)

Throop, Susanna A., and Paul R. Hyams, eds, *Vengeance in the Middle Ages: Emotion, Religion and Feud* (Farnham: Ashgate, 2010)

TOLAN, JOHN, *Petrus Alfonsi and his Medieval Readers* (Florida: University Press of Florida, 1993)
TRÜPER, HENNING, DIPESH CHAKRABARTY, and SANJAY SUBRAHMANYAM, eds, *Historical Teleologies in the Modern World* (London: Bloomsbury, 2015)
TYERMAN, CHRISTOPHER, *God's War: A New History of the Crusades* (Cambridge, MA: Harvard University Press, 2006)
VAN CAENEGEM, R. 'Government, Law and Society', in *The Cambridge History of Medieval Political Thought c.350–c.1450*, ed. by J. H. Burns (Cambridge: Cambridge University Press, 1988), pp. 174–210
VANCE, EUGENE, *Mervelous Signals* (Lincoln: University of Nebraska Press, 1986)
WARREN, MICHELLE R., 'Memory Out of Line: Hebrew Etymology in the *Roman de Brut* and *Merlin*', *MLN*, 118.4 (2003), 989–1014
WATSON, SETHINA, 'Introduction: The Moment and Memory of the York Massacre of 1190', in *Christians and Jews in Angevin England: The York Massacre of 1190, Narratives and Contexts*, ed. by Sarah Rees Jones and Sethina Watson (York: York Medieval Press, Boydell & Brewer, 2013), pp. 1–14
WERCKMEISTER, OTTO KARL, *Icons of the Left: Benjamin and Eisenstein, Picasso and Kafka after the Fall of Communism* (Chicago: University of Chicago Press, 1999)
WICKHAM, CHRIS, *Framing the Early Middle Ages, Europe and the Mediterranean, 400–800* (Oxford: Oxford University Press, 2005)
—— *The Inheritance of Rome: Illuminating the Dark Ages 400–1000* (New York: Viking, 2009)
—— *Sleepwalking into a New World: The Emergence of Italian City Communes in the Twelfth Century* (Princeton: Princeton University Press, 2015)
WIKIPEDIA, 'Petrus Alphonsi' <https://en.wikipedia.org/wiki/Petrus_Alphonsi> [accessed 21 January 2020]
YERUSHALMI, YOSEF HAYIM, *Zakhor: Jewish History and Jewish Memory* (Seattle: University of Washington Press, 1996)
YUVAL, ISRAEL JACOB, *Two Nations in Your Womb: Receptions of Jews and Christians in Late Antiquity and the Middle Ages*, trans. by Barbara Harshav and Jonathan Chipman (Berkeley: University of California Press, 2006)
ŽIŽEK, SLAVOJ, *The Ticklish Subject: An Essay on Political Ontology* (London: Verso, 1999)

INDEX

Agamben, Giorgio 7, 23 n. 3, 24 n. 6, 25, 37 n. 24, 55
Albert of Aachen 9 n. 22, 13, 37, 45–51, 54, 135
   Historia Ierosolimitana 45 n. 42, 47 n. 46, 49, 50, 54 n. 66
   Peter the Hermit 46–49, 58
   participants in the First Crusade 45–47
alterity vii, 3, 14, 17, 23 n. 3, 27, 38, 42, 60, 97, 98, 106–12, 119, 131, 132, 135
Althusser, Louis 35 n. 19, 53, 89 n. 56, 128 n. 5
American New Criticism 3, 28
Andreas Capellanus 69 n. 19 & 20, 70, 84 n. 44, 85, 88
   De amore 69 n. 20, 70
anti-Semitism 33, 39, 48, 130 n. 11, 131 n. 14, 132 n. 17 & 18, 133
Appadurai, Arjun 137 n. 5 & 6
Aristotle 7–10, 23–25, 37 n. 24, 109, 127
   potentiality 8–10, 23–25, 37 n. 24, 109
Auerbach, Erich 27 n. 11, 112 n. 93

Badiou, Alain x, 7, 10, 11, 13, 14, 22 n. 2, 24, 28, 48, 55 n. 72, 74 & 75, 56, 80, 127, 128, 129 n. 6 & 7
   the Event 10, 11, 13, 22 n. 2, 48, 55 n. 72, 56, 80, 128
   the generic 14, 127, 128 n. 2
   NeoPlatonist 11, 55, 128
Balibar, Etienne 7, 10, 14, 23 n. 3, 26 n. 8, 53 n. 64, 127–30, 133 n. 20 & 21
   materialist philosophy 7, 10, 14, 23
barbarism 11, 17, 39, 51–54, 56, 71, 75, 82, 95, 99, 106, 111, 112, 114, 117, 123
Baron, Salo 11, 45, 107 n. 87
Benjamin, Walter x, 5, 7–10, 13, 15, 19, 21, 23 n. 3, 4 & 5, 26, 57, 97 n. 74
   the angel of history 8, 9, 13, 97
Benton, John 41
Biller, Peter 9 n. 20, 133 n. 22
Blois:
   auto-da-fé of Jews 140
   Stephen, count of Blois 140
Boyarin, Daniel 129 n. 6, 131 n. 12
   A Radical Jew 129 n. 6, 131 n. 12
Bray-sur-Seine 141
   auto-da-fé of Jews 141
Burns, E. Jane 68 n. 13, 70 n. 22, 84 n. 46, 88 n. 55

Carruth, Cathy 10, 56 n. 76
   Unclaimed Experience 56 n. 76
Catholic Church 60, 61, 128, 139
   katholikos 14, 128, 131

Chansons de geste 52, 114 n. 96
Char, René x
Chazan, Robert 11, 31 n. 7, 32 n. 10, 52 n. 59 & 60, 53 n. 61, 59 n. 87, 90, 91 & 93, 60 n. 95, 64 n. 5, 73 n. 25, 141 n. 17
Chrétien de Troyes:
   as a child of Jewish converts 1–5, 9, 12, 15, 16, 20, 22, 32, 40–42, 61, 73, 101, 103, 127, 134, 135
   double consciousness 11–14, 17, 39, 79, 127
   historical identity 26, 29–31, 41
   literary identity 1, 2, 29–31, 84
   role in literary modernity 19, 22, 61, 64
   self-identified as *Crestiens li gois* (Christian the Goy) vii, 2, 32, 39–42
   Philomena:
      desire 7, 14, 66–85, 108, 116, 121, 126
      female and class solidarity 99–101, 104, 105, 106 n. 85, 117
      mutilation 10, 13, 65, 66, 72, 73, 84, 99, 100, 102, 103, 114 n. 96, 115, 117, 121, 126
      narrative structure 65–66, 70, 123
      Philomena's physical and moral portrait 70, 71, 73–78, 80
      political tale 13, 64, 70–72, 81–82, 84, 86–88, 99, 100, 106, 115, 116, 125
      rape 1 n. 3, 2, 10, 13, 15, 65–67, 70–73, 80–85, 88, 94–96, 99, 100, 102, 105, 106, 108, 109, 111, 113–17, 119, 121, 126, 127, 134
      revenge vii, 2, 3, 65, 66, 70, 72, 84, 95, 96, 100, 101, 105, 106, 113–22
      semiotic invention 8, 66, 75, 96, 97, 100–07, 113, 119
      silence 4, 5 n. 11, 12, 13, 66, 80, 97–100, 103, 126
      Tereus as evil subject 7, 66, 71–75, 78, 82, 86–88, 94, 95, 108, 109, 115
      transformation of Ovid's *Metamorphoses* 64, 71, 80–81, 95–96, 99–101, 110, 111, 119, 120–25
   romances:
      Cligès 1–3, 22, 31, 40, 63 n. 2, 67, 71, 73 n. 26, 78, 81 n. 39, 95, 112, 115, 118, 123
      Erec et Enide 2, 15, 31, 40, 64, 67, 68, 98, 134
      Lancelot (Le Chevalier de la charrette) 22, 31, 66–68, 68 n. 15, 82, 95
      Perceval (Le Conte du Graal) 3, 11 n. 26, 15 n. 32 & 33, 16, 17 n. 38, 22, 31, 41, 57, 61, 64, 75, 82, 95, 98, 106, 127, 135, 141
      Yvain (Le Chevalier au lion) 3, 15, 16, 22, 31, 64 n. 6, 67, 82, 95, 100, 101, 113, 123, 124, 134

Clarembold of Vendeuil 29, 37, 49, 54 n. 71
class politics 65, 66, 70, 84, 96, 100, 101, 106, 136
Cohen, Jeremy 11, 33 n. 11, 34 n. 13 & 16, 50 n. 56, 51–52
Council of Constance (1414) 90
'Courtly love' vii, 7, 28, 66–70, 77, 84, 87 n. 54
    invention by Gaston Paris 66–67
    as impediment to understanding *Philomena* 67
    medieval concepts of love 68–70
    see also Hugh of Saint Victor, Andreas Capellanus
Crusades 32 n. 10, 33, 37, 44, 46 n. 44, 49
cultural relativism vii, 14, 17, 78–80, 106–12, 119–21

'delingualization' 95, 101–03, 113
Derrida, Jacques 7, 23, 101 n. 78, 116, 129
dispossession 1, 11–16, 19, 20, 22, 42, 95, 96, 127, 130, 132, 135

Emicho of Floheim 29 n. 1, 49, 54 n. 71, 58
Eneas 30, 61, 64
    see also romans d'antiquité
the Event 11, 13, 17, 21, 22, 29, 34, 37, 43, 45, 48, 50–56, 58–60, 80, 85, 138, 140, 141

feminist criticism 7, 68, 70
Ferrante, Elena 1 n. 1, 3
fin'amors 77, 109, 112
the First Crusade 5, 9, 11, 13, 19, 22, 29, 32, 33, 36, 37, 45, 46, 48–53, 59, 73, 127, 133, 134 n. 23
    Pope Urban II 29, 47, 48, 54
    Jewish massacres 5–6, 9, 11, 36, 38, 45, 48–51, 58, 59, 140–41
    forced conversion to Christianity 29, 32, 33, 36–38, 43, 53, 58, 73, 78, 127, 138–40
    see also Albert of Aachen, Peter the Hermit, Emicho of Floheim
Foucault, Michel 23 n. 3, 42 n. 34, 103
French Structuralism 28
Freud, Sigmund 10, 54, 56, 57
    Beyond the Pleasure Principle 56
    Moses and Monotheism 56

Gerson, Jean 88, 90
Giles of Rome 90
Greimas, A. J. 8, 23, 32, 104, 105
Gui, Bernard 39, 40 n. 29

Habermas, Jürgen 129
Haskins, Charles Homer 43
    The Renaissance of the Twelfth Century 43
Hebrew chronicles 9, 11, 13, 32 n. 10, 37, 45, 47 n. 48, 48, 50–54, 58, 59 n. 86 & 87, 61, 117, 118, 121
    Eliezer bar Nathan's Chronicle 52, 59
    the Mainz Chronicle 9, 51, 52, 73, 121
    Solomon bar Simson's Chronicle 52, 73
Hegel 11, 139

Heidegger, Martin 23 n. 3, 37 n. 34, 55, 140
Henry II, count of Champagne 41, 140, 141
Henry II, King of England and Duke of Aquitaine 64, 93
Herder, Johann Gottfried 129
Hermann *quondam Judeus* 12 n. 29, 34, 35, 37–40, 60
history and historiography 8–11, 16, 21–23, 26, 29, 35–37, 43–35, 47–52, 54, 56–60, 63–64, 132–33, 137–40
Holmes, Urban Tigner 12, 41–42, 41 n. 30 & 32
Holocaust of 1096 vii, 5, 9, 11, 15, 19, 22, 26, 43, 48, 55, 105, 106, 127, 133, 134, 139
    as potentiality 9, 15, 19, 37, 80
    twentieth-century Holocaust 36, 45, 54, 56, 58, 59 n. 86, 60, 132
Hugh of Saint Victor 68–70, 88

infanticide 10, 13, 17, 115, 117–23
irony 2, 3, 14, 28, 40, 42, 83, 100, 103, 110, 111, 121–23
Isidore of Seville 90

Jackson, W. T. H. 27, 69
Jewish converts 5, 10, 12, 16, 19, 22, 32–35, 37–40, 60
John of Salisbury vii, 46, 88–94, 89 n. 57, 90 n. 64, 91 n. 66 & 67, 92 n. 68, 93 n. 70 & 71, 98, 115
    Policraticus vii, 46, 88–95, 89 n. 57, 90 n. 63, 91 n. 65 & 66, 92 n. 68, 98
Jordan, William Chester 34 n. 16, 45 n. 40, 137 n. 4, 140 n. 13
Judah Halévy 61 n. 98
justice vii, 6, 9, 10, 13–15, 17, 89, 94, 99, 103, 106, 107, 113–21, 128, 135

Kant, Emmanuel 10, 23, 129
Kiddush Hashem ('Sanctification of the Name') 13 n. 30, 29, 52, 53, 73, 117, 121
Krueger, Roberta 31 n. 8, 67 n. 11, 87 n. 52

Lacan, Jacques 7, 67, 68, 84, 128 n. 3
    Ethics of Psychoanalysis 67
LaCapra, Dominick 5 n. 13, 10, 57 nn. 80 & 81, 138 n. 10
law (*loy*) 17, 79, 81, 107–11, 113, 115–16, 119–21
Lenin 136
Levinas, Emmanuel 109, 131
    Difficult Freedom 131
Louis, Édouard 6
Lyotard, Jean-François 103
    Le Différend 103 n. 80

Maimonides 16, 38, 61
    The Guide for the Perplexed 61
Marie, Countess of Champagne 141
Marie de France 80, 101
    Deux amants 80
    Fresne 101

Marmursztejn, Elsa 139 n. 11
Martianus Cappella 19
Marxism 11, 23, 132 n. 17, 138, 139
Merleau-Ponty, Maurice 130 n. 9
Moore, R. I. 21 n. 1, 42 n. 34, 43 n. 36 & 37, 44, 46 n. 45, 60
Morrison, Karl 33, 34 n. 18, 57

Ovid 1, 2 n. 4 & 5, 6, 8, 10, 13, 15, 17, 31, 39, 63 n. 1 & 2, 64, 71 n. 23, 73 n. 26, 77 n. 31, 80, 81, 88, 95 n. 72, 96, 100–01, 105, 110–12, 118–21, 123, 124, 134
  Metamorphoses 1–2, 32, 63, 71, 95, 100, 111, 119
Ovide moralisé 2, 31, 123

Pajak, Frédéric 9 n. 23, 10 n. 24
Paris, Gaston 66, 67 n. 9
Peirce, C. S. 8, 104, 105
Peter Abelard 35, 60, 105
Peter the Hermit 46 n. 43, 47–49, 58
Peter the Venerable 39, 43
Petrus Alfonsi 12 n. 29, 38, 39 n. 27, 60
  Disciplina clericalis 38
  Dialogus Petri et Moysi Iudei 38
Philip II (Philippe Auguste) 5 n. 12, 44, 115 n. 99, 140 n. 13, 141 n. 17 & 18
Philippe de Beaumanoir 81 n. 40, 107
Plato 10, 11, 23–24, 55, 75, 128
Pound, Ezra 27

Rachel of Mainz 9, 13, 15, 52, 53, 66, 73, 119, 121, 126 n. 105
Rancière, Jacques 23, 130 n. 9
Raoul de Cambrai 114
Rashi (Rabbi Solomon ben Isaac) 12 n. 27, 31, 38, 76, 137
Renaissance of the twelfth century 5, 7, 33, 43–44, 58, 89 n. 57, 93 n. 70
Rhineland massacres of Jews 6, 29, 37 n. 23, 45, 48, 49, 51, 54, 58, 134 n. 23, 140

Rigord 140 n. 13, 141 n. 17 & 18
romans d'antiquité 64

Saint Paul 16, 55 n. 72, 80 n. 37, 128 n. 5, 129 n. 6
Sartre, Jean-Paul 7, 14, 130 n. 11, 131, 132
  the Singular Universal vii, 14–15, 130–32, 132 n. 17, 135
  Anti-Semite and Jew 130 n. 11, 131
  Réflexions sur la question juive 130 n. 11, 132
Schmitt, Jean-Claude 34–38, 34 n. 18, 35 n. 19 & 20, 38 n. 25
Schor, Naomi 14, 130 n. 11, 131 n. 14, 132 n. 17 & 18
  'Anti-Semitism, Jews, and the Universal' 130 n. 11, 131 n. 14, 132 n. 18
semiotics 3, 8, 14, 17, 96–99, 103–05, 119
Servius 28
The Song of Roland 3, 47 n. 47, 52, 65
Storms, Colette 67 n. 11, 87 n. 52

Thèbes 30, 61, 64
  see also *romans d'antiquité*
Third Lateran Council 140
Thomas Aquinas 90
  Summa theologica 90
Thomas of Marle 29, 37, 49, 54 n. 71
Thrace 65, 66, 71, 74, 75, 77, 82, 94, 95, 108, 110–13
trauma 5, 8–11, 13, 17, 56–60, 67, 98, 138–39
tyranny vii, 6, 10, 13–15, 26, 72, 80, 85, 86, 88–95, 98–101, 108, 114–18, 121, 130, 132, 134

universalism vii, 1 n. 3, 8, 13–17, 19, 20, 22, 28, 38, 39, 42, 44 n. 40, 55 n. 72, 60, 61, 73, 80, 83, 85, 88, 89, 105, 106, 108, 109, 111, 113, 115–17, 119–21, 126–35

Weber, Max 21

the York massacre 37, 141 n. 16

www.ingramcontent.com/pod-product-compliance
Lightning Source LLC
LaVergne TN
LVHW061252060426
835507LV00017B/2040